BLACKIE

Steve Black with Arthur McKenzie

MAINSTREAM
PUBLISHING

EDINBURGH AND LONDON

First published in Great Britain in 2004 by
MAINSTREAM PUBLISHING COMPANY (EDINBURGH) LTD
7 Albany Street
Edinburgh EH1 3UG

ISBN 1 84018 828 6

A catalogue record for this book is available from the British Library

Typeset in Din and Stone Print
Printed and bound in Great Britain by
Antony Rowe Ltd, Chippenham, Wiltshire

This book is dedicated to the greatest accomplishment of my life,
my children.
To Stephen, Mark and Emma: your mam and I couldn't possibly love
you more or be more proud of who you are.
To Mam, Nana and Roz: thanks for everything.
And finally, to Julie: thanks for putting up with me for so long – surely
above and beyond the call of duty.
I love you all.

ACKNOWLEDGEMENTS

I would like to express my gratitude to all contributors to this book. Thank you for your kind words.

Many thanks to Sharon Talbot and Ken Shepherd for looking after me so well.

To my friends John Charlton, Paul Dickson, Marten Thompson, Bob Morton, Brian Barthram, Ray Barnes, Ronnie Faechin, Chris Keith and Geoff Oughton for their help with this book.

And, of course, to my co-author and great friend Arthur McKenzie. We've had some great adventures together all over the world; this book has been another. Great job, as always.

CONTENTS

FOREWORD BY JONNY WILKINSON

I first met Blackie when I came to Newcastle Falcons just after leaving school. We had a team of people like Dean Ryan, Gareth Archer, George Graham and Inga Tuigamala, who were each about 6 ft 4 in. tall and 19 st. – big, aggressive players. Everyone was massive, but during training they would cower when this man, Steve Black – Blackie – would shout and bellow at them. I couldn't work out why, because I hadn't experienced anything like it before. The coaches at my school, physical education teachers or whatever, had always remained in the background, whereas Blackie was so well respected that players didn't want to get on the wrong side of him. It was amazing to see big guys with that kind of fear, and I couldn't work out what was going on at first. All I knew was that if they were staying on his good side, well, so was I.

Then I picked up the odd story and bit of background about him, and as I got the chance to get to know him better I started to realise that he was actually much more than just the conditioning coach; he was the true motivational force of the team. He was also a friend to the players, someone they could lean on who would give them the physical strength and mental confidence necessary to face the pressures of playing sport at this level. Also, as he puts so much into everything he does, those around him are inspired to perform to the best of their ability: there is such a strong desire not to let him down.

The amount of effort that Blackie puts in is certainly reflected in the players' attitudes. He invests so much time in every one of us individually that, while it is always about winning, there is something equally important – playing to your potential, not letting the guy next to you down and reaching your own personal, acceptable level of standards during the game, whether that be in tackling, passing, kicking or giving it your best shot. The result of this attitude is that if you don't do yourself justice, you can win a game and still be very down afterwards, still disappointed. It is those qualities of pride and integrity that he brings out in all of us.

The thing I find most difficult to accept in life and in my profession is letting people down, or the notion that it is OK to do so. I desperately wanted to do justice to my friend Blackie in writing this foreword, but I soon realised that I had put myself in a no-win situation. I owe so much to this one person for his trust, ability and unconditional support, yet I know that whatever message I write now will not cover the funnier, kinder, more incredible and more stupid things he will do tomorrow. Thank you is the best I can do.

Jonny Wilkinson
September 2004

INTRODUCTION BY ARTHUR McKENZIE

When I began my journey with Steve Black in the co-writing of his story, little did I realise it would take over four years to complete. The aim was not a kiss-and-tell but an attempt to give an honest account of what has been an extraordinary life to date.

Having had a close relationship for over 20 years, Steve and I had a mutual trust which enabled us to discuss all aspects of his story without prejudice.

Life is all about moments and without exception everyone I approached to contribute was fulsome in their love and respect for Blackie. The desire to share their moments with him was overwhelming and is a clear indication as to just how much influence he has had and continues to have on so many lives.

He has been described as 'the ultimate man for the moment' and I totally endorse this, for he has that rare quality of being able to make everyone he meets – even though it may be for only a few seconds – feel special, often when he himself is feeling low.

It has been a privilege to be able to share a rare insight into this truly remarkable person – but what a frustrating bugger he can be!

PROLOGUE

I was frustrated, bloody angry and beginning to feel coldly aggressive. I couldn't eat or sleep very well and my blood pressure was shooting through the roof, so I knew I had to bite the bullet or go home. Had I been back in Newcastle upon Tyne giving the Falcons a dressing-room roasting, it would have been easy; but this was surreal. It was only a couple of weeks into the start of the British Lions 2001 tour of Australia and I seemed to be dealing with a bunch of guys – management, coaches and players – many of whom appeared to have hidden and selfish agendas. It seemed to me that these top guns of British and Irish rugby, who were carrying the hopes and pride of our nation, seemed somehow hell-bent on doing everything wrong at every turn.

So, prior to the warm-up match against New South Wales Country

Cockatoos at Coffs Harbour on 26 June 2001, I gathered the lot of them into the dressing-room, locked the door and launched into them.

'Right, I'm going to speak to you all now, before this game, before we go any further on this tour. That includes everybody, and I mean everybody, and you're all going to sit down and you're all going to listen to me.'

As usual, Austin Healey, 'Mister Livewire', was the last to sit, so I rounded on him and screamed, 'Austin, for fuck's sake sit down!' He smiled and took his seat.

I then turned to the film crew who were on tour with us recording a fly-on-the-wall documentary. 'Turn it off, lads. This is for us only, it's got fuck all to do with anyone else. I'm not playing to any cameras, I'm not playing to the gallery. This is for us – here! Nobody else.'

They hesitated.

'Switch it off!'

They hesitated again, but whilst I hadn't threatened them, they could see my fire burning and turned the cameras off.

I was in full flow, reverting to a mindset I'd been in so many times when 'bouncing' in the pubs and clubs of Newcastle upon Tyne in the 1970s. My base instinct was to go round the dressing-room and clip a few, but unfortunately those days were well gone, even though that same violence often simmers just below the surface. Make no mistake about it, however; I could see it in everyone's eyes that my body language was screaming at them as I continued.

'We have a major problem here and we've got to turn it around. The match against Australian 'A' was a fiasco. We made a complete arse of it. We failed because our preparation was shit – and that was our fault. Ours! Coaches and management; not yours. I include myself in that because we should be operating a collective responsibility, so I accept that. For this match, though, it's going to be down to you, the players, to pull us – coaches and management – out the crap!

'What I said at the start of the tour, I meant. I said everyone was equally important and I have respect for everyone and we'll look after everyone and be a proper team. We'll support people and in no way be fair-weather friends. Those who are thought of as the best players will be treated no better than those who are not quite as good, and those in the first team will have the same treatment as those who are out of it.

'But we've all got to pull together and make it happen from now on, and we've all got to go for it, 'cos if we don't, we're fucked!'

The problem was that this hadn't been the case. Almost every famous British and Irish rugby face of 2001 stared in silence as my words drove home. They knew and I knew that this could be a defining moment for the team and tour. I stood for a few seconds in the stony silence and stared back at them, my body language roaring passion and intent. Then I turned and walked out, leaving them to digest my words and hoping they would have a positive impact.

As I sat at the side of the pitch in contemplation, some chastened players and coaches spoke to me individually. The odd one apologised, but it was scrum-half Matt Dawson who really took some of the wind from my sails and showed me exactly where his head was at when he said, 'Blackie, that's the most real thing and passionate thing I've heard from the management on this tour. Why didn't you let the cameras catch it? It would have made great footage for the documentary.'

Still simmering, I stared at him and said, 'It wasn't for the fucking documentary and the rest of the world. It was for you lot! To let you know exactly what I'm thinking, and let you know exactly what should have been happening. It's not a them-and-us thing. It's us, all together.'

Undeterred, as if everything I had said had been a waste of time, he then uttered the classic line, 'But it would have made fantastic television.'

This saddened me, because it underlined just how much some of those players were dancing to the tune of celebrity. It also gave a big hint as to why, four days later, he published a damning newspaper article about management and training. Did he take my words and decide to capitalise on them, or was the article already written?

Whatever the truth, had that camera been on, I'm under no illusion that I would have been made the villain of the piece.

So, that was the theme of my outburst, but there was no going back because I was well and truly part of a rugby circus that was consuming my life, and as I sat at the side of that pitch in Australia I began to wonder how on earth a lad from Benton council estate in Newcastle had ended up screaming at the shocked faces of the cream of British rugby.

Chapter One

READY, STEADY, GO!

Discretion is not the better part of biography.
Lytton Strachey

Embarking on the process of telling the story of your life is like climbing a mountain: there are gentle slopes, sharp inclines and incredible views, but also jagged rocks, the odd viper and danger lurking round every bend because everything is subjective and clouded with emotion. To give an honest account means exposing and confronting your weaknesses, which can be humbling and frightening. Although I regard myself as having been incredibly lucky to have had such an interesting journey to date, it certainly hasn't all been plain sailing.

While reflecting on the times and events which shaped me, however, my intention here is not to write a kind of exposé. There is little purpose in opening up old wounds, especially those relating to my family. Events stick in your mind and there were some unpleasant times – I can't paint it any other way. However, as I've become older, and hopefully wiser. I'm increasingly aware of other people's feelings, especially those nearest and dearest, and those I call true friends.

BLACKIE

So, the secret is out. Yes, I admit it, I'm a Geordie! I know the tabloids think I'm Pavarotti's love child, but I was born on 22 February 1957 in Newcastle General Hospital. It was an exciting era, as the north-east of England was emerging from a long period of depression and austerity after the end of the Second World War. My generation is now affectionately referred to as the 'baby boomers'. The industrial wealth of the area meant we were entering a period of full employment and there was great hope for a bright and prosperous future. The swinging '60s were just around the corner and it seemed that anything was possible. It was a terrific period in which to have been born.

My parents, Joan and Peter Black, were in the same class together as children, then met again some years later and married in 1955 at the age of 23. Mam was a petite, raven-haired beauty who had inherited her half-Italian mother's good looks, and my dad was a slim, athletic Gregory Peck lookalike, so they made a handsome couple.

We first lived on Walker Road in the lower east end of the city, but when I was six months old we moved to a two-bedroom council flat in Fontburn Place, Benton, a working-class area on the outskirts of Newcastle. This estate was directly opposite the Ministry of Pensions and National Insurance, a huge government complex of prefabricated buildings to which armies of pen-pushers would throng like termites on their way to work. It's still there today, but is now surrounded by razor wire and tight security, whereas back then it was a natural playground. There was a strong sense of community in Benton, and we were lucky to live a stone's throw away from my nana and granddad on my mother's side.

My early memories are of fun, happy, loving times and, although I've moved, I still regard that area as my spiritual home. I vividly recall playing outside with my friends, doing the things all kids do. I was a lively handful for Mam, who needed to keep a constant eye on me or I'd escape and go exploring the nearby streets and gardens. She'd often find me playing with my toys in the middle of the busy road outside our house, oblivious to the fact that I'd brought the traffic to a standstill.

We were a conventional family, well ordered and always extremely clean; Mam seemed to be endlessly employed at the washing machine. We were brought up to have good manners and we would always sit down to have meals together as a family. Food was wholesome: mince and dumplings, shepherd's pie, plenty of potatoes, cabbage, peas, sprouts, sausage and mash, that type of thing. Sunday mornings were reserved for a traditional fry-up.

Television programmes that stick in my mind from that era were *The Lone Ranger, Zorro, Wagon Train, Rawhide, 77 Sunset Strip* and *Tales of the Riverbank*. I was never a big *Crackerjack!* fan, but I loved Johnny Morris, a clever man who introduced children to the world of animals, in which I became intensely interested. I had a tortoise and a guinea pig called Queenie, though it turned out to be a bloke! There were always plenty of toys – Meccano, a Hornby railway, soldiers and animals with a plywood zoo. My imagination was always overactive and it hasn't stopped since. Sometimes I even dream I'm a fitness coach!

Family unity played an important part in those early years, and while later events shattered that ideal, the principles I learned from my parents and grandparents were the vital foundation on which I was to build my life. Like everyone else, my parents worked hard to provide a good home for their family. They both had a basic education, but at that time few people from their background went on to further education. The priority was to get out there and find a job. So, on leaving school at 15, Dad began work as a warehouseman at the Co-op and later he went to work as a stevedore at the docks in Newcastle with his two brothers, Tony and Dennis.

All my dad's family had been good sportsmen. He played football quite well, but really excelled in the boxing ring and got himself a reputation within the fight fraternity. His brother Dennis took his love of the sport a step further and turned professional. Unfortunately, Dennis was put in the ring with experienced fighters too early, and because of that, didn't fulfil his potential. Interestingly, years later, when I had a dabble in the world of professional boxing, my manager's father, Herbie Jackson, had actually worked with Uncle Dennis and rated him very highly. Unfortunately, the hard world that is professional boxing didn't compensate Dennis from a financial standpoint and he worked all his life. That life ended tragically at the age of 48 when, after returning home from the Corner House pub one night, he tripped over an electric fire and burned to death.

BLACKIE

Mam's home background was solid working class. She had led a sheltered existence and on leaving school her parents wanted her to go into the garment trade, which she did for a while, but found it boring and ended up working in Fenwick's Newcastle store. When I was born, she did what all mothers were expected to do at the time and became a hard-working housewife. My sister Roz came along five years later, so her hands were pretty full, though my nana was a constant source of support. When my sister arrived, we needed a larger house, so we shifted round the corner in Benton to Fairways Avenue on the Fairways estate.

My happy childhood continued on the Fairways estate until, dramatically, when I was seven, my parents separated and everything changed, most noticeably my relationship with my father. Up until then my dad would take me to football matches and other sporting events when he was playing. He was a fine athlete and obviously my physical attributes come from his side of the family, but, in those early years, the more he tried to involve me in sport the less I was interested. It's a typical story, really: a father pushing his child into those things which give him most pleasure and the child resisting, developing his or her own interests in life. I just hope the success I have had in my recent years has given him some pleasure.

Dad didn't drink until he was in his mid-20s, which in Newcastle is incredible, but at that time his circumstances changed. When he went to work at the docks, I think, he, like many before, and after, fell in with some bad influences. Up until that time, he'd been fit and active, but he was soon to change, and not for the better. The routine at the company he worked for was very much empty the ship, then off for a pint. He soon got into the habit of blokes together doing their wages in and coming home with very little to see the family through the week, which not only put the pressure on the family budget, but also severely strained relations between him and my mum. I've no doubt he was a victim of his environment and that social time, and who am I to cast judgement, but his change of behaviour had a profound influence on all of our lives and that continues to this day. Anyway my mum, sister and I upped and left Dad, though we only moved along the street to my nana's. After that, I only ever had minimal contact with him.

From then on I became naturally protective of my mam and younger sister Roz. I can't think of Roz in any other way than being my little sister even though she's now married to Kevin with two lovely lads of her own, Tony and Paul. Tony is a very talented, nationally-ranked go-kart racer, while Paul can be seen racing around the golf courses of the North-east with his dad, Kevin. Neither of them are nationally-ranked golfers . . . allegedly! In all seriousness, I'm immensley proud of her and her family. I am immensely proud of her and her family. She inherited my parents' good looks and was much sought after as a model when she was younger. Being naturally protective, and probably because my dad wasn't around to make these decisions, I once prevented her going to Paris for a modelling interview at a critical time in her life because I was worried that she would get mixed up with 'the wrong types'. When you see what I got up to in later life, it shows both how astute and equally hypocritical I was at that time. Though it was done with the best of intentions, it's something I often regret.

My nana was one of the finest human beings I've ever met. She was a very strong, intelligent woman, extremely practical and able to manage on very little money. The house was always spotless and she would leave little humorous notes all over the place saying, 'Please put towels back on the rack after use', that type of thing, which was really for my benefit as I was the only messy one. My nana had strong principles and faith, and said her prayers every night before going to bed. She brought my sister and me up to do the same and taught me to pray that all the family were safe and well. Due to my Catholic upbringing, my Christian faith has always played a very important role in my life and I have been able to put it to good effect in my approach to fitness coaching. For international rugby games, it's a ritual for the management to go for a drink and a pleasant meal together the night before a match. While that's an important social tradition to bind the coaching team together, it's something that I've never participated in as I don't want anything to deflect or cloud my mind, and silly as it may sound, I worry that the coaches might have just too good a time, which could take the edge off the next day's performance. Even to this day, wherever I am in the world, I will make time to visit a church to sit there in the peace and quiet, and enjoy the solitude. It probably has less to do with religion now and is more of a method which I use to help me focus. Simplistic, perhaps, but it works for me.

I was extremely close to my nana, and in some ways, because of the family situation, she was more like my mam while my mam was like another sister to me. My nana and I could argue like hell, but never fell out and my respect for her was, and still is, immense. She had an enormous influence on me and I adored her. Just before she died in 1990, I managed to take her on a week's trip to Italy as a special treat for us both. Even though her roots were in that country, she'd never been before or even been on an aeroplane, and we visited Venice, Rome, Florence – the lot. It was marvellous and I treasure every minute I spent with her. When she passed away, I was shattered, and even felt angry and guilty that I was unable to do more for her. I still think of her every day. She comes into my head to remind me of the path I am attempting to follow in life and I miss her.

Both my parents are still alive and I see Mam as often as I can and phone her daily. She's done so very much for me in my life and I could never begin to repay her, other than to say that I love her very much. I've been trying to look after her ever since my dad left. I don't really have any contact with Dad, and only wish we could have developed a better relationship. I do bump into him occasionally and we smile and are civilised, then we both get on with our own lives. Sad, really, because I know deep down that the situation isn't going to change. I genuinely wish it could, but as Sinatra said, 'That's Life!'

I'm talking about my son here, and yet he's still my real hero. Ever since he was little he's been a big emotional softie, very caring. When he was a boy, he was small and thin, but always like greased lightning. When the family split up, he said, 'You don't need anybody else 'cos you've got me.'

When I was working late in Newcastle, he would come and wait for me without asking so that he could take me home. My friends used to say they wouldn't put up with it, but I thought it was great. I loved it! Stephen has always been very protective of his family, especially his sister Roz, and he used to guard her pram, walking round and round it in case anybody came near. A lad in the neighbourhood used to taunt him from the other side of the road and shout, 'Stephen Black's sister's got a face like a monkey.' Stephen would chase him, but could never catch him. If he had, goodness knows what would have happened.

Later on, when Roz got older, if she wanted to do something, it was no good me agreeing to it, because Stephen made all the decisions. That's how much of an influence he has always had on the family.

When he left the Welsh rugby team, it was very sad, because he'd given them everything he'd got. I watched the Scotland–Wales match on telly and, even though they won, I knew what he'd be going through. At the end, everybody was celebrating, but there was no Stephen to run out and give them all a big cuddle – he had already quietly left the ground. But that's what he brought to the team – a sense of family and love.

I'm always amazed at the number of people who know him. When we were coming out of Macy's department store in New York, a man stopped Steve, clapped him on the back and told him what a wonderful job he had done at Wales. When I asked Stephen who it was, he said, 'I don't know. It happens all the time.'

As a son, I couldn't ask for anything more because he's always there, come rain or shine, with that marvellous sense of fun. It just seems natural for him to make silly jokes about anything. He brightens my day. He's lovely!

Joan Black – mother

After my parents separated, everything changed and, instead of rejecting it, sport became my life. From that moment on, I was consumed by every aspect of physical achievement.

St Stephen's Primary School, Longbenton, was great. I couldn't get enough of it and always got on well with the other pupils and the teachers. On sports day in junior school, the priest, Father Crumbly, would hand out packets of sweets as prizes, and I used to win everything. The other kids would whinge, 'Sir, sir, Stephen Black's winning all the sweets, sir . . . it's not fair.' But it was fair, because even at that age I always saw myself as a winner. In one football game I had scored six in the first half and the teacher came over and whispered, 'No need to score any more, Black.'

Looking back, I believe this is why many kids nowadays don't have the killer instinct . . . it's been bred out of them. I would set up street Olympics, pretending to be Kip Keino in the mile and win it, just like him, in the last 100 yards, or David Bedford, running away from the rest of the pack early in the race. My dreams were always big, and still are, because without dreams we might as well be dead.

BLACKIE

At the age of 11, I was awarded a scholarship to the best Catholic grammar school in Newcastle, St Cuthbert's, which was a major family success. I remember that first day well, as I proudly set off for school in my cap, blazer, nice tie and short pants. My cherubic demeanour lasted for about 45 minutes until a kid at the back of the class began taking the mick because I was the only one wearing short pants. I calmly walked to the back and chinned him. Father Walsh, head disciplinarian, said, 'You've made a lovely start, son.'

'Thanks, Father,' I said, but I don't think he meant it that way.

That auspicious introduction aside, life at St Cuthbert's continued in the same vein as it had at St Stephen's and again I got on with pupils and teachers alike, though there was a brief spell when the spectre of bullying reared its ugly head. Some lads came from another school to wait for me outside, so I developed a way of dealing with them. I recognised if there were three or four of them and they were older than me, there was every chance I wasn't going to win. So I would either talk my way out of it or run away. Then I would work out how I could find them one on one, when the story would be different. This method of quiet planning served me well in later life when fighting became an obsession. I was never a bully, though; in fact, I was always ridiculously over the top in trying to be the good guy with the white hat, always a hero. That's the way I justified it to myself, anyway. I got into loads of scuffles, supposedly trying to help people, but that was probably an excuse to fight, 'cos I loved it! My heroes were Muhammad Ali, Sonny Liston, Floyd Patterson, people like that, and when I got into a fight, I'd pretend I was them.

Boxing was my first passion and I got so into it that I began taking a pair of gloves to school, coaching other kids in 'the noble art'. It caused bother, though. The headmaster eventually summoned Mam and told her to stop me running my boxing academy in the schoolyard because parents were complaining that their children were returning home with black eyes and bloody noses. Unfortunately, I had a tendency to punch them in the face as soon as they started putting the gloves on!

As well as boxing, I loved football. I watched Newcastle United and was a huge fan, but I also just loved the game, whoever was playing it, especially the greats of the day. George Best was my favourite. He was such a gifted man – the stuff dreams are made of. As a young footballer, I modelled myself on him. With his ability to beat people then change angle with flair, he was the most skilful player I had ever seen. I used to practise moving one way then the other, turning back on myself, surging and changing pace in an attempt to emulate him. Incredibly, his early influence on me helped Jonny Wilkinson, the England and Falcons fly-half, many years later to develop his movement drills.

The sports masters at St Cuthbert's were very good and I soon settled into a cycle of football in the winter months, and cricket and athletics throughout the summer. During my first couple of years in senior school, Stan Eardley coached our football squad and we were very successful. We worked well as a team, but not in a way that stifled individual flair. As a result, everyone enjoyed the games and our winning results reflected that positive state of mind. His encouraging approach to coaching definitely struck a chord with me and I still believe that most people respond better to a kind word than a kick up the backside.

When Tony Knox took over the team, it was a different story. With the benefit of hindsight, I now realise that his tough approach probably helped focus my sporting competitiveness and that he was trying to stop my ego getting out of hand, but at the time it often felt as though he was singling me out unfairly. The following incident, during my early teens, illustrates our relationship perfectly.

The Newcastle Boys had played Berwick. We'd beaten them 3–0 in the Cup and I'd scored all three goals. I got a great write-up in the local 'Football Pink' and was excited because influential club scouts were asking about me. The form teacher stood me up in front of class to say how well I'd done and everyone was treating me like a star. Later that week, the team against Rutherford Grammar School was published and I looked at it in amazement. There was the team, then a line, then the substitutes, and another line . . . then Black! So I went to see Mr Knox.

'Excuse me, sir, the team's on the board, but I'm not injured.'

'And why would you think I would think you're injured, Black?'

'Well, I'm not picked, sir. I'm not even a substitute.'

'Exactly, because we want to keep your feet firmly on the ground, son.'

And with that he walked off. I was stunned, but his attitude actually fuelled my determination to do even better. It may well be that Tony Knox was right after all, even though his management techniques left a bit to be desired.

Heroes and role models such as teachers are vital in shaping young lives. They have an enormous influence on the youngsters who look up to them, and the responsibility that goes with such influence is therefore equally huge. It clearly comes with the territory, so when I witness behaviour unbecoming of icons it makes me shudder, as I believe it can only have a knock-on effect in society as a whole. To give an example, Muhammad Ali, as I've already said, was a major hero of mine when I was a young lad, so when I saw him being interviewed by Michael Parkinson I was extremely disappointed and shocked when he began bullying Parkinson verbally and talking about white devils. I didn't want to see him like that; it tarnished my image of this fine athlete.

Today, sport has become the new religion in many people's lives. Those who are successful can make incredible amounts of money and many sportsmen have been elevated to iconic status. Their image is used to sell everything from sunglasses to drinks, but in many cases it seems to be money in, brains out, as, with monotonous regularity, they end up on the front pages of the tabloids for behaviour totally unbecoming of a so-called hero.

The responsibility doesn't only lie with them, however. To take footballers as an example, many of the young kids who enter the game are inexperienced, poorly educated and ill-equipped to deal with the money and fame suddenly thrust upon them. The clubs who sign them therefore have a major responsibility to educate their players and be clear about the standards of behaviour expected of them. Surely it isn't beyond the wit of man to work that one out?

Heroes can also be found closer to home and three other figures who played a major role in shaping my attitude were my granddad on my mother's side and his sons, Uncle Billy and Uncle Keith. Granddad was a bricklayer and stood for all the things that were right in life. He died when I was three years old, but the image of him the family portrayed and the stories they told about him turned him into a hero in my eyes. He was apparently a really tough man with a heart of gold and I wanted to emulate his James Cagney style. He was fair-minded and lived according to his principles about what was right and wrong. He saw life clearly in terms of black and white, and I tried to follow that approach, though, now, many years later, I realise life isn't like that and there are lots of shades of grey. He possessed an uncompromising work ethic and never took a day off sick. He shaped the man I have become today, and the principles passed down to me were honesty, reliability, the importance of taking pride in everything you do and always trying your best.

Uncle Billy and Uncle Keith, the other prominent male figures in my life, were obviously highly influenced by the same legacy. Both were hard-working and had made excellent progress in their chosen careers. Billy worked in the building trade and was responsible for the building of the Odeon Cinema in Leicester Square in London; Keith held a senior managerial role in the mining industry. They provided me with concrete examples of succeeding in a competitive environment and their influence extended into my early forays in sport. Unlike some dads or uncles, Billy in particular would never let me win anything if we played any games. He made me fight for every goal, every run, every inch. Even when playing makeshift golf with a lump of wood, I always had to win on merit.

I've always been close to Stephen. He is the most emotional human being I've ever known, and that's what makes him so special. I'm absolutely delighted at his success, because if anyone deserves it, it's him. He works so hard, too hard at times, but can't say no to anybody. One of these days he's going to have to say no or his desire to please and give of himself will catch him up.

Ever since he was a child, he's had a thirst for knowledge. My wife Eva and I would take him camping and I can vividly remember him sitting on a little chair outside the tent at night going through the football results. When I told him to come in, he would refuse until he'd finished them off. It was amazing, as he'd commit all the information to memory: who'd scored, in which minute. He was always reading books and had this incredible desire to be a zoologist. At night, we'd sit up late arguing and debating, and if he thought he was right, he would rush to find a book with a reference to prove his point.

I always taught him to be a winner on his own account and when we were playing games I would never just let him win. He hates losing! He takes it personally if the team lose, as if it's a slight on his character. My father was his real big hero, though. A real hard man who stood as a good example in the rules of life, as did my mother, whom Stephen dearly loved.

One of the most incredible things about Stephen is the way he is loved by people right across the board. Perhaps this little story illustrates what I mean. A few years ago when he worked at the YMCA in North Shields, a lad called Jason got into a load of bother. He had some major psychological problems, and he was immensely big and strong. One day he went berserk with a gun and a siege took place in the YMCA. It was an extremely dangerous situation, but Stephen talked him into giving up the gun and saved the day. Some time later, I met this lad at Rake Lane Hospital and he told me Stephen was the only person who could deal with him, and went on to say he loved him so much and asked if I could get some photographs of him. I managed to get some cuttings and took them down and as we sat on a seat in the grounds of the hospital he looked at the cuttings and started to cry. It was an extremely traumatic and touching moment, but it just shows the effect Stephen has on people.

Stephen has always given me and Eva incredible pleasure and he continues to do so. He hasn't reached the limit of his powers as a person or a coach yet, despite his success, and when he finds his real niche I think he'll go on to even greater things. When he finally decides on what he wants to do, he'll go for it full belt . . . no half-measures with Stephen.

Billy Hall – uncle

Another big influence in my young life was my mates. I still see some of my pals from that time and was best man to both Peter Ashcroft and Lawrence (Lar) Fawcett. Other friends included Tommy Hunter, Ian Mutire, Des Smith, Harry Craggs, George Burgess and David Welford. Rob Shields and Michael Cairns were both close friends and sparring partners as I sharpened my fighting skills on a regular basis.

We played a lot of football outside of school in those days as well, honing our skills while using jumpers for goalposts. The games were very competitive and used to go on for hours, and there was an amazing age mix of players, from kids of ten up to guys who would have a game before taking their girlfriends or wives out to the pub! There was no quarter asked for or given and it was great for building your confidence. From impromptu games in the park, some of us eventually made our way into youth and pub teams playing in formal leagues.

I made my first foray into senior football at the age of 13, playing with my mate Peter Ashcroft for Benton Club, a Sunday morning team run by Bobby Shields. It wouldn't be allowed now, but I'd always hung out with lads older and bigger than myself. It seemed natural to me and I relished the challenge.

One of my friends at the time was a lad called Jimmy Bradford, who has gone on to fame and fortune as the actor and singer Jimmy Nail. I'm glad to say, and I know Jimmy won't mind, that I'm pleased his acting/singing/writing talents far exceed his football skills! It's great to see what he's made of himself and I'm proud we shared the same background. It shows that if you are determined, dreams can become a reality. I occasionally bump into Jimmy on the celebrity charity fundraising event circuit. It's always great to see him and have a chance to reminisce about our youth on the Fairways estate.

I first met Steve – little Steve, as he was then, though of course I wouldn't dare call him that today! – when we were kids growing up together on the Fairways estate in Benton. He was about seven, I guess, and I remember a kid with a permanently quizzical look on his face. He wanted answers, wanted to know. He had dark hair, an open face and a friendly smile. Thick-set. He looked a handful even back then! The main thing that sticks in my memory, though, is that, apart from being a really pleasant lad, he was obviously very smart. The big lads didn't like that kind of thing – a nipper with more savvy than they possessed. It made them all nervous. Steve would go on to make them even more nervous.

Life took us off on our own separate odysseys and, like a lot of old friends, Steve is someone I don't see very often these days, but that's never a problem when we do meet; the fun's in the catching up.

I'm often asked about Geordie characteristics: the mental make-up, the mindset, what is it exactly that makes us the way we are? Difficult one to answer, that, but if you're looking for the physical embodiment, for the real deal, Steve Black fits the bill pretty well.

Jimmy Nail – childhood pal

I was doing well at the football when a guy called Nobby Hall spotted me and took me for a trial at Hull City when I was 13. He had concerns about my size as I was quite small at the time, and both he and Cliff Britton, the manager, decided not to take me on. Their argument was that my mother was small so there was little chance of me growing, despite the fact I told them my dad and his side of the family were well built.

After the Benton Club, therefore, I played for most of the other teams in the Benton and Longbenton areas: The Benton Black Bull, The Innisfree Social Club, The Viking Public House, The Newton Public House, The Killingworth Arms . . . the list is endless. I then graduated to teams like North Heaton Sports Club, The Byker St Peter's Middle Club, Wallsend Athletic, Stanley Limited and Longbenton Football Club. Come to think of it, I've had more clubs than Jack Nicklaus, but this provided me with great experience and taught me how to integrate with different people, how to fit into a team, how to get a team to play as a unit. I was learning constantly, even if I didn't realise it at the time. People began saying I was the best talent they'd seen since George Best. Unfortunately, for whatever reason, I didn't reach that potential as a player.

Inevitably, as I'd gained a reputation for being not only a decent player but also a good, hard trainer, the teams I played for generally asked me to do some coaching for them as well. It was never a chore and I found that I had the knack of controlling a bunch of guys while training, even if they were several years older than me. Looking back, it seems as though this path in life was always mapped out for me, as one time when my Uncle Billy took me on holiday to Staines I went on the wander as usual and got lost. A bloke approached Billy and asked, 'Are you looking for the little lad?'

'Aye,' said Billy.

'Well, I've been watching him. He's in the middle of the football field over there, telling the two teams how to play.'

Sure enough, there I was, aged seven, directing the two teams in a forceful way with total belief in what I was saying. So the coaching bug was in me even then!

As the lads I was coaching started to get fitter, their wives and girlfriends asked me if I would start a fitness class for them, too. It soon escalated and I was coaching groups of men and women all over the North-east in youth clubs, church halls, pubs and schools. All this started when I was in my late teens and continued until I was in my early 30s. The lessons I learned during this time would prove invaluable in my later career.

One thing I realised early on was that humour, if used properly, can be a very effective device in most situations. It can be part of the subculture of a team, used as a way to bond the players together, or it can be used to defuse stressful situations and relieve tension. I have to admit, though, that sometimes my mate Lawrence Fawcett and I did take things a bit far. Lar was probably my closest friend, one of the hardest and most honest workers I've ever known. We got on well because we shared a ridiculous sense of humour and did the craziest things together. Once when we were playing in a Cup match, there were only seconds to go and I went to take a corner. Lar and I had it all planned. I picked up the ball and ran away with it. Lar had the car engine running and we took off. On another occasion, playing for Wallsend Athletic, the manager asked us to pick up two new players for a six o'clock start. We did so in Lar's car, put them in the back seat and clicked the child locks on. Then we stopped, took a couple of deckchairs from the boot and began reading newspapers at the side of the road. The two lads went daft in the back, and when we eventually got to the match we were 20 minutes late. They tried to explain to the manager what we had been doing, but we convinced him they were a couple of crackpots.

When I was asked if I would like to contribute a few words about my relationship with one Stephen Peter David Black, I was of course delighted to do so, as it would be an honour to share some moments from my friendship with Stevie, which has spanned some 35 years. However, after thinking about it, when you are talking or writing about Blackie, a few words are never going to be enough.

With those sentiments in mind, I do believe I am in a position to observe, through the written word, that Blackie is without doubt a complete and utter raving lunatic. The reader may think, 'What an awful thing to say'; however, be assured, Steve will accept it as the compliment of compliments. To explain this, one must understand that he is just different from the ordinary guy on the street. He will do the opposite to what the mainstream of opinion will expect. He has done so all of his life and will continue to do so for the remainder. That's what makes him so special. Here are just a selection of some of the capers he and I got up to over the years.

Whilst driving back from Sunday morning football, we would pick our 'victims', pull up alongside them and proceed to introduce ourselves as scriptwriters for some then in-vogue comedy programme on TV. We would explain that we were in the area carrying out research and ask whether he or she had any new jokes we could use on the programme, with the promise that if they were used we would send them a cheque for £20 a joke. The 'victims' would then either immediately reel off joke after joke, mentally counting up £20, £40, £60 and so on, or stand embarrassed for a little while until greed got the better of them. We would then thank them very much indeed, enquire if they had ever considered a career in show business, and take their names and addresses for the expected cheque.

Which football manager would serve his players large slices of fruitcake and tea in china cups at half-time after a 'not so good' first-half performance? Blackie would – and did!

For a short while, the 'professor' decided he would become the great white hope of the professional boxing world. The scene is set – a packed house at the Mayfair in Newcastle. The gladiators enter the arena to deafening applause. The adrenalin is racing through Blackie's body. This is the moment he was born for (or so he thinks). Formalities over – ding, the bell goes for round one. 'Remember what you have been taught,' he thinks to himself. Jab and move, jab and move, feel your opponent out, look for an opening. Those thoughts last as long as it takes for the other guy to land a blow, then the dreaded red mist comes down over the great white hope's eyes. For the remainder of this round and the next couple, Blackie is attempting to detach his opponent's head from his body at every single opportunity. More by luck than any great boxing skill, this guy evades every torpedo thrown at him. Eventually, tiredness seeps through Blackie's body. He is now walking through a sea of molasses, his gloved hands now blocks of concrete down by his side. The opponent, sensing this, moves in for the kill – BANG! – Blackie's huge legs bambified in an instant, a swarm of bees buzzing in his brain. For a second he can't understand why the world looks different. The referee starts the count; Blackie tries to drag himself from the canvas to no avail. One would think at this juncture he would be down in more than one sense of the word. Not at all. Steve peers through the bottom rope to a guy in the ringside seats and calmly asks what time it is because there is a great late-night film on and tells him he doesn't want to miss it. Priceless!

On a more serious note, Steve Black is without doubt the greatest exponent of his profession in this country, if not the world, today. I truly believe this is no exaggeration. What Steve has achieved so far is truly amazing and there is no end in sight. The greatest compliment I can pay him is to say that if there are any professional sportsmen/women reading this, irrespective of what stage of their careers they find themselves at this moment in time, do yourself the biggest favour of your lives and get in touch with Stevie. I guarantee he will achieve for you improvements in yourself that you never thought possible.

Like I said, when talking or writing about Stephen Peter David Black, a few words are never going to be enough. From a personal point of view, I am immensely proud of him. He is a wonderful, kind and caring human being and a fantastic friend.

Lawrence P. Fawcett (Lar) – childhood friend

I seemed to have been playing football since I came out of the womb and became very skilled at it, but I also had this quality of rubbing people up the wrong way. My biggest problem was my volatile short fuse. Playing the game itself didn't present any problems at all. There was no need to become too physical. I used skill, but this would annoy other players and the only way they could stop me was by kicking me. Normally I could avoid their efforts, but sometimes, on an off-day, they hacked me and I retaliated the only way I knew – by knocking them down. I would then lose control and was sent off many times.

I played as much as I could at that time for lots of clubs . . . have boots, will travel! Everyone thought I was much older than I was. I was approached by Billy Todd, manager of Stanley United in the Northern League, who seemed impressed and invited me to meet him in the café of Parrish's department store on Shields Road. It sounds crazy now, as a cup of tea and a bun wasn't exactly the greatest incentive in the world, but my stomach dictated and I signed for him. Actually, to be fair to Billy, I could have had any cream cake and a piece of quiche had I demanded it! Billy 'Big Time' or what?!

On my first day at the club, Billy gathered everybody together in the dressing-room and told them, 'I've brought Blackie along. He's an experienced player who's done it all and will provide the steadying influence we need.' I thought he was kidding because I had just turned 17 at the time. I did look a lot older then. In fact, I look younger now!

In addition to all these other teams, I'd been playing for Newcastle Schoolboys throughout my teens, then for the county, and was finally picked up by Newcastle United, playing for the youth team at 17. I stayed there for a year and really thought I was on the brink of making it . . . but unfortunately it wasn't to be and I was offered the opportunity to play either at Hartlepool or Darlington. No disrespect to either of these teams, but neither of them seemed the best location to launch the career of the next George Best, so, with my pride hurt, I declined the offer, turned my back on the prospect of being a professional footballer and got on with the rest of my life. Little did I know that years later I would return to this famous club as a conditioning coach under Kevin Keegan during their renaissance period.

I'd left school at 16 with two O levels in my back pocket. From 11 to 15, I had serious ambitions about going to university, but eventually decided it wasn't to be, with the associated financial implications and the fact that the job market was pretty buoyant at that time. With hindsight, I probably decided against it because my career ambitions were changing all the time.

St Cuthbert's had a reputation for moving their pupils into white-collar employment as opposed to manual work, so in November 1973 I was taken on as a trainee accountant at British Engines in the east end of the city. I don't kid myself – I only got the job because I'd attended the same prestigious school as the chief accountant who interviewed me and who had also been in my house at that school.

British Engines was steady, respectable employment. Unfortunately I found accountancy boring, but working at British Engines did provide an opportunity to further my education on day-release to Newcastle College in Bath Lane. There I passed the equivalent of a further five O levels and an ONC (Ordinary National Certificate) in business studies. Even after two years' study, I was psychologically no closer to making it as an accountant because my focus was always on sport. But there was also another side of my life that was to intervene and interrupt this fledgling academic journey.

Education is a marvellous thing. I tried it once, as did Blackie. I don't think we were meant for the esteemed corridors of Oxford or Cambridge, on account of the fact that the general consensus of the teachers at St Cuthbert's Grammar School was, 'You boys will amount to nothing.'

I was the after-lunch comedian on the day that the new stand at the Falcons Rugby Club was opened in 2003. I entertained the builders and their management, and I was proud that they laughed and enjoyed my routine. When I was done, I looked over to the other side of the pitch to see Blackie working with top professional sportsmen on a top professional sports ground, a man revered in his chosen field, and I was proud of him.

I am fairly sure that I am good at what I do and I am damn sure that he is. Education is a fantastic, important thing, but moulds must be broken. It's a fine thing to say, 'If I had my life over I wouldn't change a thing!' I personally wouldn't, and I'm guessing that Steve Black would probably say the same.

Brendan Healey – (failed O level Spanish) performer and lifelong friend

Chapter Two

THE BLACK (AND BLUE) YEARS

When shall we live, if not now?

M.F.K Fisher

Similar to the time when I walked away from the Millennium Stadium after resigning from my position with the Welsh rugby team, I can pinpoint the moment in my youth when my life changed forever. Even though I was only 16, I was gaining a reputation in Benton for various reasons . . . boxing; football; being able to handle myself. In many ways I was probably regarded as a bit of a character. The guy who organised the disco at the local Corner House Pub in Newcastle approached me. He said he had a gig on Sunday night and asked if I would come down to make sure there was no trouble. It seemed like it would be a good laugh and a good way of earning a few bob, and, of course, in my mind I was Sugar Ray Leonard and well up to the job. It was a new adventure and I wandered around the pub all togged up, feeling important, but without a clue about what was expected of me.

Most of the evening was pretty uneventful, though there was a bit of a fight during the dancing. I didn't really know how to stop it, but figured if I chinned both parties pretty quickly that would stop it and hopefully others would recognise that if they started similar trouble, they would get the same treatment. I jumped in with both feet, sorted it, enjoyed it and a style developed from there. Actually, the guy who employed me, Jimmy Roe, is a good pal to this day but he tells me that, instead of stopping trouble, I used to cause it. I'm sure he's joking!

The Corner House soon became a regular gig and as time went by there were parties and lock-ins to which I was invited. The local 'faces' used the pub as an after-hours watering hole and though at first I didn't realise who they were, I noticed that others seemed to be in awe of these people. I got to know them when I became established on the doors, but at the time I was probably just regarded as just some canny young kid hanging around.

I began to develop a reputation for being able to handle myself and everything took off from there. On one particular night I chinned a load in the Corner House, then went to a party/disco in Jesmond at the Imperial Hotel and had to sort out a fight there. Then it was on to a club called Billy Bottos on Shields Road to continue the process. Things were getting out of control, but, hand on heart, I loved the attention and the power that came with the reputation I was beginning to acquire.

I was working at British Engines during the day and I became a close friend of Geoff Watson, a terrific judoist. We both had a barmy sense of humour and got along like a house on fire, so we began training together and generally egging each other on. He knew I'd been on the door at the Corner House and asked if I fancied working with him at a place in Newcastle called the Playground on Westgate Road. Naive as hell, I was definitely up for it, and, next thing, there I was preening myself among the bright lights with the really big lads.

The Playground disco was regarded as one of the most notorious spots in town, where villains and various other characters gathered, and I soon found out there'd been a vicious gang murder there not long before. Here was me 16, Geoff 17; we didn't know anything or anybody and we were setting ourselves up for trouble. Due to the fearsome reputation of the place, any intelligent person, hard or not, would have made an informed decision not to go near it with a bargepole, but as we didn't have a clue, we didn't know there was anything to be scared of. It didn't take long for us to suss the situation out, though, when two members of what turned out to be a very well-known, violent family approached the door.

'Is "X" in?'

I knew the name of the man they wanted because people had been speaking about him. Apparently he'd been involved in a recent murder. 'No,' says I. 'He's not allowed in.'

But they persisted. 'We think he is in.'

'Look, I've just said he isn't,' I smiled at them. After all, I was telling the truth and didn't know them from Adam.

Then came the magic words: 'Just tell him I've got a bullet for him, will you?'

I giggled and thought, 'Bullet?'

He then opened his coat, produced a handgun and pointed it straight at me. 'Just tell him, son.'

It was a surreal situation. I was just a kid who'd never faced anything like this before and couldn't really comprehend what was going on. It turned out that the man I'd had the conversation with actually shot and injured somebody outside the Waterloo pub just across the road that same night. The police came and asked if I'd been threatened, but I realised that discretion was the better part of valour and said I didn't have a clue what they were talking about. My instincts served me well and the next day a stranger came to the pub and asked, 'Is Steve Black here?'

'Aye, that's me,' I answered.

He handed over a large bottle of whisky. 'From the lads, to thank you for last night.'

'But I didn't do anything,' I laughed.

'Aye, and that's why y'getting it.'

As a postscript, the two men in question went on to continue their life of violence, committing atrocious crimes. Both went to prison and one of them came to a horrible end after being battered with a baseball bat.

I was learning the rules very quickly and came face to face with a reality I never knew existed – a reality that was to dominate my life for some years to come. One night as a doorman stretched to two, three, then six nights a week. It was fascinating meeting all these different characters. It was an extremely heady, exciting atmosphere and I was totally seduced by it. I think being so young at the time I was able to burn the candle at both ends, although I'd be looking at that time through rose-tinted spectacles if I didn't say that once in a while I was so tired that British Engines had to get by without me for a couple of days as I recuperated. It was a strange situation, really, as I was very much the junior office worker during the day, and became the 'main man' at night. I remember one occasion when the order of those personality characteristics got a bit mixed up. It was during the works' five-a-side football competition and I was representing the softies from the office. We played a team from the factory, one of whom was viewed as the hard man of the works. During the course of the game, he kicked, barged and punched everyone on our team other than me. I knew it was only a matter of time before it was my turn and so it came to pass. I instinctively turned into my night character and remember the astonished looks on everyone's faces when he tried to bully me and I knocked him out before carrying him to the side of the pitch. I also recall quite theatrically telling the referee, 'We can get on with the game now. I don't think he'll be causing us any more trouble.' There was a recognisable difference to his attitude pre- and post-knockout whenever he visited to borrow a chair for a union meeting or simply to pass the time of day.

I also found at this time, whilst being the same loving relative and friend, I didn't suffer fools gladly and was probably more confrontational than I'd ever been. But a consequence of that was that people stopped provoking me, whoever they were.

Then someone came along who was to become a major influence in my life. I'll diplomatically call him 'John'. He turned up at the door announcing himself as 'CID'. Confident, smartly dressed, he put the act on well so I allowed him in. John can only be described as a wonderful character who lived, and still does live, life very much on the edge, and when the boss saw him he wanted to know why I'd allowed him in. I explained that he was CID.

'Balls, that's —, he's big trouble and barred, so get him out.' I was angry at being conned, so I went over, told him I knew who he was and asked him nicely to leave. John gave me a long stare, then a toothy smile – which I got to know so much better later on. He patted my shoulder and left. I'd have tried to put him out by force if necessary, but luckily my strategy worked. He must have wondered who this upstart was and under normal circumstances probably would have nutted me.

In months, and then years, to come, he became a sort of mentor, even though he had a reputation in Newcastle as a real cold, tough guy. To me, he was a warm and friendly pal. He reminded me of an old sea dog coming back from long trips abroad and telling yarns. We would meet in various pubs and clubs, and he would sit with half a lager and tell me tales about his days in London when he not only knew, but had also had physical confrontations with, the Krays. I was a more-than-willing listener.

Of course, while guys like John were charismatic, others were not. They were out-and-out bastards, but the whole mix was part of the intoxication of it all. Looking back at all the characters I met, I realise the bulk were extremely likeable people with terrific personalities, but their dark side tipped the scales against them.

Generally, dealing with people who were awkward or drunk wasn't really difficult. Confident I could match them physically, I always felt that if you looked people in the eye and talked to them properly, it would normally do the trick. By and large, I never had any real bother. Naturally there were fights and fracas, where I saw guns, knives, baseball bats and the rest, but, in reality, nothing I couldn't handle, and over a couple of years, I gained enormous respect for being able to resolve anything that came my way. With a guy like John marking my card about this one and that, it made things run a little smoother.

Of course, when firm, reasonable talk didn't work, there was the final solution and that was based on my fighting prowess. I probably trained as hard to become as good a fighter as I could, just as Jonny Wilkinson trains to become as good a rugby player as possible. That's how serious this career became for me, and that's how much pride I had in my fighting and efficiency to win as quickly as possible and remain unscathed.

I was training hard, living harder and becoming so self-confident that, quite frankly, I must have been a pain in the backside to those who knew me. The arrogance of youth is natural, but I seemed to have more than my share, and knocking about with these twilight people gave me an extra edge. This confidence grew firmer when I saw so-called hard men operating at close quarters. Watching them fighting, taking liberties, I'd think, 'Well, that's that myth exploded.' They seemed to be living on reputations wildly out of proportion with their real ability.

I remember one fight starting in an east-end nightclub where one of the supposed leading lights in this hard guy fraternity, a guy I knew well, began beating up one of the local troublemakers, who was just dying to get knocked out and was putting up little or no resistance. It became embarrassing when the guy couldn't even act that he was hurt and was even beginning to contemplate hitting back because he couldn't think of anything else to do. I remember turning to my pal and working colleague at that time and saying, 'Should we step in and stop this before he loses any more face?'

This happened a few times and made me even more determined that if I found myself in a similar situation, the best thing would be to give them one, knock them out and get on with my life. There's fighting for real and fighting for effect. Real is the only one worth bothering with and should only be done if it is absolutely necessary.

Not long after that episode, I was back in Bottos standing at the bar one night when this fella, dark eyes, dark hair, Neanderthal-looking, hit me for no reason – bang, bang, bang, bang! It didn't really hurt, but I was a bit put out. I unleashed a couple of firm ones on him and down he went. I didn't follow up or anything, because there was no call to. It was sorted as far as I was concerned and I returned to the bar. But he recovered, jumped on my back and tried to gouge my eyes out. I had to chin him. He went down again and the whole thing broke up.

Next day it was all round the town, because this guy was yet another 'face'. People were coming across to shake my hand and there were messages of congratulations coming from villains and other hard men. That one punch-up really secured my reputation, though, of course, at the time I hadn't had a clue who he was. John marked my card again and said to watch my back because he was a dangerous guy and would never forget what had happened. He was the sort who would only ever fight straight on if he was drunk, and when he was sober he would come in from behind, biting and gouging.

John taught me a lot about the strategy of streetfighting and I had a lot to thank him for. I had enormous respect for him and saw a side of his character others didn't know existed – his intelligence, wit and the loyal friendship he gave to me and my family. I watched him and saw how he commanded situations: if something was going to kick off, he always got the first one on and never gave the other guy a chance. The fight wasn't finished until he'd decided the other person was rendered harmless. John taught me how to behave appropriately in different places and circumstances. Not like which knife and fork to use, but how to enter, make your presence felt, the way to look at people with conviction and totally take control of a situation.

Our relationship was always a good one and I think he liked me enormously as well. We never ever had a wrong word and my respect for him was total. Our lives naturally drifted apart when I left the doors and changed the course of my life, but on odd occasions when I do meet him in the town it is always a joy because he is still the same character with a wicked sense of fun.

So there I was, a junior trainee accountant at British Engines; one who knew his place, by the way – 'Yes, sir. No, sir. Three bags full, sir' – and was very respectful, because that's the way I'd been brought up. But then there was this other side of my life. I was two different people and it became a bit ridiculous. I could walk into places where all hell was breaking out, where everything was being smashed up, and I could hold my hand up and shout, 'That's enough! Don't spoil my night!', and incredibly it would stop. I have to say that power was extremely intoxicating, and it went further. Restaurants could be jam-packed, but a table was always found and I wasn't allowed to pay. I wasn't into protection or anything silly like that, and certainly never had a bad reputation with the police, but I can fully understand how easily that situation could have arisen, given the heady atmosphere. I knew most of the villains and was accepted by them, but never became involved in any of their capers and, whilst I couldn't know what was going on in their heads, I would like to think they probably respected me.

Word got round that I was a safe pair of hands and at one time I was looking after no fewer than 40 bars in and out of the centre. It was becoming big business and I remember saying to a pal that, if we wanted, we could take over the town. It seemed too easy to be able to create a private army. At any one time, I could have upwards of 30 people out there in the pubs and clubs working for me. I looked upon it as a proper business and managed to persuade myself that I was still the good guy, still wearing a white hat, because I genuinely thought these pubs and clubs should be places where people could enjoy a night out without bother. I still do, by the way, and 'bouncing' is now a legitimate calling and very necessary.

Again, looking back, the control I had over the lads who were working for me was the result of the mythical status I had acquired, built up from stories about my exploits – some of which were true, but many of them total fabrication. I used that status and reputation to good effect on many occasions, taking the sting out of potential trouble before it really got started. I would visit places for the first time and see the looks if they didn't know me. The crack would come, 'Who are you?' But as soon as I introduced myself and shook hands, the change was comical: they couldn't do enough for me.

On one occasion, I was even threatened with myself! The bar was called Filthy McNasties Liquor Emporium in Whitley Bay. There was a bit of an altercation at the door and a queue was building up. I was called to sort it out and went to the door where a rather belligerent individual was giving it what we called 'the bit' with his gums. I was my usual pleasant self.

'What's the problem?'

'I don't pay.' He stuck his chin out invitingly. 'In fact, I don't pay anywhere.'

'Ee, well, that's unfortunate, because everybody has to pay here. Sorry.'

'Listen, pal, I don't pay. I'm coming in and you're not going to stop me.'

'Sorry, but it's the rules.'

'You don't know who you're talking to, do you?'

'Well, who are you?'

'All I've got to do is pick up the phone and the lads'll come down from the town and tear you and this place to bits.'

'Oh, we don't want that. Exactly who are you going to phone?'

'Steve Black.'

'Not him – oh, no.'

'Yeah, well, him and me did time together and we're big pals – so I'm coming in.'

'Hey, I don't want any trouble with that nasty bastard, you'd better come in.'

'Thought that would change your mind.'

Very gently, I led him into the pub, bought him a drink at the bar and told the staff to look after him. I then went to the other side of the room to watch developments, because I'd seen a kid from Benwell at the door who'd been watching and knew who I was. He approached the guy now drinking and preening at the bar and began whispering in his ear. It was comical watching him get redder and redder; he'd dug himself into a hole and was desperate to climb out.

He came over full of apologies. 'Look, I'm sorry. It was just a joke, I knew who you were all the time.'

'No problem, just enjoy your drink and we'll not fall out over it.'

He drank it in double-quick time and left, but it illustrates the way stories and reputations can get totally out of hand and exaggerated.

As with everything else, I had a strict set of rules for the guys I used on door control. Some of the lads were a bit questionable, but I knew if they were controlled properly and got paid, they would do a good job. The rules were simple: working for me meant no silliness, no threatening people, no taking liberties and, in particular, no demanding lock-ins. They were my responsibility and, even though we got on well together, if they stepped out of line I told them we would fall out, stressing 'fall out'.

Everything went well for a while until I was given the whisper that a group had been putting pressure on for a lock-in at a particular pub. So I went along to see them on the Sunday morning when I usually paid them.

'Right, lads, I've a special surprise for you today . . . you're not getting paid.'

They were shocked.

'And the reason I'm so pleased is that I've got extra money in my pocket this week.' After which I walked out. There was no need for me to say any more.

Their main spokesman followed me, saying, 'Hey, Blackie, come on, I know you're famous for your strange sense of humour, but you are paying us, aren't you?'

'Am I laughing?'

'Well, no, but . . .'

'Hey, look, if I make rules and you don't take any notice of them, people will start to think I'm soft. Do you think I'm a soft touch?'

'Oh, no . . . no, never.'

'Well, I think you do, I'm nearly positive about it. In fact, I'm just thinking I might not pay you all next week as well.'

'Ah, come on, Blackie . . . howay, that's not fair.'

'No, it isn't, is it?'

I'd won the day, but rumblings and rumours started circulating on the indestructible grapevine that it was actually me creating trouble at the bars, so the moment was fast approaching for me to knock it all on the head. Like I say, I was never a villain, but the line was a thin, jagged one, and after years in the game, I had probably made enemies who could have manipulated events which would topple me into that pit quite easily.

It just shows how luck plays such a big part in your life because by that time I was definitely changing and didn't like what I was becoming. If the truth be told, I was sick of myself, really. My thought processes had started to treat as normal behaviour that which any average person would have considered as anything other than 'normal'. Having fights when your heart rate doesn't change at all can become a little frightening. The associated coldness just isn't very attractive. One close pal, Bob Morton, talks of that period as when he 'lost me'. He was dead right, and not the only friend from whom I'd become distant. But, thankfully, once that period was over, we picked up our friendship again. It is now stronger than ever.

I first met Steve by chance in 1976, through a mutual friend, when he was about 19, and we hit it off right away. We both had a great love of training and football in particular. At that time he was playing for good-quality teams and in later years, when he stopped playing, we went on to manage teams together like The Black Bull Pub and Bedlington Terriers.

Anyway, at that first meeting he was looking to do some work as a doorman, so I spoke to a pal of mine and he got a job at the Eldon Grill in the centre of Newcastle. On his first night, I went to see how he'd got on and there were bodies lying everywhere. Apparently there'd been a team of yobs in who'd been taking their time to drink up after last orders. Steve had asked them nicely to be quick about it and they had refused, so that was it . . . sorted!

We got very close after that and the thing that attracted me to him was his personality, always full of fun and daft carry-on, you couldn't help but like him. Most important of all, though, he was an extremely loyal, loving lad and it all came from the heart, but sometimes he takes on too much and gets things wrong.

We'd socialise and I'd meet him about ten o'clock, after he'd finished his late shift at Newcastle Breweries, where he worked in the bottling plant. From there we'd go for a couple of drinks and end up in Grey's Club. It was silly. He'd be wearing his boots and brewery bib and brace, then get up onto the stage and sing. When he gets into that mood, though, you can't stop him. One night a taxi driver told us Bing Crosby had just died, so Stephen stopped everything and made everyone sing Bing Crosby songs all night. It was hilarious, but more or less sums up what he's about.

You could put your house on Stephen, whatever the situation; he's always 'master of the moment', and always knows what to do in a crisis. I'm extremely lucky to have the relationship I've got with him. We've never really had a wrong word except once when he tried to substitute me in a football match. I wouldn't go off and there was murder on! If you ever had to go over the wall with somebody, he'd be the one to go with, and he'll always fight other people's battles.

A total one-off, he constantly surprises me with some of the things he does, like giving the man of the match a Mars bar, or just before a game he starts reading passages from the Bible. You never know what's coming next with Stephen. He's self-taught, a revelation and without doubt one of the finest, most original coaches ever born. It all comes from his head and his heart, but he also has that unique quality of making everyone he comes into contact with, even if it's for a few minutes, feel they're special. He's a rare pal and it's a privilege to know him.

Bob Morton – friend

Incredibly, all the time this was going on, I was still going to day-release, night school and reading voraciously, trying to improve my education through courses in accountancy, business studies and law. I was even taking an Open University degree in art history and became obsessed with the Renaissance period from Giotto in the thirteenth century up over, past Michelangelo, Titian and that type of thing . . . right up to the Romantic period. I went into it in great detail and, just to show how complex a person I really am, I've seen me and some of the lads involved in a bit of a skirmish at the Waterloo pub – they've gone on to celebrate and I've shot off to the library to study Leonardo da Vinci. Fortunately, however, I made the right decision to get out of the business when I could, and that's when Lady Luck really kicked in because I met my wife Julie.

I was looking for some stability in my life. I had none and couldn't really see a future in a lifestyle that was now scaring the hell out of me. I'd turned cold, become inured to the violence that was now becoming 'just a job'. When I was younger, I'd been a passionate fighter, but now I'd turned into a callous machine and instinctively knew this was wrong.

No question about it, Julie was my saving grace. When I met her, I was actually going out with a friend of hers. I'd seen Julie before, when she was about 16, and thought she was nice, but that was it. Anyway, I went to a wedding function at the North Star in Longbenton, where her mam and dad were the relief managers. Julie was behind the bar and I remembered her. I was probably at my most outrageous and began showing off, hosting an impromptu cabaret evening I decided was going to take place. We got chatting, I asked her out and took it from there. I knew straight away she was the right girl for me and we were married within four months. At 22, I now had a whole bag full of real responsibilities.

We moved into a flat in Camsey Close, Longbenton, not far from her mother, and I was now working at NEI Parsons, in the office, as a pretend quality-control administrator. My education drive was continuing, but I was away from the twilight world of the doors and glad of it.

Julie has unconditionally supported me for 25 years and anything I have achieved has been a testament to this support. In late 1980, she fell pregnant with twins. The day she told me could have been yesterday, it is so clear in my memory. She met me at Parsons at lunchtime as a surprise to give me the news. I was gobsmacked and we were both overjoyed. I was completely elated, as it meant I could now field a couple of wingers with maybe a centre-forward later on. I'd always wanted a family, and now I could concentrate on that change in my life, with my priority now being the search for proper stability.

The pregnancy was a very stressful time because Julie had to spend 16 weeks in hospital, but there were humorous sidelines. Still working, training hard and running the house in her absence, quite frankly I needed the rest more than she did at times. The consultants would come in and I'd be lying in bed while Julie sat on a chair holding my hand!

Everything went off well in the end, though. It was an incredible experience when Stephen and Mark were born on 21 July 1981 and I was present at the delivery. They were born on the same ward as I had been in the Newcastle General Hospital, and even though I would try and make the odd joke, when they arrived I went to pieces.

When I left the hospital, I was desperate to tell somebody about our miracle and incredibly there was no one around. Normally I only have to step out of the house and I'm bumping into folk who want to clap my back and wag my hand, but on this day there was nobody. So I had to manufacture the situation and stopped a guy in the street. 'Excuse me, have you got the time, please? Oh, by the way, I've just had twins.'

He looked nonplussed. 'Yeah? Good. Twenty past two.'

The stability I was looking for had arrived and we moved to a bigger house in Shiremoor, which isn't too far from Longbenton. Julie obviously got a bit of the flavour of my former existence in some off-the-wall situations that arose. For example, on one occasion, there was a knock on the door and a woman was standing there with a teddy bear under each arm.

'Steve Black live here?'

'Yes, that's me. What's the problem?'

'Well, you don't know me, but my name's such and such and my husband's been beating me up. I've heard you've got twins and I'd like you to have these,' she said and handed over the teddy bears. Then I was expected to sort out her domestic trouble.

Something like this happened nearly every day, with complete strangers, sometimes even in the middle of the night. Once, when I opened the door, there was a guy standing there with a pick and a knife covered in blood, saying his brother had tried to chop him up and he was terrified of going back home. I searched the streets for the brother but never found him and the lad went back home satisfied that he now had me to call in any further emergencies.

The various scenarios that cropped up were pretty surreal, but illuminate just how far I had become immersed in the subculture. Julie couldn't comprehend what was happening and told me she just didn't want to know anything about it, for which I couldn't blame her. I must admit, though, that giving up that position of power on the streets wasn't easy as it gave me status and respect within my beloved North-east. As I've said before, there's only one set of people that Geordies revere more than their sports stars and that's their hard men. When people have said to me over the last 20 years, 'How do you deal with so many people knowing you?' and I suppose the associated fame of sorts that goes with that, I've always secretly answered that my infamous notoriety beforehand probably made me better known long before my sporting achievements were recognised. Julie used to ask how I could give loyalty to people who came for my help, especially when I didn't know them. The problem was that if I built up such a huge reservoir of goodwill across the North-east from these vigilante-like escapades, I knew my popularity would stand me in good stead in all aspects of life as the years went on. Still, I knew that rationale still had enormous risks and dangers attached to it, so I decided to change the face of Mr Stephen Black.

After Julie and I were married, I only ever went back to the doors if we were desperate for money. But it was a bad decision to return even on those few occasions. I shouldn't have gone back because to be master of your own environment you have to be confident and you must want to be there, and the simple truth is I didn't want to be there. I tried to compromise in too many situations and left myself very vulnerable. These were indeed dangerous times for me and the fact that I came through them unscathed surely meant somebody up there liked me. Two particular incidents really brought things to a head because either of them could have gone disastrously wrong. The first involved an incident at the Gallowgate Club, which was a meeting spot for the Newcastle United Supporters Club, very much in its infancy as an organisation. They had been having a lot of trouble, so I was asked to come in to try and settle things down.

On the very first night, this lad came in and began making derogatory remarks about me being on the door – 'You're not big enough', that sort of thing. I laughed it off, but he continued with his unnecessary behaviour so I gave him a warning, a few body shots and threw him out. No big deal – a short combination did the trick and he was, as far as I was concerned, all mouth and no action. He certainly didn't cause my blood pressure to rise. About an hour later, however, he returned. I knew it wouldn't be to fight, so I went out to talk to him. 'Look, we got off on the wrong foot, you've felt the weight of yourself and got a clip, so let's forget it and you go in and finish your drink.'

Suddenly I was hit from behind with an iron bar and I went down on one knee. A couple of cars screeched up and a man with something of a reputation stepped out holding a shotgun and said, 'I'm going to blow you away.'

I didn't give him time to think, but leapt up and caught him with a lovely left hook – and that was the end of blowing me away. My pal on the door dragged me back and all of a sudden the mood changed. The guys with the gunman were all apologetic, saying they hadn't realised who we were. One minute they wanted to kill me, the next they were having drinks with me. It was all very strange. My antennae were out because these particular people were more than capable of carrying out their threats. Bells were ringing loudly in my head as guns seemed to be becoming ever more prevalent and I was in the front line. I trained like a man possessed in order to be able to handle any street situation of a physical sort, whether it was one to one or if the odds were overwhelmingly against me. My mate Paul Tucker always used to say, 'I'd rather fight four or five than one, as with one you've got too much to think about.' But I couldn't put together any training drills to dodge bullets. Believe me, you can't do it, no matter what they show you in those low-budget Hong Kong martial arts classics.

The real crunch came that same Christmas and completely stopped me in my tracks. It was the worst situation I had ever been involved in, the blackest moment of my life, which haunts me to this day. We needed money for presents, to buy a couple of bikes for the twins, and I was asked to do the door at a pub for £100, which was a lot of money then. It was the normal rowdy sort of night, but it kicked off and turned extremely nasty when a kid tried to stab me. It was one of those situations where serious measures had to be taken, and had to be taken instantly. He went through a glass door and ripped his neck wide open. He was taken to hospital and I was terrified he was going to die. I was convinced I was going to be arrested and sent to prison, but somehow or other he was all right and there were no comebacks.

I need to thank a few people who played a full supporting role and allowed me to survive this period of my life. In various guises for their loyalty and friendship Paul Tucker-Grant, Harry and Brian Barthram, Willie Palmer, Larry Moat, John Hudson, Paul Downs and Eddie Higgins all need a mention. Special mention to my one-to-one coach and mentor Dave Findlay, a good friend throughout my adult life.

In no way am I attempting to make these incidents sound glamorous, because they weren't. And whilst my natural instinct is to try and justify what happened, there's no way I was in the right, because I know what was in my mind at the time. On the spur of the moment I'd completely lose it. I can't say I enjoyed the violence, but the power that came out of the success of winning these fights did have an addiction of sorts, and it was definitely corrupting me, with that last incident showing how I was prepared to seriously injure someone without hesitation. I went home deeply upset about what I'd done and become. It was a defining moment that made me completely take stock of my life. Again, I'd been lucky. I'd been given a warning and I never went back to it again . . . thank God and everything that is good!

Chapter Three

STRIVING FOR ABNORMALITY

Winning isn't everything, trying to win is.

Vince Lombardi

Leaving that last chapter was like hurtling from the scene of a road accident where there is a lot of wreckage but fortunately no one has been badly hurt. I'm not into weird ideas such as guardian angels, but I honestly feel that something has kept me on the right track, as I've been so incredibly lucky. I'm not superstitious, but over that wild period, even though I was locked up a couple of times for daft fights, I was never charged, don't have a police record, and this despite the fact that I must have been involved in thousands of punch-ups. It could have been so different because I was definitely walking a thin line. But that something keeps coming back and one or two strange things have happened which make me wonder.

For example, I was filming a programme about Sunday football some years ago. It was a simple idea: taking a run-of-the-mill pub team to see if a top-class coach could make a difference. Malcolm Allison volunteered to come in on tactics and the dancer Lennie Hepple gave them advice on balance and movement. It was a terrific experience, especially for a bunch of rough-tough players, and it made a huge difference to their performance. However, I was the one who learned the most from it. A remarkable thing happened during filming. One day when the programme narrator, Bobby Whittaker, was standing beside me he suddenly gave a terrific shudder.

'What's the matter, are you having a wobbler?' I asked him.

'Look, don't laugh, but sometimes I'm a bit psychic.'

'You're psychotic?'

'No, seriously, I've just had an unbelievable feeling go through me, and I just know you're going to be so successful.'

I laughed. 'You're crackers, but you can send the cheque to this address.' We all had a good giggle, but he was dead serious.

Steve Black is a legend in his own tracksuit. Master motivator, brilliant tactician and incredibly charismatic, I've never met anyone else who can bring more out of a sportsman or woman than Steve. He simply has that amazing ability to make athletes go that bit further or bit faster. His abilities were in full focus for all to see when I filmed a television programme in the '90s on an experiment to see whether first-class coaching could improve an average pub soccer team. Well, his dedication led to the dramatic transformation of the team into a squad of winners. Winning is what Steve Black is all about!

Bob Whittaker – TV executive

Some time later I was in the Hale Clinic in London, now renowned as one of the most famous alternative therapy clinics in the world. I was walking down a corridor when Theresa Hale came towards me and I must stress we had never met each other before. She stopped, grabbed my arm and said, 'You've got an incredible aura.'

I laughed and made a crack that I'd had a bath or something like that, but she continued, 'No, you're going to be incredibly successful in everything you do,' before walking on. I know it's silly, but the number of times I've been in serious scrapes that could have gone wrong, but didn't, have made me take these kind of events and statements seriously.

I'd somehow managed to continue with my coaching commitments while working on the doors and I actually learned quite a lot from bouncing that I could use to good effect. Organising a team, dealing with owners and directors, helping set codes of behaviour – these were all skills that I could utilise in coaching.

Attempting to put the origins of my coaching career into a nutshell isn't easy because it grew organically. As I've explained, it probably started when I was about 15 or 16. I was training all the time, taking the lads at Killingworth, then they started bringing wives and girlfriends, so it spread from there. The number of women attending the classes grew much faster than that of the men, which reflected the worldwide trend in aerobics and ladies' fitness at the time. I began taking classes at church halls, places like that, and it mushroomed at an amazing rate. It would go something like this: Wallsend Town Hall ladies' fitness class, then one at Hazelrigg, then two at Shiremoor, then the lads' football team, then another squad in Gateshead. Then somebody would ask me to take another one here and another there. I even started kids' classes, and my mate had a garage up at Shiremoor which we'd done out with punch bags and bikes. The women's class on a Sunday morning would run to the garage, do a circuit and run back.

The extra income from all these classes was a bonus, but my real motivation for taking on all this work was the coaching, and I truly valued the relationships I built up during that time. Like most things in life, I don't really have a very conventional attitude to money. I don't have any comprehension of finance: whether it's ten grand in my pocket or a fiver, it doesn't really make much of a difference, because I'll just spend it anyway.

I began formulating my own training methods very early on. All the books I was devouring were absolute nonsense, about kids not using weights till they were a certain age and all that crap. Stephen and Mark started off when they were three and when I told people this they said it was stupid. So I took time to evaluate it properly. Put your finger into a baby's hand and it will grip on and you can lift it from the pram, so the capabilities are naturally present. Look at it this way, the councils build parks and climbing frames for kids of three, four, five, six years of age to play on. This involves all aspects of physical activity: strength, balance, awareness; the whole thing is built into the play premise. If a kid of six or seven is pulling himself or herself up and swinging on bars, this is the equivalent of lifting 35 lb or 40 lb, but nobody in their right mind would give a 35-lb dumb-bell to a child – it wouldn't be allowed. It was simple principles and ideas like this which I began to explore.

I realised early on that simplicity was the absolute key. Even now people ask how they can become quicker and I tell them. How to increase their speed is simple. They must run faster. How to get stronger – simple: lift heavy things. You're not going to get stronger by lifting light things, or run faster by running slowly. It's common sense, if you stop to think about it. You can't become evasive on the field of play if you don't practise it. You can't develop the stamina to do a particular task unless you practise holding at the intensity that you're going to have to work at in that particular environment for that length of time. I think it's absolutely clear, but people don't seem to want to hear it.

In evaluating anyone's ability, I look at what kind of person they are first, try to find out what makes them tick, their ambitions, what switches them on. Then I work on the principle that you can make everyone faster, but you can't turn him or her into Maurice Green. You can make everyone stronger, but you can't turn them into Geoff Capes. You can improve anyone's endurance, but you can't turn him or her into Paula Radcliffe. It is possible to make the fastest improvements aerobically. Anyone can run a marathon. Anyone can become more flexible if they work at it, but in the end not everyone has the capacity to become a champion . . . that requires something special.

One particularly interesting concept I did embrace was hypnotherapy, which I taught myself from books and videotapes. I thought, 'I know what this is about,' and found I could do it very successfully. All you need is to talk to someone, gain their confidence, block all outside influences, engage their concentration and off you go.

I used it in coaching sessions as a form of relaxation, and in later years when I was at Newcastle United I told Kevin Keegan hypnotherapy could be a marvellous tool to develop a positive attitude and make the players feel good about themselves. There's been a lot of valid research in this area and Kevin gave in, probably thinking it was another one of my hare-brained schemes. John Carver, who is still at Newcastle United, was supposed to be coaching with me, but when I put the lads into what was really only a deep state of relaxation, he was more susceptible than any of them. As soon as I began speaking to him in soft tones, he went straight out for the count.

Anyway, the best little ditty about this was in 1993, when I was general manager at the YMCA in North Shields, as well as pursuing all my other activities. Scott Sellars, who was at Newcastle United at the time, had been put with me by Kevin Keegan, not just to train, but to pick up on the coaching and fitness side. So I took him to a class of elderly ladies all over 65 at the YMCA – lovely women to work with, and we had a smashing session, at the end of which I put them under for 20 minutes. Then came the moment to bring them round and they all responded except for one. She wouldn't wake at all, then started squealing and moaning in a regressive state. We later found out she'd gone back to an operation for cancer and the situation became extremely distressing for everyone.

Scott thought she was going to snuff it – I must admit I wasn't too hopeful either – and despite the fact he was supposed to be injured, he began running up and down the stairs in a panic trying to get some assistance. An ambulance took her to hospital, where they couldn't work out what to do, and I stayed with her, biting my nails down to the quick. It was eleven o'clock when we took her to hospital and about half past four in the afternoon she suddenly came round, stretched herself and said, 'Ee, I'd love a cuppa tea. What a lovely sleep. What am I doing here? I've never felt better in my life.'

Just like that . . . nothing wrong with her . . . right as rain. It terrified the life out of me.

That alarming experience made me realise that hypnotherapy is a tool that has to be used pretty carefully and it isn't the only one in the box. All types of mind games can be dangerous in the wrong hands and, although they have enormous positive potential, they should always be treated with the utmost respect. That's not to say I don't still use hypnotherapy as a basis for relaxation, focus and concentration, for it's excellent in eradicating short-term anxiety early on with a new subject, but other methods have largely overtaken it.

While fulfilling all these extra commitments, I got hooked on a hectic lifestyle, which has never really stopped since. That particular week was a classic. On the Monday I was organising a creative-writing class. Then the 'You are going to sleep' episode, and on Thursday I introduced a day of morning prayers. Kevin Keegan asked me in passing how I was doing and I said, 'I feel as if I'm Robert De Niro and I've been in the films this week.'

'Oh, how?' says Kevin.

'Well,' says I, 'on Monday it was *Only Fools and Horses*, on Wednesday it was *Casualty*, and on Thursday I was Jesus of Nazareth.' He just gave me a quizzical look – as well he might.

If someone sat me down and told me they were doing what I was doing, I would say it was nonsense. They say if you want something done, give it to a busy man, but as I pushed myself harder and harder it was a miracle my energy held out and I didn't suffer some kind of breakdown.

Looking back on my home life at that time, I probably kidded myself that I was doing a good job, but truthfully I wasn't spending the quality time with Julie and the kids they deserved. It just wasn't possible. But Julie never complained, God bless her, and she'll tell anyone that I was a worrity father. I fretted about everything involving the bairns. The health visitor said it was generally the mother who worried more than the father, but not in our case! Having twins was a revelation – some actually have a language of their own, up to a certain age, that others don't understand. I began thinking there was a problem that they weren't talking properly at six months – or doing advanced calculus! – and I wanted to take them to a speech therapist. I continually pushed to take them to see the doctor, but it was all in my head. Julie, being the sensible girl she is, realised they needed nothing of the sort and kept my feet on the ground.

I was also continually terrified that something would happen to them, or that someone would hurt them. I'm sure this stemmed from my experiences on the doors, when I had been exposed to the lowest forms of human life. As Mam said, 'Trouble with you is, you treat people from all the horrible people you meet,' and she was dead right. Again, it's still with me. I worry about everything, and if there's nothing to worry about . . . I worry about that.

Due to my many extra-curricular activities and family duties, I needed to be more mobile, so decided it was time I was able to drive. In 1981, I bought a car, nothing flash, a battered old Morris Marina for a couple of hundred quid. Looking around, I felt most people with a modicum of intelligence could drive, so I thought there would be no problem in teaching myself. I planned my strategy carefully, learning how to turn the engine on, studying the Highway Code and practising simple driving techniques – easy!

In Shiremoor, there were some lovely long stretches of road, so I managed to get the car started beside the Metro station, and jerked and stuttered down the road without hitting anything. The problem was I didn't really know how to turn it round, so I stopped at the bottom of the road and luckily saw a mate of mine.

'Davy, do us a favour, mate?'

'Yeah, what is it, Blackie?'

'Turn this car round for us, will you? I haven't a clue how to do it.'

'What's the problem, like?'

'I've just bought it and I'm teaching myself to drive.'

And that's where it started. I bought books on the subject, as you do, and in my own 'fol-de-rol' way broke the fundamental skills down into units, gradually becoming more adept at starting, stopping, turning corners, everything. I had to plan my first attempt at overtaking with military precision, though. I selected a spot on old Benton Road, a nice straight stretch beside the hypermarket, and waited. It was a wintry day and the condensation inside the windows made it difficult to see when I attempted to overtake a tractor. Unfortunately, I pulled in too sharply and hit it. The driver wasn't overjoyed, but I persuaded him to put it down to another interesting experience of life.

After nine years of practice, I considered myself to be a safe and competent driver. I took the test and, obviously, passed first time. Once again, luck had played a big part, as I'd never been involved in any serious accidents or been stopped by the police. The quality of my practice must have been OK, but if there is anyone reading this who is tempted to try my nine-year self-learning course . . . forget it! It's definitely not to be recommended.

As well as my crazy schedule working, studying and coaching, I was still training like a mad dog myself at Killingworth sports centre. Anything involving exercise – weights, boxing, judo, running, trampolining, basketball – you name it, I'd try it. I'd been mesmerised by boxing since my schooldays and really fancied my chances, so in 1984 at the tender age of 27, I decided to try my hand. As an amateur I couldn't get anybody to fight me and only had 3 bouts. The first was at Chester, and I was supposed to be fighting a lad 6 ft tall and 14 st. 2 lb, but when I got there I was told there had been a change of opponent and faced a guy 6 ft 5 in. tall and 17 st. 12 lb, when I was only 14 st.

In the first round, I battered him – like a whirlwind. I threw everything at him, but it wasn't like getting things sorted on the cobbles, because the referee kept standing in the way. I couldn't reach my opponent and ended up hitting his arms, elbows and the top of his head, but I kept throwing the punches in. I was butting, hitting him with my elbows; it was very ungainly and anything I did which resembled the noble science of boxing was totally coincidental. He went back to his corner after the first round and said to his corner man, 'He's butting me.' To which his corner man replied, 'Well, butt him back.'

In the second round, I was absolutely knackered after throwing him all over the place, so I bit him all around the shoulders in traditional style.

Again he complained, 'He's biting me now.' But the corner man was totally unsympathetic and said, 'Well, bite the bastard back.'

In the end I beat him, but only marginally, and was probably given it on aggression. I was knackered. I'd never felt so tired in my life. I actually came out in a rash all over my body with the effort.

The next fight was at Lemington Social Club, where I fought a big lad from Alnwick, then I had another one over at Chester Moor. My opponent, Steve Brown, had apparently been touting about what he was going to do to me, or so some of the other boxers told me, and prior to the fight he swaggered into the dressing-room asking, 'Who's this Steve Black?' as I was sitting trying to get ready.

'I am,' I replied.

He laughed. 'You're not fighting me, are you?'

He dismissed me out of hand and I thought, 'Well, if I was going to get beat before, I'm not going to now.' I shrugged and gave him a friendly smile. 'Well, we're down to fight each other, so I'll just have to do the best I can, won't I?'

He put his arms out, appealing to the room. 'Surely this can't go ahead?'

To be fair, he was a great big lad of about 6 ft 5 in. Unfortunately for him, I hammered him . . . in fact I lifted him off the ground with a left hook in the second round. It was over and done, no problem.

Before the fight, another big heavyweight guy had wanted to fight me. His coach nipped over with a confident look in his eye, 'Fighting heavyweight, are you?'

'Aye.'

'How do you cope with us big fellas?'

I could see what he was thinking. 'I do the best I can.'

He indicated his boy. 'Can we fight?'

'Yeah, do you want one now, like?'

'No . . . but there's a free show in Lobley Hill in three weeks' time, what about that?'

'No problem.'

After the fight, he came rushing over to my coach Norman Hatton, who looked after me as an amateur, and said, 'Look, I don't think he's ready for it yet.' Would I be right in thinking his bottle had gone?

I was so confident in my ability that I decided I should turn professional and beat Tyson. In fact, I started getting a bit of a cult following because after fights I would grab the microphone and break into song, encouraging the audience to join in. It was normally a Barry Manilow number or something like that. Again I was emulating one of my heroes, an Irishman called Rinty Monaghan from the 1930s.

Had I trained properly, I think I would have been more successful. The problem was I was a 5 ft 9 in. tall, short-armed, maniac streetfighter pretending to be Muhammad Ali. Had I changed my focus slightly to become Rocky Marciano, it may well have been a whole different ball game, because I was hitting really hard with both hands and if I ever connected, that was the end of the story. The problem was that I wanted to please my coach Ron Jackson, who took over my professional prospects; again that 'wanting to please' flaw reared its ugly head.

Ron was a real character and a lovely person. He had been a solid pro in his time and I respected his experience, but I must have been a nightmare to train. While well intentioned, Ron's determination to train me in the best possible technical manner was doomed due to the quality of the raw material he had to work with. Sorry, Ron!

Nevertheless, I trained my socks off for nine months in the build-up to my first and only pro fight in 1986 and I really thought I was going to take on the world. My entire running was done at kennels at Ponteland, with the ringwork in a room above the Grey Horse pub in Burradon . . . all very traditional. I was sponsored by the landlord, Jimmy Sample, a colourful character who had once been the proprietor of a notorious pub in North Shields nicknamed 'The Jungle'. Jimmy's support was total and I had a lot of affection for him because he was a genuine guy. He would take me to high-profile fights of the time, such as Bruno v. Witherspoon in London, and I'll always be in his debt.

I was battering my sparring partners, breaking their ribs and flying high. On the night of the fight, everything had gone to my head. I was beginning to think I was real show business. Cocky wasn't the word for it. While being interviewed by the press, I foolishly said, 'Give me five minutes, will you? I just want to deal with this fella.' Ludicrous! I must have been crazy and the fight was soon to confirm it.

The Mayfair Ballroom was packed with over 3,000 fans. The full contingent of Newcastle's criminal fraternity was there to see me get beaten while the rest of the crowd was there to support me. There were other bouts on the bill, but mine was the main attraction because it had been given such a build-up. My opponent, Tony Hallet, was a lovely lad, but I didn't consider him to be a problem because I was so hyped up. I rushed at him from the bell like a mad dog. Miss! Swing, miss, jab, miss, miss, miss. I couldn't hit him with one and I was trying to make every blow a knockout shot . . . Whoosh! Miss by miss, I grew more and more tired and, no disrespect to Tony, but as long as he could just stand up he was onto a winner . . . and of course he could do more than just stand up, so he won with plenty to spare and deservedly so.

My old mate, the respected sports journalist John Gibson, described my efforts as crude and vulgar, and I think he was being kind. I wasn't hurt at all but extremely disappointed and very embarrassed. It was the first time I'd ever lost in a fight situation and I didn't like the feeling one little bit. I obviously put a brave face on, genuinely congratulated Tony for his victory, gave his dad, Paddy, a long-time friend of mine, a hug, thanked Ron and my other cornerman, his dad, Herby, and left the ring to an unbelievable standing ovation! I kid you not. Maybe something to do with the amount of effort I'd put in, but certainly not for the quality of the performance, I assure you. I went straight to hospital and found out that I'd broken my left hand early in the fight.

Over the next few weeks I needed to decide whether this had been a complete one-off, and the occasion had got to me . . . or I'd started this boxing odyssey too late in my life, and the skills I'd learned in a low-key sports setting just couldn't hold up under the pressure that is a professional ring. I instinctively knew the answer, but my pride wouldn't let me quit. I thought that if I could control my aggression and treat the next bout as a sparring session then maybe I could relax and use some of the skills I'd acquired in training.

Come fight night, I entered the ring as laid-back as Dean Martin, absolutely aggression-free. Talk about from one extreme to the other. I fought – sorry, shadowed – a lad from Manchester, Jimmy Cropper, who, to be fair, seemed bemused by the whole situation, as he had to put up with me singing 'Everybody Loves Somebody Sometime' to him throughout the course of the fight. A stupid thing to do, really, as I later found out that he hated Dean Martin. A second defeat . . . and you'll never guess what? It didn't hurt so much. What on earth was happening to me? The world's most competitive person accepting defeat, it just couldn't be true. I was obviously using this mindset as a defensive strategy to offset the emotional embarrassment of my almost comical ineptitude inside the ring. I had one more fight, against Tony Hallet again, and after five rounds found myself lying on the canvas under the bottom rope. I leaned out of the ring, lifted a pint glass off a nearby table, took a drink and told the audience, 'This wasn't in the script.'

Ever the clowning crowd-pleaser, but I'd been taught a very difficult lesson; I'd been well and truly beaten, and realised my days as a professional boxer were over. Of course, the villains loved every minute of it, all the while saying nice things to my face . . . part of life, isn't it? The one surprise that did come to me about boxing was it never ever hurt, even when I got caught, the adrenalin must have been so high. So, unbeaten as an amateur and disastrous as a professional seems to sum up my boxing career. Yet again, to give that time the respect it deserves, I was so very, very proud to have earned a professional boxing licence at the age of 27 after my limited amateur experience. I gave it my best shot, but I was the wrong person at the wrong place at the wrong time and that's bad time management.

There's a marked difference between professional boxing and streetfighting. In the latter, there are no rules and when my opponent was thinking of starting I was already finishing it. Outside the ring, I'd have fought Tyson in a telephone box; in the ring . . . no way. Within those ropes all my strength and street guile were a complete waste of time. The only common factor between the street and ring is that you have to be ruthless to win. But I did enjoy the experience and it made me recognise that I had serious limitations in the noble art.

Getting back to my 'abnormal life', I was married with twin boys, playing a lot of sport, coaching the company football team and what seemed like most of the North-east. My day job in quality control at Parsons was bringing in a steady wage, but my real priority was developing my coaching ability. My boss at Parsons, a very likeable former rugby player called Geoff Ward, knew of my love and obsession with sport and, because he had a similar passion, probably supported my efforts more than he should have done considering the circumstances, for which I'll always be grateful.

Eventually, however, the axe fell and I was made redundant in 1986. I'd had a bit of an inkling it was going to happen, because I was a cheeky bugger. Believe it or not, I was the most passionate and committed shop steward in the union and would get into many arguments with the gaffers over their condescending attitude to some of the lads. I even had the temerity to defend staff at internal tribunals – with limited success, I have to admit – but if I felt an injustice had been done, once more I was wearing the white hat.

I enjoyed my time at Parsons and was fortunate to work with some great guys, who also happened to be sports mad as well. One good friend, Andy Kinchley, is still the most knowledgeable person I've ever met concerning soccer strategy. I loved his company and enjoyed the hospitality of his wonderful family on so many occasions during my formative adult years. His son-in-law, Davie Short, was a big pal of mine for many of those years also, along with Micky Cogan, Paul Dixon, Peto Stephenson, Micky Quinn, Joe and Ned McClaine, Bryn Pringle, Billy Cawthra and the Colwell brothers. We'd inevitably end up at Andy's house for an impromptu party and his wife Mary would always produce a feast fit for a king.

Two other big pals at Parsons were Chris Keith and Ronnie Feachin. Chris is a very talented sportsman, with a great work ethic that manifests itself in the world of engineering, and Ronnie has been my pal since junior school and is a lovely lad. Tommy Scott, the funniest lad in the world, was a great mate. I miss them all.

Although I was partially expecting it and wasn't really enjoying my job, redundancy still came as a blow. I had a family to support, we had no money behind us and I didn't really have any qualifications to my name, unless anyone wanted to hire me to talk about the methods used to paint the Sistine Chapel. I was facing another major turning point in my life and was I about to take a leap in the dark.

Chapter Four

DEBT AND EDUCATION

Energy and persistence conquer all things.

Benjamin Franklin

Newcastle Polytechnic, or the University of Northumbria as it's now known, had begun a degree course in sports studies and Steve Cram had been one of the founding student recruits. The course sounded too good to be true as far as I was concerned, but I rang the college and made an appointment to see the head of the department, Ian Elvin. Ian was the driving force behind the course, which had been established by the charismatic and slightly eccentric George Wilkinson. George, who sadly passed away a few years ago, had pioneered a similar degree at Liverpool Polytechnic and was the inspirational presence in the department, while Ian was responsible for the day-to-day management. Ian was also chairman of Newcastle Sports Council and he has done a marvellous job through the years, becoming one of the foremost managerial forces in sports education in the UK and making the sports studies department at the University of Northumbria one of the most respected in the country.

At the meeting, I sat down and basically told Ian my life story to date. I outlined my extensive experience in sport and physical training, and explained that I had recently been granted a professional boxing licence from the British Boxing Board. I think the fact that I had continued to gain educational qualifications in a wide range of subjects since leaving school also counted in my favour. I told him that if he gave me the opportunity to join the course as a mature student, I would work hard and wouldn't let him down. Thankfully, Ian was prepared to take a chance on me, for which I'll always be grateful, and I can only hope that when I was elected to the university's hall of fame in 2004, he felt his faith in me had been rewarded.

Embarking on a three-year, full-time education course was a terrific gamble, especially as we had no money whatsoever. I quickly realised that, whilst I'd made a fortune from working the doors, I'd squandered the lot. Stupid extravagances meant I had no security behind me, no house, no savings, and I agonised over how I could make some money. The boys were growing fast and bills had to be paid, but Julie continued to have confidence in my ability to come good and never wavered in her faith. So, as usual, I put myself about doing other jobs to make a few bob and soon an opportunity arose to make some money in the black economy – there was a building boom at the time, and I would go down to London to organise labouring work. I would get out of lectures on a Friday, fly to London, graft all weekend and then travel back for Monday's classes. Sometimes we would get Wednesdays off for sport, so I would leave on Tuesday night and be back first thing on Thursday. I had other guys working for me on the 'black' and after picking up the money for the job, I would pay them their share.

It was extremely lucrative work for a few years and once I even managed to clinch a million-pound deal in Ireland fitting out a group of hotels. I decided not to go ahead with that job because I didn't have local contacts there. The building work trade in general had by now served its purpose and I decided to expend my energies elsewhere and get on with my life.

I took on a lecturing job at Newcastle College and worked on a rota supervising the sports centre. Peter Black (no relation), Tony Fielding and Pat Memry all helped me enormously at this time, not only giving me as many hours as I could manage but also, in Pat Memry's case, by giving me the chance to explore my theories and practices within the environment of an educational and community sports complex.

This was a tremendous time for me during my coaching development.

Week in and week out, I'd be coaching top non-League football, a host of community sports and leading an increasing number of health-related fitness activities that would mostly take the form of community exercise classes. This wasn't just at the college but in an expanding base all over the region. The insight and experience I gained was amazing.

I realised at this time that, from a safety point of view, sports preparation was stuck in the Dark Ages. So many of the exercises used to get athletes/players prepared for their activities were dangerous and in many cases ineffective and inefficient. At the other extreme, the aerobic dance movement had begun to put guidelines in place that excluded most of the fun and excitement from the classes. I basically decided to mix the two approaches in an attempt to come to a happy and effective medium: to incorporate exercise regimes that worked for the individual into a class situation, ensuring that they were as safe as possible while generating the best possible results. This strategy proved extremely successful at the time and has been the basis of my work over the last 20 years at elite level.

I also became an examiner for the Northern Council for Further Education (NCFE) and enjoyed moving around the colleges of the North-east evangelising about the benefits of good exercise and the hazards of bad exercise. I also took on the role of course leader in exercise studies at New College, Durham, and Northumberland College, Ashington.

All of this activity still wasn't enough to keep the wolf from the door, however, and the arrival of baby Emma a year into my course, while a wonderful addition to the family, highlighted how precarious our financial situation was. I began to get into more and more debt, and without the help of Barclays Bank and a particularly caring manager – a smashing bloke called Ken Thornton – I don't think I could have got through. On one particular occasion, I remember having a one-to-one meeting with Ken at the bank and asking him, once again, for an increased overdraft to allow me to continue with the course. I was determined to barter hard to get what I needed to survive and really did my best to sell myself to him. The sweat was pouring off me as I drew on all my powers of oratory and spoke straight from the heart, explaining that if he wasn't able to help me out, my family were really going to struggle. After 45 minutes, I ran out of breath and Ken said, 'Time-out, son. You're trying hard today, Stephen, aren't you?'

'Ken, to be honest, I've nowhere else to go at this moment in time. You and Barclays are my only hope. I know I am going to be very successful in my chosen field, but I need you to back me as a person. I promise I'll not let you down in any way. You have my word.'

I couldn't believe it when he said: 'I suppose I shouldn't really do this, but I'm going to say that your word is good enough for me. Good luck.'

It was clearly a risk for him and I hope he knows how grateful I am to him for his support. As the years went by, one loan stretched into another, and I actually only recently paid off all my debts after all those years!

Despite the financial pressures, I thoroughly enjoyed my time at college and made many good friends whom I still see to this day. One of them, Marten Brewer, has become our physio at Newcastle Falcons. Marten, Craig Gordon and I must have broken all records for coffee drinking during our three years together. Marten tries to get me to keep stopping for coffee breaks when we are together at the Falcons now, but I just say 'NO!' in no uncertain terms and he has to reluctantly get on with his work. Marten is a top professional, with a first-class work ethic, who really is an unsung hero for us at the Falcons. I'm such a hero to him and, whilst this is understandable, the lengths he'll go to to emulate my achievements are beyond belief. He even forced his lovely wife Jill to have twin boys, Thomas and Daniel, just to keep up on the family front! It was Marten who first introduced me to rugby as I used to go and watch him play wing for Gosforth Rugby Club when we were at college. I used to think that in certain positions it was almost pointless playing, as you never got to touch the ball! Marten was mad fit, powerful, fast but nobody ever passed him the ball . . . strange game . . . or a poor team? Marten would have been a very effective player in the modern professional game, but he'll have to settle for being the best physio on the block!

The course itself was like a dream come true. Every day I got to talk about sport and test the theories I had been putting into practice in my coaching career. I have to say that many of the ideas I had already formed before starting this academic journey proved to be well founded.

I don't believe in magic potions or faddy training devices, but in the interests of staying ahead of the field I still explore the potential of everything that comes on the market (or give my opinion before it comes on the market).

The major lesson I took away from my course was the importance of treating each athlete/sportsperson as an individual. The only reasons for not training everyone slightly differently in their chosen sport or activity are the constraints of time or laziness on the part of their coach/trainer. Whenever you work with any athlete/sportsperson, it is of paramount importance to find out what makes them tick, what turns them on, what works for them, and then to focus your collective efforts around those elements. The utilitarian principle of a safe programme that everyone will get something from is OK from a health-related fitness standpoint, where the collective social aspect of the activity is important, but in the world of sport, especially at elite level, this is the wrong approach. Believe me, there is no shortage of natural talent out there. What is often missing is the environment that will allow that ability to flourish.

Over the years, at the many talks I've grown fond of giving, a question I've been asked repeatedly is how I've been able to move between so many sports and had so much success in all of them. Well, apart from the luck factor that no one ever likes to acknowledge (but let's not kid ourselves, we all need it), I tell people that I don't focus on the activity or sport; I focus on the person or people within a team environment. I try to keep an open mind, have no real preconceived ideas about what 'tools of the trade' I'll use in any given circumstance and let the relationship, and therefore the preparation programme, evolve. It's a philosophy that will always work, because you focus on the ever-changing needs of the specific situation. Keep collecting knowledge and thereby improving the tools at your disposal, and if your intent is strong enough to improve the athlete, coach or team, you will do it.

I did have some difficulties conforming while at college. I don't know if it was because I was older and thought I was wiser than the lecturers, but at times I felt as though they were trying to turn out a production line of sports instructors who would all follow exactly the same routines and never challenge the status quo as handed down from on high. I thought this was terrible, as it stifled my natural ability to approach problems from an original perspective.

The fact I was obsessed with the training side of things also probably got some of the other lecturers' backs up, because I would badger them, asking if they'd read that book or this article. I can't really blame them for switching off from my fanaticism, but I knew instinctively I was pursuing my vocation and really put my back into studying.

It took four years for me to pass instead of three, but the real reason for that was a very personal one. My nana was getting older; I loved her very much and wanted to do something for her before she passed on, so I decided to take her to Rome, Florence and Venice. I went to the tutors to explain the situation and ask for their permission to take some time out. I wasn't a young kid trying to get out of doing the work, I was a mature bloke with three children of my own, but some didn't want to listen. Their answer was, 'So, you think going on holiday is more important than your exams?'

Of course, that was like a red rag to a bull. If they weren't prepared to listen to what I was trying to say, then I'd do what I wanted anyway. And I'm bloody glad I did, because the time that Nana and I spent together in Italy was very precious to both of us. She was such a huge part of my life and I know I would always have had regrets if I'd bowed to the pressure from the college instead of taking her away. We had a wonderful time, but as a partial result of the trip, I failed my degree, though only by a slim margin, and had to stay on an extra year.

I eventually graduated in 1990 at the age of 33, but of course this was never going to be the end of my forays into the academic world. In an effort to build on my qualifications, I started a correspondence course with Fairfax University in New Orleans, working towards a PhD programme, sponsored by my old mate Bob Morton. But I found that my extra-curricular activities gave me little or no time to pursue it fully. Unfortunately, it was a step too far at that time, but it is a goal I hope to resurrect as soon as my work situation allows.

To be honest, apart from no longer having to attend lectures five days a week, my life stayed pretty much the same after I graduated. The only major difference was that I started to be approached by all kinds of people, including several successful athletes and sportspeople, who wanted me to help them individually by giving them some advice concerning their training. By this stage, the motivational aspect of my coaching had started to come to the fore and be in more demand, and I was beginning to realise that you can't separate the physical from the psychological, as one invariably drives the other.

One outlet for this counselling work was Bob Morton's gym in Gosforth, a nice leafy suburb of Newcastle. It was during one of my classes there that Bob told me that a very successful business entrepreneur, Stan Henry, was going to open the first of a series of upmarket health and leisure clubs, and would like to speak to me concerning their design and programme content. Stan had bought Gateshead Squash Club from Bobby Moncur, the former Newcastle United and Scotland skipper. His idea, as he'd done with some of his other very successful business ventures, was to get a working blueprint at this first venue and then copy it at an ever-expanding number of outlets countrywide.

Stan put together a marvellous facility. There was an excellent gym with an increasing focus on top-quality cardio-respiratory-enhancing exercise equipment; a super pool and spa complex; a programme of fantastic classes mostly run by two girls I had worked with at Newcastle College, Carol Harrison and Cath Turrell; and a great social area incorporating a bar and restaurant. My main role was to hire the fitness staff and set up the fitness programme in what was a bold venture. I focused on ensuring staff adhered to solid principles in customer care, which is vital for the success of any organisation.

Stan was a consummate businessman and tough character to work for, but I learned a lot from him. His knack for spotting a niche in the market was second to none and I had the utmost respect for his ability. In the end, however, it didn't work out because he reckoned I was too nice to people and should be far more ruthless. I understood what he meant, but it didn't sit easy with me as I felt my style of management was working. Eventually I felt I had to resign on a matter of principle. Principled or stubborn? Depends on which side of the fence you're sitting at any given time.

I thoroughly enjoyed putting that blueprint together with Stan and he went on to use and improve it at a number of clubs he opened throughout the region. He eventually sold his Springs Group of leisure clubs for around £20 million, though I've since heard that he bought them back again at a vastly reduced rate. I wasn't surprised to hear this as Stan is a very astute businessman and a great proponent of doing what works. He knew effectiveness rather than efficiency is the key to a successful business and that also sums up my coaching philosophy.

After leaving Springs, in April 1991 I went to work for another local entrepreneur who was to have an enormous influence on my life. Charles Buchanan was another major player in the leisure industry in the area. Unlike Springs, the emphasis at the Ivy Court Group was more on the actual physical training side of things, even though, as I've already said, you can't divorce the mind from the body. Charles took me on as general manager, to ensure everybody, staff and clients, was kept in shape within his clubs. Here was a man hell-bent on success, very much turned on to business in the true sense of the word, and I loved it because I was right into that psychology. Although he could be a bugger to work for because of his belief in his own methods, he became a true friend and I thoroughly enjoyed my time working with him. We still get together and swap Jerry Vale records, and we once formed a fantastic impromptu three-piece combo with me singing and on keyboards, Charles on drums, and the great American jazz singer Nancy Wilson harmonising. On another night our partner was the late great Buddy Greco . . . I know he's not dead, but he was late for our meeting. Oakland, California, will never be the same.

It was Charles who encouraged me to really express myself in my methods of fitness conditioning and as a direct result I began making big strides and gaining credibility in the fitness game. I concentrated on making people feel good, as I consider this is the most important aspect of any success, be it sport or any other line of business. Because my ideas were new, they opened doors. I was gaining a reputation and being called upon to move on from general conditioning and aerobics to other aspects of strength and fitness. Getting the best physical results had never been a problem. I'd always been able to take athletes to places to which they'd never been before and many thought they'd never go. But I was starting to realise that the deciding factor in any relationship was the strength of the psychological interaction and the mental focus that came out of that. My diaries from that time show a sharp upturn in the application of general sports psychology principles. Case histories from the individuals and teams I was associated with invariably showed the main catalyst in any successful coaching situation had a people-skills bias, i.e. understanding what the person or group of people really wanted to accomplish and trying to allow them to meet those goals in a manner that best suited their personalities and the environments in which they operated.

I applied the same principles in running my exercise and sporting classes as I had used while working the doors. For example, I'd be approached to set up a class somewhere, but I was so busy I would have to employ somebody to do it for me. It didn't take long to build up a huge client base and the feedback I got was terrific; whether it was the elderly woman down the street saying she felt great, the kids' football team, or the businessman earning millions, I got a buzz out of everyone feeling better.

I first met Steve in 1987 when he was working at Rye Hill Sports Centre in the west end of Newcastle and my son, who was a promising boxer, was recommended to contact him to see if he would be interested in coaching him. They both had a ridiculous sense of humour and a firm friendship quickly developed. When Mark became seriously ill, the compassionate and extremely sensitive side of Steve's personality was also shown to me. A couple of years later I needed a fitness director for my health club chain, and it was Steve's personality and charisma, together with his enthusiasm and ability as a motivator, which drew me to him.

I saw him operate with high-profile sportsmen and women from all areas and his energy and success were amazing. One of his subjects was Ken Redfern, the Premier League referee, who introduced him to Kevin Keegan at Newcastle United, and from that point he continued to flourish.

We enjoyed a great working relationship and friendship, travelling to international fitness industry trade shows together. In Chicago, I introduced him to the legendary bodybuilder Bill Pearl, who was astounded at Steve's natural strength, and yet another strong friendship was formed.

Steve's ability to be open to and absorb new and revolutionary ways of training paid off, as athlete after athlete came under his wing and then went on to success. At another trade show in San Francisco, Steve was extremely interested in how the 49ers American football team trained, and so he visited their camp, looking for innovative ideas to add to his portfolio. However, the highlight of that week was a visit to a smoky jazz club to see the legendary Nancy Wilson perform, and she joined us for a drink, telling us her life story. Another jazz legend, Buddy Greco, also joined us and I'm sure these encounters were more enjoyable than the meetings he had with representatives from the fitness industry on that trip, for Steve believes he is a talented Frank Sinatra soundalike.

Steve has great people skills, is extremely knowledgeable, witty and inspirational, and was a major influence in helping my company to grow. Motivational speakers such as Zig Ziglar, Brian Tracy and Anthony Robbins kick-started Steve's deep interest in the psychological aspects of training and performance, but his true guru is the great American football coach Vince Lombardi.

As a younger man, Steve had a reputation as a strongman/strength-athlete/boxer and unassuming hard man, and one confrontation that will remain in my memory forever occurred at Castle Farm Tennis Club (now David Lloyd's) in Newcastle. I was delivering some heavy gym equipment and the owners wanted it installed quickly. However, the site contractors were behind schedule and due to incur penalty payments, so they point-blank refused to cooperate or allow us access and a stand-off developed. The aggressive foreman indicated that there were ten East End of London labourers in the Portakabin who would physically throw us off the site. It was a tense and nasty situation. Steve remained cool, but I could see his eyes blazing and he insisted on going into the cabin to confront them. Against all advice, he stormed into the Portakabin alone and within five minutes they all walked out laughing and apologising, and insisted on helping us unload the equipment. The foreman later confessed that Steve was the most fearsome and intimidating person he had ever met.

My fondest memory of him is that after the British Lions beat Australia in Melbourne he immediately rang me to talk about the result, his feelings and the

general mood in the UK about the match. I was so flattered and honoured that
at the peak of his sporting achievement he should contact me.

Steve is a one-off person who I am proud to call a friend.

Charles Buchanan – company director

As Charles says, we travelled a lot together and this made me realise how important it is to be aware of changes going on both within your own industry and in the wider business world. You need to be a step ahead of the competition to keep your place at the top. He introduced me to the work of a lot of inspirational management gurus such as Harvey Mackay, Tom Peters, Anthony Robbins, Peter Drucker, Rosabeth Moss Cantor, Ken Blanchard and other hugely influential figures from the world of business and self-improvement. It was also through him that I became more interested in the work (and style of work) done by great American sports coaches such as Vince Lombardi, Tom Landry, Bill Walsh, Mike Ditka, Pat Riley, Phil Jackson, Lou Holtz and the great basketball coach John Wooden. I found their writings supported what I was doing and what I deeply believed in: namely, that people are your real differential, not the weights you use or how you use them, not the food you eat or the training regimes that you follow. No, it's the characters, personalities and attitudes of the people in your organisation that determine your success or failure in any given situation.

The current world champion England rugby team need to further individualise their preparatory programmes if England are to have a chance of retaining their number one status. I am genuinely concerned about this at this moment in time. If we use a utilitarian principle to underwrite all our methods of personal preparation, no matter how scientifically valid those principles are, we are failing to make a differential. If we give all our players individual attention and put together regimes that bring out the best in them, it will give us the chance of perennial success. You can't use computer programmes to give exercise and psychological preparatory advice at an elite level. Well, you can, but it's not the best way and, ultimately, it will cost you potential glory. The great American football coach Lou Holtz once said, 'I find my players listen best to my advice when it coincides with their opinions!' I need more

British conditioners/motivators/coaches/managers to get on my wavelength. Arrogant? Not when you passionately believe it to be the truth.

More well-known faces from the sporting world now began to approach me for help, for example Glenn McCrory, who had lost the world cruiserweight boxing title. It was my mate Lar Fawcett who introduced us, though Glenn and I had, in fact, met before casually at the boxing in South Shields. I'd been beaten once again and as I came out I put my hand on his shoulder and said, 'I don't think you've got anything to worry about.' Whilst many others would have snarled at me, he laughed and it broke the ice, and from then we got on really well.

Glenn was an artist, a martial arts boxer, tall and rangy with a superb physique. He had great skills, fabulous movement, balance and, as with all elite sportspeople, an unquenchable thirst for success. This mindset was what had brought him the World Cruiserweight Championship in 1989.

Glenn was one of the most talented athletes I have ever encountered, but in my opinion he'd had so much ineffective training in the past he could have gone into any ordinary PE department in any school in Britain and received better advice. His dedication and determination were top-notch, but the guidance he'd received didn't match that. Glenn is probably as gifted a world cruiserweight as there has been in the last 25 years – only the great Evander Holyfield could be discounted from that remark. But when I met him, the problem was that he lacked the body strength to match his undoubted skill. Determined to regain his title in 1992, he was due to fight for it against Alfred Cole, a tough New York fighter. This was the first-ever professional world title bout to be held in Moscow.

We worked on all aspects of his physical and psychological preparation. I've got to say, he took to it like a duck to water. His strength levels improved, his power improved and his stamina could never have been called into question. By the time he got to Moscow, he expected to win. As the great Henry Ford said, 'If you think you can or if you think you can't, you'll probably be right.' I was so very proud of Glenn's performance that night. He showed the heart of a lion against a very, very good world champion, and had it not been for an unfortunate clash of heads that concussed him, I think he might have just sneaked a points victory. But, the fight itself was a victory of sorts for Glenn as he'd come through a renaissance as a fighter of true grit and no little ability.

Having been a fighter and so-called boxer, I was more than impressed with his attitude, determination and skills. 'Beautiful' is the only way to describe him in all areas. Had I got hold of him at 14 or 15, I'm convinced he would have retained his title for many more years than he did. As it is, he remains the most successful boxer ever to come out of the North-east, and his training partners for that Russian experience – the Newcastle United footballers, notably Lee Clark, Steve Watson, Alan Neilson and Robbie Elliott, along with Newcastle Gosforth's legendary Geordie Kiwi Richard Arnold and former Gosforth captain, Rotherham coach and now head coach at North Walsham in Norfolk, Jon Curry – should all take credit for the superb shape Glenn got into for that fight. Kevin Keegan even used to welcome Glenn along to join in our fitness sessions with the Newcastle United first team at Maiden Castle in Durham.

Glenn has gone on to be extremely successful as a television commentator for Sky and I am delighted to be classed as one of his friends. The experience with him, a world-class athlete, not only confirmed but also reinforced my view of physical and mental conditioning, making me more determined to inculcate my ideas into as many people as I could.

Steve Black is the most inspirational person I have ever met. On the surface he appears to be one thing, but there is a lot going on underneath and because of his personality he can be seriously underestimated. In a period of my life when I had lost my world title and then been beaten by Lennox Lewis, I was at an all-time low. Steve pulled me back into the best shape physically and mentally of my life, but what is more important he gave me back my confidence and self-belief. He has the amazing ability to make people feel they can achieve and apart from that he is a bloody good bloke.

Glenn McCrory – former world cruiserweight boxing champion

I was still working for Charles while advising on conditioning work at Newcastle when out of the blue my career took on a new direction. Whilst I got on extremely well with Charles, I felt my chances of progress within his company had expired. My expectations about my developing role in the company just weren't being fulfilled and, being my usual dramatic self, I knew I had to look for a brand-new direction to keep me stimulated. Browsing, as always, through every obscure publication I could get my hands on, I spotted an advert for a senior managerial position at the YMCA in North Shields. The title of the position was centre programme manager.

The YMCA is a Christian organisation but welcomes everyone, whether religious or not. It has also developed a deep commitment to exercise and I'd read a lot about the marvellous work they do. Having grown up as a committed and practising Catholic, and evolved into a less-structured though no less committed Christian as I entered adulthood, and with my lifelong obsession with exercise and its positive effects, working with the YMCA seemed to be a natural move.

The interview went really well and I felt totally comfortable in the setting. The panel asked me about my Christianity, how I handled people, what I expected from them and what contribution I had made to the community. I was able to tell them that I had always been passionate about getting involved at community level, from working in schools right up to holding classes for old-age pensioners – my priority is to get the message across about the importance of health and fitness, and how it can make a really positive impact on people's lives. I have always believed in the importance of the development of a person's spirit. One of the greatest things anyone can do is do a good turn for a complete stranger and get nothing in return. No one but you will ever know. Obviously there is an element of self-gratification involved, but it is very rewarding and, more importantly, a private thing between you and God.

I must have had all the right answers, as the general secretary at the North Shields YMCA, Colin Stanbury, took me on as his programme director. I thoroughly enjoyed the opportunity this gave me to work with the public and provide leisure activities for them. I fitted in well and it was a wonderful job. North Shields is a rough but honest town, and the YMCA is regarded as a sanctuary where anybody can drop in for a cup of tea, a bite of wholesome home-made lunch, a game of snooker or just a chat. They would come from all over – the Meadowell estate, Preston,

Tynemouth or the middle of Shields itself. There was a terrific mix of people from every walk of life: professionals, unemployed, talented people without an opportunity and those who had wasted it, criminals, Christians, non-Christians, people who didn't get on with their family and saw us as their family, people who just came in for a chat or a snooze, and endless combinations of all the above. On one table there'd be a group of lovely older folks who liked a laugh and a bit of a carry on, on another a group of local 'characters' with lively reputations, while on another table a group of kids. It brought people from diverse backgrounds together and in many respects was regarded as the heartbeat of North Shields.

My remit was wider than exercise provision. I was responsible for ensuring that people felt welcome and that there was something on offer for everybody. I therefore introduced classes in creative writing, painting, sculpture, music, dancing and drama, and we encouraged the growth of discussion groups.

As my coaching base was still increasing, my clients would also come and use the YMCA facilities, leading to some wonderful interactions. The likes of Jonathan Edwards, Gavin Peacock, Glenn McCrory, Lee Clark, Robson Green, Steve Watson, Paul Lister and Warren Barton all came to the centre as part of their training routine but also got involved in other activities. I remember Scot Sellars sitting in on morning prayer groups; Jonathan and Gavin giving their time to help some of the local children's groups; and Lee Clark and Steve Watson giving a lot of their time to the kids who came to the centre. They were really appreciated, so I felt I was actually doing something constructive, albeit in a small way. The days were uncomplicated: religion is more about attitude than ramming it down anyone's throat. We had daily prayers, but it was low-key and an excellent opportunity to motivate everyone for the day ahead, and I must admit to taking great comfort from the whole experience.

I also loved the theatrical side of the job. For example, I would go into the gym, put 400 lb on the bench press and, from cold, knock out several repetitions, just for effect. The effect was to keep the clientele from fighting one another and that bench-pressing strength allowed me to keep the peace. It gave me status, because to be frank that was the only language some of the characters who came to the centre spoke. Perhaps this seems a little shallow, but people understood it. It took the place of eloquence and it even broke through to some whom I persuaded to come to church.

Bearing in mind some of the 'characters' who came in, I never had a peck of bother from any of the opposing factions. It was amazing, because I would get to know everything that was going on: that this group were going to go out on Friday night to turn another group over, despite the fact that earlier the same day they had all been training in the gym together. These opposing factions never spoke to one another, but my rules were that the building was neutral territory and I demanded they had respect for it, never allowing a bad atmosphere or anything to kick off. It proved to me that people can get on together, given the right circumstances, and it is up to all of us to not only create that feeling but also build on it.

I really enjoyed my life within the YMCA organisation and became chairman of the national YMCA's Pathway committee, which was a group of senior personnel from the YMCA who were brought together to look at the standard and direction of exercise provision throughout the YMCA movement in England. I also travelled to flagship centres in San Francisco, New York, Chicago and Frankfurt on the YMCA's behalf.

There was only one incident during my time at the YMCA that, had it gone wrong, could have been disastrous. It was a lovely day; I'd been to the library and was in a terrific mood coming back into the building, not a care in the world. I was beginning to get to know everybody in Shields and was starting to feel really at home. But on this occasion, as I walked through the door, a knot of apprehensive visitors were peering into the canteen, where standing on his own was this massive young man. When I say massive, I mean massive, about 22 st., and he had that look which told me he was for real.

I kept walking towards him and said, 'Hello there, how y'doing? My name's Steve Black.'

In response, the young man said, 'I've got a gun and I'm going to kill somebody.'

I started talking to him, trying to calm him down. 'Look, don't kill them here, man, 'cos the cleaners have just finished and they're lovely women and we don't want to upset them now, do we? Look at the lovely shiny floor and that.' I knew I was rambling, but I was having to think on my feet.

'No, I'm going to do it.'

'Never mind about shooting people, man. Howay, have a cup of tea or something with me, man. We can talk about it.'

Then he pulled this handgun out of his pocket and I reacted instinctively. Grabbing it off him, I moved in and hit him with a flat open hand, lifting him off his feet. It took him totally by surprise and he fell to his knees crying.

I put my arm round his neck in a comforting way and led him into the café like a child. I put the gun on the table between us just to let him know there was no threat, and just kept talking to him. Looking back, I must have been nuts to take that kind of a risk, but it worked. He calmed down and it was sorted. It turned out he was a troubled lad with serious psychological problems. He needed medical assistance, so I didn't call in the police.

The gun eventually went into my drawer, then to the police, who disposed of it. Through Social Services we got him a flat and when I went round to see him it was immaculate, like a show house. He was always clean and tidy, with his shirt pressed, a nice tie, and his shoes highly polished; he must have spent hours on his appearance. The poor kid never really had a chance: his proper father left when he was young, after which his mother had a succession of partners and he was left to his own devices. He'd had no education and wasn't really socially adept enough to hold down a job. Massive psychological problems mounted up over the years and his violent behaviour has continued to terrify many people in some serious situations since. I believe he is now in hospital. God bless him as I know he's a good person at heart.

Whilst at the YMCA I was still involved in all my other sporting activities and I was approached to go into partnership to open up a health club called KICKS in Wallsend with my good friend Greg Wallace. The premises were just off the High Street, on three floors. It wasn't a big club, but it was a good location. I went at it with my usual energy, training up the staff, getting the right equipment and even building a small pool. The membership grew steadily, but unfortunately it didn't work out, costing me several thousands to withdraw. Buying and selling small businesses is not an environment that has been kind to me, either financially or emotionally, as invariably everybody thinks they are getting the short end of the stick and maybe, in many cases, they are. Instead of Stephen Covey's idealistic concept of WIN–WIN, in my experience it's been more LOSE–LOSE! I am proud, though, that the club has since expanded and is still thriving. Ian Knox, the guy we bought KICKS from was – is – a great ideas man and I hope he eventually gets the rewards he is due for his innovative vision within the leisure industry.

My own health was also beginning to suffer as I was continually pulled in a multitude of different directions, and it became obvious that I should streamline my efforts into one specific area. The choice of which area was easy and I decided that professional sports training was to be the way forward for me from now on. All my experiences up to that point had provided me with the best possible background to launch a full-time career in coaching. I had been involved with all age groups, all abilities and had dealt with all kinds of people from my time on the doors to running classes at the YMCA . . . and it seemed everywhere in between. I seemed to know everybody involved in the very broad definition of sports, recreation and leisure throughout the North-east, and whenever I needed to formulate my CV, I used to purposefully miss so many things off from the practical experience standpoint as I thought nobody would believe someone had got through all these things. But on a very practical level, these experiences now combined to formulate my coaching style and in 1995 I was given a wonderful stage to put all this into practice at the Newcastle Falcons.

Chapter Five

MAGPIES AND MACKEMS

I am delighted to make my contribution to Steve Black's autobiography. Blackie has a lot of qualities, but his main asset was to bring colour in the training sessions and into the lives of people with whom he worked.

Kevin Keegan, Manchester City FC

Charles Buchanan was once again a potent catalyst for my career when he introduced me to Kevin Keegan at Newcastle United. Being a Geordie and being interested in sport generally means only one thing: a lifelong love affair with Newcastle United. I was no different and after flirting with professional soccer as a youngster but failing to make the breakthrough to the level I thought my talent deserved, I believed that my chance of success with the club had long gone. Fortunately, however, as my reputation for success with individuals, and groups of players and teams grew throughout the region, I had attracted Kevin's attention. Kevin had just been appointed manager of the team by Sir John Hall and was putting together a backroom team that he felt could contribute to the renaissance of this great club which, at this point, towards the end of the 1991–92 season, was languishing at the bottom of the Second Division and fighting hard to avoid relegation.

Initially I joined the club on a three-month trial as a conditioning consultant, but after two weeks Kevin asked me to sign on. I was very proud I'd made such a good impression, and was excited and determined to make a difference. Suddenly I was pitched into the perfect environment and I loved it.

The moment I met Kevin I was captivated by his infectious personality. He is a bouncy, positive man with a huge passion for football. He had been used to almost constant success in his life and that, plus his tremendous charisma, really made me want to work with him. Remember that when he came back into football he had been away from the game, living in Spain for eight years playing golf with the likes of Sean Connery and living a superstar lifestyle. In fact, just about the last competitive thing he had done was *Superstars* on television, where he had shown his indomitable competitive spirit. So, after all those years in retirement, it was a coup for Sir John Hall to persuade him to come back to the club, first of all as a consultant manager for the remaining months of the 1991–92 season, which was then to develop into a longer-term contract. His return could not have been more timely as it really looked as though Newcastle were in great danger of sliding into oblivion.

It was no easy challenge facing Kevin, as he had never been involved in football management before and the game had changed rapidly since his playing days, but he rose to the occasion and brought in a solid team around him. Terry McDermott, a good friend who had played with him at Liverpool, was first on board as his second-in-command and it was very much a case of where one was . . . so was the other. Most importantly, they understood and trusted each other, which set the foundation on which he built his new team.

I can remember first going through with them to their training ground in Durham. It was evident from day one something special was going to happen and Kevin was going to lead the club back to success. He seemed to make decisions very quickly about people and as soon as he made a positive assessment he was fiercely loyal to them. As long as people delivered what was expected of them, gave as much as they could or had delivered for him in the past, he supported them. Kevin had a nice balance to his coaching team, which included Derek Fazakerley, who had been round the block with a record number of appearances for Blackburn and is now back with Kevin at Manchester City.

Kevin was highly respected as a good, honest professional by everyone around him and we got on well together. I always thought he was a very practical man with a good football brain. He brought through sound young lads like John Carver, who is still at Newcastle, and Lennie Hepple, a marvellous coach and totally unique in his approach to balance and the development of natural ability. Everyone he brought in round him had different skills and this amalgam of experience was always galvanised by Kevin's passion. His team talks weren't bogged down with technical advice. It was all about enjoying the game; he didn't believe in practising set plays but expected players to react instinctively to the situation at hand and very much followed on from the Liverpool method he'd enjoyed as a player, which embraced the players, using their natural flair and talent. I saw at close quarters the effect Kevin's passion and infectious competitiveness had on the players. They saw in him the person they would like to become in their own careers.

We worked hard, but we also had an enormous amount of fun and I think this was reflected in the way the team played the game. The media referred to us as 'the entertainers' and we certainly were. But, importantly, we also won the vast percentage of games that we played over the next couple of years. All our training was done with the ball and done in a competitive environment at a high pace, with an almost zero tolerance of errors. We just didn't expect passes to go astray and, to be fair, not many did. My main contribution was to ensure the lads warmed up properly, were in the right frame of mind collectively to get the most out of their main football session of the day and then to ensure they warmed down correctly and were individually aware of the positive effect training properly could have on both their personal career and the effectiveness of the team.

I didn't try to impose anything on any of the players, I just chatted and took one-to-one sessions. As the majority of the more influential members of the team seemed to enjoy and benefit from these, it had a positive effect on the younger element at first-team level at the club. Players like Barry Venison, Scott Sellars, Rob Lee and particularly Paul Bracewell were all regulars, and their subscription to my programme definitely enticed the likes of Lee Clark, Steve Watson, Robbie Elliott, Alan Thompson, Steve Guppy, Andy Cole and others to work closely with us.

The first-team coach, Derek Fazakerley, was an experienced pro and a good coach who had the respect of the players at the club. The fact that he obviously supported my input also helped from a credibility standpoint – an absolute necessity at this level. Colin Suggett, John Carver and Derek Wright were also part of the coaching and medical team, and altogether I felt a good working environment had been created.

I had a special relationship with Len Hepple and, although he was some 70-odd years of age, we were on exactly the same wavelength and got on famously. I'd say, after some 30 years around the elite level of professional sport, I've met only one true genius in the field of coaching and that was Len. He had a great eye for seeing how a player moved and could always devise a drill or series of drills that would make a significant difference to the efficiency of movement of his chosen client, whatever position, whatever sport. He was also strong and confident enough to say, 'Carry on with whatever you're doing, because it's working and I don't want to tinker with your unique movement,' or, 'At your age, whatever input I make could carry a risk that might outweigh the benefit, so I'm sorry, I can't help you.'

But there were so many instances when Len's help proved invaluable. I loved working with him as he helped to cement my confidence that my understanding of the requirements of any player was being formulated from an objective and rational standpoint. Before meeting Lennie, I'd never really known anyone who formulated their strategy along similar lines to myself. Now I'd found someone who had a lifetime's experience as a professional dance-movement coach and had an almost identical mindset.

Basically we did what worked. We watched players training and playing, and analysed their movements. We then asked both the player and his technical coach what it was they wanted to achieve and made a decision as to whether we felt that was feasible or not as a goal. If it was, we then set about adding and subtracting movement from that player's repertoire until we ensured a more fluid and effective movement pattern than had formerly been in place. This would take the player ever more quickly towards their achievement of the target standards set by themselves and their coaches.

Kevin also used me increasingly for special one-to-one projects, such as my work with Lee Clark, now captain of Fulham, and Steve Watson, now with Everton. One major success I had was with former Liverpool goalkeeper Mike Hooper. Hoops had returned for pre-season training almost 60 lb overweight. Kevin told me I had my greatest challenge yet and told Hoops that he had six weeks to get his weight down and, more importantly, to get to a fitness level normally associated with a top-flight football club. Day by day we worked: early morning at the beach, after training in the gym, along with the Newcastle Gosforth Rugby Club, playing basketball and doing countless agility drills. In six weeks, Mike Hooper lost 56 lb, came out in the top 10 per cent of the entire squad during fitness test results and didn't pick up any injury. We worked together for sometimes three or four short sessions a day at a very high level of intensity. We ensured that he ate small amounts of good food in a balanced diet, drank lots of water and took only two supplements every day – a multivitamin/mineral tablet as well as a gram of vitamin C. Kevin was astonished at the transformation he saw in Mike Hooper and I felt an undeniable pride when I heard Kevin refer to me as the best one-to-one coach in the world during an interview on BBC radio about Mike Hooper's progress.

Kevin also supported my inclusion and increased 'weighting' in the programme of resistance training. He'd experienced the benefits correct weight training could bring when he'd joined Hamburg from Liverpool and, over the course of his time, there put on around 10 lb in muscle weight. Most of the team began including muscle training into their weekly routines. I think it really did help give us a little more confidence on the ball and probably helped our collective sharpness.

I never make wild claims – those who do are invariably talking nonsense – because I know weight training or a correct agility programme, or an all-encompassing holistic approach by coaches to support the player on and off the park may help a little, but it will not turn a bad player into a good one. But all those elements, as well as an incorrectly balanced diet, could take the edge off a good player if they are not specially tailored to suit that player's needs and natural abilities. If formulated correctly and specifically, however, they can have a positive effect on an already talented player. Especially if you can keep them on the pitch and injury-free.

If you look back at Kevin's successful era at Newcastle, you will find we had few injuries, which allowed Kevin continuity in his team selection, vital in order to achieve success. I despair when I see players out injured with strains and pulls – there's no need for a team to get many, if any, soft-tissue injuries if they are prepared properly.

Many coaches nowadays impose a world champion boxing-type regime as a goal for the team as a whole. The only players who escape this approach are the ageing senior pros, who refuse to join in, do their own thing, and probably benefit because of it. The others are subjected to a regime laced with 'fads' that look to continually increase the fitness level of the player at that given time. This is disastrous. Why? Because if you get to an Olympic-level of fitness, you can't maintain it week after week. You'll break down, get injured and need time off to recuperate. Olympic athletes need to peak once every four years, while footballers and rugby players need to be match fit every week for nearly 40 weeks of the year. To achieve that you need your players to live healthily, so that they are alert and bright mentally, and can walk around at a constant level of 80–85 per cent optimal fitness. This will ensure they are fit enough to play successfully as an ongoing contributing team member for just about as many games as you need them.

Members of our industry continually harp on about the number of games players have to turn out for in a season and how debilitating that is. I say nonsense! It's not the games that are tiring, it's the inappropriate training being formulated and delivered by people who are under enormous pressure from the powers that be to get the team performing better and better (or so they perceive) that they do too much on the training field and in the gym.

Since more and more management teams are following this trend, there are in reality fewer and fewer teams who are actually capable of challenging for honours, not because their players aren't good enough, but because their preparation is just awful. And because this disease is so widespread, there are fewer and fewer people who have the actual knowledge and experience to put it right.

I don't know whether Kevin trains the same way now or if he's succumbed to the ways of the masses. All I know is that he didn't do it then and he was rewarded for the training subculture that underwrote all the performances that led to the 'entertainers' label.

It was a great feeling to be associated with him and it is no surprise that some of the kids brought up in that environment have gone on to have excellent careers, especially local lads like Lee Clark, Steve Watson, Alan Thompson and Robbie Elliott. Others, like Andy Cole, John Beresford and Barry Venison, thrived in this attacking and exciting environment more than at any other point in their careers.

Over the period of time Kevin was with the club, his cast improved to fit the requirements of the League, the team and the way he wanted to play the game. He inherited Mick Quinn, who, effective as he was, would eventually be replaced by Andy Cole, Les Ferdinand and then Alan Shearer, which is not a bad list of leading strikers. Add to this providers such as Kevin Brock and Franz Carr, who were also exchanged over a period of time for the excellent Scott Sellars, David Ginola, Keith Gillespie and Ruel Fox. The 'leadership' role was always strong and this was bolstered by Kevin Scott through Brian Kilcline and Paul Bracewell to Rob Lee and Alan Shearer. So there was good solid leadership, good providers and top strikers who were prolific goalscorers. Added to this, his goalkeepers were also top-notch, from Pavel Srnicek to Shaka Hislop – popular and talented players, big personalities who became heroes at the club.

I was very surprised later on when Lee Clark fell out of favour because I thought he was Kevin's type of man. He was a great passer, worked very hard, was totally unselfish and a good man in every respect. However, Lee was a larger-than-life character, young and full of himself. In one particular match against Southampton, Kevin pulled him off the park. Lee was playing a good game and didn't deserve to come off, but upon reflection I think Kevin did it for all the right reasons. He wanted to show Lee that he was boss, but I don't think he dealt with it properly at the time and the only thing Lee did wrong was to show his dissent by kicking a bucket on the touchline. It did create some friction between them. In many ways, I wonder whether Kevin was in fact punishing himself a little because he could see in Lee some of his own traits – when he was a player, I remember him being sent off along with Billy Bremner, and Kevin ripping his shirt off in a temper.

Steve and I have been friends for over 15 years. We first met when Kevin Keegan, then manager of Newcastle United, brought Steve to work with the players. We hit it off straight away. This was because of his training methods, personality and terrific humour, but probably the most significant factor was our upbringing and past were very similar.

Steve is extremely highly rated and respected by people in my profession whether they have worked with or just met him. He has been a massive influence on my career, especially in assisting me to recover from injuries. It's no coincidence that I have had my longest time out through injury when I can't work with Steve on a regular basis.

This sums up his importance to me as an individual. Thanks, mate, and I'm glad to call you a friend.

Lee Clark – Fulham FC

The important thing is that Kevin made firm decisions and during his time at Newcastle United he was, without a shadow of a doubt, even taking into consideration Sir Bobby Robson's impact, the best manager they've had, because he lifted the team to a different level altogether. His ability to galvanise a team to entertain the crowd on a regular basis, but not be so high risk that from a results standpoint it would be foolhardy, was a huge achievement and forward step within the world of sports management. He was trying to balance the emphasis on winning at all costs with aesthetics. It just so happened that the best way to gel and play all those exciting players Kevin had at his disposal was as a team that lived up to its 'entertainers' billing.

In the early days we had the winger Franz Carr, a lightning-fast athlete who'd come from Nottingham Forest, one of the late Brian Clough's exciting prodigies. I can remember doing a little stretch with him in the dressing-room, preparing for a game, when Kevin came over and said, 'I'm really looking forward to seeing you play today. I'm really excited, because

I'm not particularly sure about what you're going to do. And I don't think you know either. So, if I know you really well and I don't know what you're going to do, and nobody knows yourself better than yourself and you don't either, we can rest assured the opposition will have no flippin' idea what you'll do. So let's get out there with that unexpected spontaneity because that will win us the game, son. Get out there, enjoy it and show your best qualities.'

I can remember thinking at the time that that was marvellous management and motivation, because when I was a player I would have loved the manager to have said that to me. That was a typical example of his leadership qualities, but he also led by example on the training pitch because he was playing every day and loving it. Make no mistake about it, Kevin was a tremendous player and all this stuff written in the media about him being manufactured is absolute nonsense. You can't achieve what he did, which included being European footballer of the year twice, by accident. He was revered all over the world and much of the work I do with Jonny Wilkinson has been influenced by him. I constructed a lot of Jonny's movement drills after watching Kevin play. He was a nightmare to mark in games. He ran defences ragged and that was evident every day on the training field even after he'd retired. He'd twist and turn, and defenders couldn't leave him for even one second. Their attention was constantly engaged. Even good players found him almost impossible to control and said he was a nightmare to mark. He would do three, four or even five shimmies when only one would have done for other players. They hated playing him in practice matches. His energy was terrific and his strength very surprising. In one training session we were carrying on and I got everyone to climb round their opposite numbers' bodies whilst they were standing up. I was with Alan Thompson and 16 st. at the time, and as soon as I started climbing he not only fell down, he crumbled! Kevin rose to the bait and offered himself up, and I climbed round him and tried like hell to get him to fall over. To my amazement, he was so strong he stayed up, and this showed me yet another dimension to this incredible sportsman. I remember coming away impressed.

Kevin also liked the hierarchy within the players' structure. He felt the older players should be given respect for what they had achieved. This is seen as an old-fashioned approach now, but he had traditional standards. If there were two players of similar prowess, he would go with the older one out of respect. I think his tactical awareness of the game was almost innate for him as a player. How he developed was how he saw the game and wanted it played – instinctively. He wasn't a 'let's sit down and talk tactics' type of coach, but on a one to one with a player, explaining what he wanted out of him, there was probably no one better. Footballers loved playing for him and you can't ask for more than that.

Kevin had a major impact on my life and career, and I can't thank him enough for what he did for me. I feel he could have benefited more if he had subscribed to various innovative ideas on preparation and coaching from sources other than the playing staff, but when I worked with him he was a fledgling manager. Had he been a little older and more experienced, he would have listened to other ideas, even if he might not have put them into practice.

Kevin Keegan took Newcastle United forward and his greatest signing, Alan Shearer, continued that momentum. I know Alan through Jack Hickson, who discovered him as a boy, but haven't had the pleasure of working with him on a one-to-one basis. Alan had a terrific impact not only on the team but also on the whole city of Newcastle. A totally committed professional, he is apparently very vocal when necessary in the dressing-room and leads by example on the field of play. He is supportive of players, but at the same time tells them exactly what is expected of them, and if they don't meet those expectations he will call them on it. By the same token, if he doesn't come up to scratch, he expects the same treatment back.

I do know he liked playing for Kevin and there was a mutual respect there. In many ways their footballing skills are similar: both are big on the fundamentals – good first touch, quick movement, supporting others and doing the job well. As a team, Kevin and Alan were a revelation to Newcastle and that impact can still be seen today, despite the fact Newcastle haven't won any silverware recently. Shearer brings hope to the city even in the twilight of his playing career.

Another side of Alan is that when my son Stephen broke his leg, he actually phoned my home to wish him well. Alan had been through almost exactly the same injury and offered advice. He is a role model for anyone who aspires to success in sport. A happily married man who plays hard and always gives 100 per cent, and never a whiff of scandal about him. If every player leaned towards his approach and professionalism, the sport would be in excellent shape.

Looking back on my spell at Newcastle, I can see that Kevin and the others occasionally regarded my enthusiasm and unusual innovations with more than a little suspicion, but again they gave me the support and encouragement necessary for me to continue a professional coaching odyssey that had only just begun.

All I did was to try to establish the right environment for each individual player in order to obtain the best from them. Nothing complicated about that! Work out what situations players were likely to find themselves in and practise, practise, practise that particular skill. If that's off the wall, I had, and still do have, problems. Everything a player performs in training has to correlate to the game itself. Different skills and movements may make them fitter, but won't necessarily turn them into better players if the movement has no relevance to the task in hand. If they're not even getting the benefit, then why are they doing it? Invariably I believe many coaches are doing it for themselves . . . to enjoy the experience of power and control.

A problem with many football clubs is that they appear to be stuck solely in the traditional ideas of training and even when they do embrace some new alleged advances from the world of sport science, invariably they do it in a traditional manner, i.e. everybody does the same and so nobody gains a true advantage. This can be compared to my approach which is to break down different movements and game situations, and specifically stress the athlete in those environments . . . over and over. Jonny Wilkinson, of the Falcons and England, is the finest example of the success of this approach. He's become the best player in the world and made his most dramatic gains by employing this training philosophy.

My approach encompassed the training methods employed by the most successful teams at any sports worldwide. Invariably the methods I saw at the football clubs I was involved in consisted of running round the field for a warm-up with some fun games thrown in, then a small-sided game followed by shooting practice. Now, you can obviously get so far by employing these tried-and-tested conventional work regimes, but by making the training programme more specific to the individual and then becoming 'conventional', you'll get that bit further. The conventional was fine in essence, but the modern game has moved on in physical and psychological terms, in areas of diet, relaxation and most of all technique. There seems to be very little emphasis on strength training or examining the game for what it really is – now a fast, reactive sport requiring skill, speed, physical and mental strength. By training for football by playing football, which is fair enough, you'll develop to the level of the skills of the players in those games, but there is so much more you can do to add to what each individual player will bring to those games.

An example of innovation: most matches kick off at three o'clock, but very little attention is paid to training at that specific time, which is crazy because the body clock needs to be specifically focused for that task. Of course, every other club trains at the wrong time as well, so they get away with it. Other innovations include exercising in the pool, weights, little changes of game emphasis to make it fresh and interesting. You can't be successful if you don't have enthusiasm and by keeping it fresh and interesting it is easy to maintain that enthusiasm. One-off moments of success can occur by accident, but you can't have a whole season, or a whole career, by accident. Attitude and motivation linked with dedication, skill and determination are everything. They bring their own rewards, but unfortunately many well-paid sportsmen, especially jobbing footballers, treat training as 'just another day at the office'. They turn up at the right time, do all the training, get a good sweat on, get a shower, get something to eat and go home . . . day-by-day . . . week-by-week. But very few of those days and weeks bring with them a high excitement or a sense of using those sessions to become as good as you can be, i.e. pushing yourself beyond the norm. There are 92 professional soccer teams in England with between, say, 20 and 30 professionals in each team. There are about 10 per cent of those teams in any one year who are genuinely striving for competition success. Unfortunately too many of the other players don't have a differential to their play or their environment and therefore end up living their professional lives in a type of limbo . . . fairly safe but very rarely in danger of winning anything.

From what I can see even now I don't think things have changed that much, and I believe that if given a subtle change of attitude to training and conditioning work, teams who have the fourth-, fifth- or sixth-best squads still have a chance of winning the Premiership. Most clubs adopt the same approach. In general terms, I do have strong views about football clubs and their conditioning process. I think there's an influence from athletics that can be dangerous. Again, like I said earlier, athletes, in the strict sense of the word, maybe only need to peak once every two or three years whereas footballers need to be fit to get the job done week in, week out for nine months every year. If you train an athlete as a footballer needs to prepare, then that athlete will never fulfil his/her potential as the fundamental philosophy behind weekly peaking definitely detracts from the one-off test. If a footballer is trained like an athlete, as is becoming increasingly the case, they actually get too fit and invariably break down in one way or another and end up playing very few games during the course of a season – acceptable for the athlete who competes in one or two selected athletics gatherings throughout a season, but no good for the footballer who needs to play successfully every week.

If I had to give my opinion as to whether players are overpaid, I would say the good characters, top professionals in every respect, deserve what they earn, but so should the best bricklayer, policeman, accountant or architect. I honestly believe that, for it reflects my values on life in every respect. However, there are those who aren't particularly skilled or dedicated, and not great professionals or good role models, and I think many of them are overpaid. There is a myth that all players are on massive wages, but football players in the English Leagues One and Two sometimes don't get paid as much as a plumber. So, putting it into perspective, many of them at the age of between 30 and 35 are knackered and, having existed on normal wages, leave soccer with very little to fall back on and poor job prospects. Contrary to popular belief, these players are in the majority. We only hear about the Beckhams and the other glamour boys, but the elite level is a very narrow band. I do think, though, there should be parity between those who play in the same team. Their wages should be closer together and incentives similar, because that inequality can be disruptive and create tension amongst players.

Make no mistake about it, football is in a major transition and the business side of the game in general, apart from teams such as Manchester United, Chelsea and Newcastle United, hasn't been handled all that well. Certain clubs have paid out vast amounts of money in the hope of success, but it hasn't worked because they haven't bought well . . . and that is establishing a clear two-tier system. Clubs are now going into administration and many are sweating week to week in order to maintain their position in the Premiership. Those who are successful in maintaining their position in the Premiership will continue to succeed because of the business acumen of their management and the efficiency of their playing staff, and those who don't will go to the wall.

Football is evolving and in the future I can see it following very much the same lines as American football and basketball, with the Premier League in a class of its own and teams coming up from the First Division suffering from an even bigger gulf, struggling like hell, then going straight back down. The future at elite level is bright, but below that I see it working more towards recreational sport for all. We can't maintain 92 English professional football teams businesswise. It's impossible!

I have known Blackie for a number of years and, as he comes from the east end of Newcastle like myself, we understand each other. I'm pleased Steve 'Windmill' Black has given up boxing to concentrate on what he does best – coaching and motivating the top athletes in his profession to become world-class performers. People don't realise how much he has helped middle-of-the-road athletes to achieve goals higher than their ability would have taken them had they been coached by anyone else.

I am particularly proud of the fact I was instrumental in signing Jonny Wilkinson for the Falcons in the early days, and that Blackie has been the motivational force that has transformed him into a world-class rugby star.

Freddy Shepherd – chairman, Newcastle FC

It was during this period, in 1993, at Newcastle that I was put on the shortlist to become manager of Blackpool. While at Ivy Court, I'd begun training Ken Redfern, a top referee. He had to keep fit to remain on the refereeing panel and found that the programmes I was setting enabled him to keep on top of his game. Basically, they consisted of cardiovascular work, some light circuits and motivation through conversation, relaxation and positive thought. We often had long conversations where I used to expound my theories and on one occasion I told him of my obsession with taking a smaller club from a lower division into the Premier League. It must have sparked him off because he knew the then owner/chairman of Blackpool before he ran into a few 'difficulties'. They were looking for a new manager and Ken took me down to meet Owen Oyston, which, when you think I had no track record in management, was very brave of him.

I had an interesting time showing off my responses to Billy Bingham's practical questions which gave me not the slightest problem. I was confident I could do the job standing on my head. Contrary to my expectations, the interview was extremely simple and I realised I was more than up for the job. The management side was something I was wired into and felt that, given the right backroom support, this could be a marvellous opportunity. Billy Bingham offered me the job that day, but was a little apprehensive because I wasn't a big name. He said, 'I'll probably get harassed to hell in the press for this, but I want you for the job.'

It's interesting to note that the names on the shortlist included Peter Reid, Lou Macari and two or three others. In the next few years, I was to work closely with Peter when he was managing Sunderland, but I never told him about the Blackpool offer. I can just see his smile when he finds out.

I agonised over the decision with Julie for several days, but finally turned it down because I would have had to move the whole family to Blackpool, a factor that hadn't been mentioned at the start as I was initially told I could commute. Moving lock, stock and barrel would have meant a huge disruption to the kids at a critical time in their schooling. I also suspected that all was not well at the club – nothing I could put my finger on, but my instincts were telling me it wasn't the right course of action to take. It was all supposed to be hush-hush, but Julie, bless her, let it out to the press without even realising. She received a telephone call, that went as follows.

'Oh, hello. Alan Oliver here.'

'Oh yes?' Alan Oliver of the *Evening Chronicle* was talking to her as if he was in the inner secret circle concerning the proposed job. 'Apparently Steve's been down to Blackpool for the manager's job?'

'Yes.'

'Did it go well for him?'

'Very . . . they've offered him the job.'

Next thing I know, it's all over the headlines . . . very embarrassing, but it's the way things go now. To be really honest, I was also still harbouring romantic dreams that I would get my real breakthrough at Newcastle United. There can be no ifs or buts about it, Blackpool would have been a challenging job in my number one sport and I do have major regrets about turning it down, but the past is gone. What the offer did reinforce, however, was my faith in my own abilities.

Meanwhile, at Newcastle United I was working with some good lads with a solid base of Geordie blood who enjoyed playing together on and off the field. They played exciting, almost cavalier football, but, my word, it was wonderful stuff. Kevin was often accused of being too emotional, but again it was that emotion which galvanised the team. There is no doubting his passion and I hope that marvellous enthusiasm continues to be rewarded throughout his managerial career, as a game without the Keegan passion would be poorer for it.

Paul Bracewell, who was playing for Newcastle United at the time, is one of the most honest, hard-working and likeable people I've ever met, not just in professional sport but in any walk of life. He was a superb player with a top attitude and complemented superbly his three midfield partners in that great Everton Championship-winning team (Peter Reid, Trevor Steven and Kevin Sheedy). He played with his heart on his sleeve; what you saw was what you got, and you got the lot! His fierce, brave style meant he was in the wars continually and I think he had something like 14 operations during his playing career to help repair structural damage. I worked closely with him during his rehabilitation from one such injury at Newcastle United and we became good friends. I loved his work ethic and he played well when he got back to playing.

Paul then went to be assistant manager to his old Everton midfield partner Peter Reid at Sunderland. In July 1994 he asked me if I'd go along and help out at the club. Since Newcastle United and Sunderland were in different leagues at the time, I had a unique situation whereby I trained both teams because interests didn't conflict. In fact, from November 1995 until August 1998 I trained Newcastle Falcons, Newcastle United and Sunderland all at the same time, surely a unique situation that could never be repeated.

Blackie is a great character, in fact larger than life (no pun intended). He has a great ability to get the best out of players and can both physically and mentally condition anyone for every sporting occasion. Obviously I only talk with regards to football, but he was a valued member of staff and a very, very professional person.

Having said all that about Steve, it is an injustice to him. He is a tremendous character and the best to work with and I would have a drink with him any time.

Peter Reid – ex-manager, Sunderland and Leeds

Peter Reid had gone to Sunderland at the right time, just as Kevin had at Newcastle United and Rob had at the Newcastle Falcons. Peter had (has) a great passion and surrounded himself with solid characters who worked well as a team and who all supported Reidy 100 per cent. He had, apart from Brace, some really good football men there, through and through professionals who knew the game and their jobs inside out. Coaches Bobby Saxton, Pop Robson and Ricky Sbragia were joined by my old mate and Pop's father-in-law, Lennie Hepple, to form an outstanding group of people.

Former Roker idol Jimmy Montgomery was goalkeeping coach, as he'd been at Newcastle United before. I liked Jimmy and enjoyed watching his work. I also enjoyed my work there and whilst we didn't have the same quality of player skillwise that we had at Newcastle United, we had some great characters. My personal emphasis was to try to bring those players a little closer to their optimal physical potential, certainly from a quickness standpoint, than I would at most other clubs. Yes, it was a risk, but it was one I felt we could take and if it was managed properly, and it was, we would get the just reward for our optimism.

Marten Smith and Craig Russell were two young players who had potential for years and years! I worked one to one with them and tried to resurrect their ambition and confidence. In one game we played against Millwall at Roker Park, Craig scored four goals. I really believed that, given a long enough run and the right support, Craig could have ended up a top-class Premiership striker. Smithy had equally good potential and actually has had a good career, playing most recently with Huddersfield.

Kevin Ball, who is back at Sunderland in a coaching capacity now, was a marvellous character for the club: fiercely competitive and honest as the day is long, tough man, super competitor.

Niall Quinn, Kevin Phillips and Kevin Kilbane were also top-class pros who were more than capable of delivering quality at the highest level on a regular basis. When Quinnie was on, at his best, he was unbeatable. He was big and awkward physically, but had a great touch and was the perfect foil for Kevin Phillips, who had a season where he was as good as anything in Britain, scoring lots of goals in only a slightly better than average team. It's a pity he didn't have an opportunity at one of the really successful clubs like Manchester United, Arsenal, Liverpool or Newcastle United under Kevin Keegan, because I believe he had the qualities which could have made him an excellent, and regular, international player. Kevin Kilbane contributed more as a very valuable team man than the media and certain sections of the crowd gave him credit for. A big, strong lad with a good turn of pace when he backed himself, a strong shot, good in the air and an unselfish hard worker. I enjoyed training 'Killer'. He was very professional and that attitude helped bring out his quality on the world stage for the Republic of Ireland, for whom he played very well.

My old mate Micky Holland once took Peter Reid into the Geordie heartland that is Scotswood for a drink with some of his mates. You have to remember there is a huge rivalry between Sunderland and Newcastle, so he was going into the enemy's camp, a bit like me. Now this was a really tough place and Peter going in there was like a red rag to a bull. It was certainly not the best location for a Sunderland manager, yet he won them over when they had a go at him. He gave them as good as he got and their attitude was 'Yea, he'll do for us' and as the weeks went by he called in again. That's the type of bloke he is – plenty of bottle. Peter is a good person and though the expression 'a man's man' is old-fashioned, it fits him like a glove for he is extremely loyal to those who work for him. His strengths are his great passion for the game, his toughness, tenacity and honesty. A hard worker with an intrinsically good understanding of the game, he has a good rapport with his players and a devilish sense of humour.

A very humble and well respected guy with an immense knowledge of sport. He will willingly share his experiences within the game and it is without any doubt that I have benefited from these meetings and that has helped me in my ongoing career.

A true friend to whom I owe a lot.
Ricky Sbragia – Manchester United FC

Of the coaching staff, I particularly liked the style of reserve-team coach Ricky Sbragia. The players liked and respected him as did the other coaches. But underwriting that popularity was a pragmatic and effective coach who organised his teams well and taught his individuals not just the rudiments of their chosen profession, but also the tricks of the trade! Ricky regularly brought his Sunderland reserve team across to train with our Newcastle Falcons side and some of our inter-team basketball challenges were legendary. Seeing Julio Arca, Kevin Kyle, George McCartney and the rest of the Sunderland lads up against Jonny Wilkinson, Mark Wilkinson, Jamie Noon and Liam Botham was great entertainment for any sports fan and the boys loved it. I wasn't at all surprised when Sir Alex Ferguson signed Ricky up to his coaching team at Manchester United two seasons ago as his reserve-team manager.

The most impressive part of that entire coaching team's background for me was their willingness to learn and work hard together daily to keep improving the team. Reidy was a charismatic and knowledgeable leader whose passion totally engulfed the club at that time. I really believe that if Peter had kept that entire coaching team together and allowed them to grow together as a management unit, then he would have been rewarded for it for years to come with a genuine chance of regularly qualifying for Europe.

'So much effort is wasted for the sake of giving a little more,' said the famous Chicago Bears coach/owner, George Halas, and how right he was.

When Sunderland were seventh in the Premiership that would have been the time to invest in the team, show real ambition and go out and sign a couple of big names who could have taken the team to the European zone qualification position. Easier said than done! I know that, but the team's acceptance of their position in life, believing they were doing well for the resources they had, ultimately cost them their Premiership status.

'If you stop trying to improve you stop being good,' is a saying that I felt subconsciously underwrote the Sunderland ambition. Pity, because they are a big club and will assume that status as soon as everyone associated with the club really believes how good they could be. Success is sometimes only about deciding to be good. A club like Sunderland need to think they can achieve not only from a stadium standpoint, but from the terraces to the dressing-room, and mostly by way of the pitch! If the team are to achieve, they must expect to achieve.

A huge influence on me at that time was Lennie Hepple, as I've mentioned before. Now Lennie came from a totally different standpoint as a dancer and it was he who introduced me to the benefits and necessity of body awareness. A wonderful old guy who had been a world champion ballroom dancer in his day, he was a revelation to the players. It was he who made Pop Robson quick as opposed to being fast and there is a distinction between the two. Lennie was extremely brave and I qualify this in the following terms. When Ken Knighton had Frank Clarke at Sunderland as manager they asked Lennie to have a look at a particular footballer. Their view was that the lad walked wrong, was slovenly and didn't have good movements. They wanted Lennie to change him completely. Lennie had a look at the player and then straight from the shoulder told them that if he attempted to change him in any shape or fashion, the boy would be totally destroyed. Now many coaches would have tried to justify their position and given lip-service to the management, but not Lennie, and he was right because that player was a young Chris Waddle, one of the most successful players ever to come out of the North-east.

So Lennie was for me – that is the honesty I respect. His knowledge was incalculable. He could look at an athlete and immediately identify strengths and weaknesses, and you can't put a price on that. It was a shame Lennie wasn't allowed to influence the game of football even more, but because he hadn't come from a football background, people were scared of his training methods which came from outside the square.

At this time I'd got to know a television producer, Ian Lennox, at Tyne Tees when we were making a boxing documentary called *From Russia With Gloves* and we got on so well we talked about taking a Sunday football team, giving them professional help, seeing what effect it had on the team's performance and turning that into a television documentary. We took Killingworth, where I had strong connections with the manager Frankie Law, and persuaded Lennie and Malcolm Allison to take them on. It was a great exercise and what amazed me was not what the players learned from Malcolm Allison, but what he learned from the players. Having been in professional football all his life, he thought, like a lot of others at that level in sport, that everybody's worth outside that scope was negligible. When he saw the skill levels of some of the players he was staggered and had to admit that he never realised just how much talent there was out there. He was an extremely biddable person and opened his mind, proving to me that the paths I was treading were the correct ones. The documentary was a success.

In my job I've come across literally thousands of people and if I had to single out one person whom I'm grateful to have met, it would be Blackie. There are two reasons for this. First, every time I speak to him he lifts my spirit with his sense of fun and life. Second, despite my best efforts I failed to meet Brigitte Bardot in my youth.

Ian Lennox – TV producer

BLACKIE

Recently, Ian has published a novel called *The Sixties Man* and one of the lead characters is based on me. Billy Latimer, he's called . . . unfortunately Ian kills him off in the book. Thanks, mate!

Chapter Six

FALCONS

At the top professional level of all sport, not just rugby union, but also that other-shaped ball game, football, just about all the players are in the same ball park concerning actual talent. But the guys who come out on top are invariably the ones who want to, believe they can, and decide to make those thoughts a reality. Whatever sport or job you're in, try this approach and you'll make quantum-leap gains in your chosen environment.

Steve Black

When I first arrived in Newcastle to take over as director of rugby at Newcastle Falcons, it was obvious to me that this was going to be a terrific challenge. I was confident of good support from the likes of Dean Ryan, Steve Bates, Doddie Weir, Gary Armstrong, George Graham, but realised that if we were to make any impact in what was a new phase of rugby it was going to take something special.

On going to the training ground one evening, Dean and I suddenly saw this man called Steve Black and thought, 'This guy is a little bit unusual, but he certainly craves attention.' From that moment we recognised that indeed he was such a special person apart from his ability in the physiological field. He jumped out of the pack as a motivator and from that moment I knew I had to build the team around his 'one-off' abilities.

Our success in those early days was in no small part due to his drive, personality, motivation and ambition, for he is a man who simply does not like to lose, and for that I will always be indebted. When he went to Wales, I didn't really want him to go, but recognised that he had to leave for the experience and I feel that he is now a more rounded coach for his time there.

Five years ago, everyone looked at Newcastle Falcons and thought that what we wanted to achieve was impossible. You only have to look round at our magnificent stadium, our squad and fan base to recognise that we have proved that we have both the determination and ability to become a force in Premiership rugby.

Blackie is very much part of that energy and ambition, and continues to be an inspiration at this club.

Rob Andrew – director of rugby, Newcastle Falcons

I was standing at the foot of the stairs when the telephone rang . . . I can't believe it was October 1995.

'Hello, Rob Andrew here.'

'Hello, Rob.'

'As you know, I'm coming up there and I've been talking to various sources and been told you might be a good person to chat to about contacts in the area and training.'

Rob Andrew, one of the most influential men in rugby, wanted to talk to me? Who in their right mind would have said no? We met at Kingston Park a couple of weeks later and I was immediately impressed. Right from the start I liked his winning personality and attitude. He was smartly dressed in a blazer and tie, and he exuded confidence. A good first impression doesn't always mean everything, but psychologically you can give a tick in the positive box straight away. I'd always had enormous respect for Rob as a sportsman. He had bottle on the field and epitomised everything good about sport. His attitude and ambition were exciting. He looked like someone I could do business with, so I had no hesitation in accepting his offer to become part of his team.

Newcastle Gosforth RFC had just become one of the first teams in the country to turn professional. I'd got to know Jon Curry, a larger-than-life character, former Gosforth captain and Under-21 International, whose career had been cut short by injury. Jon, an excellent motivator, knew rugby inside out and we worked well together. He'd actually been the person who recommended me to Rob and I'll always be indebted to him for having the confidence in my ability to succeed when it wasn't my game. Of course, a whole new structure was being implemented now money was coming into rugby, and with it a whole new generation of titles. Whereas I'd been regarded as a fitness coach/motivator, I was now being classified as a 'conditioning coach'. The term is now commonplace, but there is a misconception about the role, as most people, even still, regard the position in terms of fitness. Whilst in some respects it does have a bearing, the responsibility and terms of reference of the role go way beyond that. At this point in my life, I recognised that all the experience I had must be quantified to tackle the immense job I had just been given, so perhaps this is the right moment to address it, because it has a bearing on everything from this point. Exactly what is a conditioning coach?

Blackie is the most innovative and inspirational coach I've ever had the pleasure of working with, a coach way before his time and not afraid to take risks in his pursuit of that edge. More importantly, everyone that worked for him considered him their closest friend and I'm very proud to be one of that select group. Cheers, Blackie.

Dean Ryan – director of Gloucester rugby

Bearing in mind this was my job within the framework at Gosforth, it is important that I set out my own take on what is an extremely complex and demanding role. It involves preparing the team physiologically and psychologically for competition, at the same time embracing management in the equation in the quest for success. Over a period of time I take the individual and appraise where that person is at any given moment. In other words, find out how they tick. Having done that, it is necessary to carefully consider a number of interim goals, then a final objective considering that person's natural abilities in attaining those goals. I also have the responsibility of having to say, 'Sorry, we're not going to achieve those goals, I don't think they're realistic and we should reset our sights.'

Of course, there is a far bigger picture to take into account, for assessment is not solely an individual focus, but also involves a collective set of team goals. Like the pieces of a jigsaw, it is always better to get the framework right, then build from there. On individual assessment there are many aspects to be considered. Initial size, strength, speed, flexibility, power and agility are paramount considerations for the athlete to be in sport anyway. Over and above that there are psychological, emotional and spiritual factors, which until recent years have been universally ignored. In these areas I work hardest because, balanced correctly, they produce confidence, belief and knowledge. Every individual is unique, therefore a different mix of those factors is required. Some require more emotional and spiritual support, yet only a modicum of time on the physical. The combination is endless; I have to be all things to all men, with a sound knowledge of all of these areas. Percentagewise, the psychological and physical, on a bed of emotion and stability in a given area, are probably the most important. By that I mean if you feel good about being there and you want to be there, there's more chance of success. It's impossible to engage one of these factors without the others. Otherwise you become an aerobics teacher, psychologist, psychiatrist or priest. I see myself as all of these wrapped up in one.

The greatest art is being able to absorb everyone's needs at all ends of the scale. One moment I might be dealing with an intense Christian, the next a blatant philanderer, but I have to get close to all of them, give total support, provided their actions and beliefs are not destructive to the task and goals. If so, I will endeavour to steer a different path for them. A true conditioning coach has to be well read, with a genuine interest in all matters that may arise, to be chameleon-like, but at the same time not just act – it has to be Stanislavsky method acting rather than a Sir Lawrence Olivier style. It is incredibly rewarding if you get it right, but there are down sides, so the balance is always fine. There are times when you tell players you are for them and want to support them in every way you can. Then there are those that, whilst they have potential, will never achieve.

There are others who will listen, but will break ranks either by their own will or be influenced to do so by other forces, and I personally find both of these latter cases emotionally distressing. I feel their failure becomes mine. To choose someone for their ability and then have to tell them they are not capable of hacking it is a massive responsibility and reflects on both my judgement and that of the management.

It is therefore vital that I not only respond to the team, but also to the needs of management. I am a conduit for communication in both directions, and this is the most difficult area because I have nowhere to run, no one to play me. This role can be a hard one to bear, but I am fortunate in having a solid and understanding family to absorb part of the negative aspect. It isn't a healthy situation, but I know I am a one-off, flaws included, and can't change my personality. I have no illusions that, whatever effort I put in, it is always going to be a one-way relationship. Nothing back. If I dropped dead tomorrow someone would fill my place, start again and survive. They may not be as successful, but everything is about perspective. Knowing and understanding all this, I still can't change my approach because I consider it to be the best way forward for those with whom I work.

Often, when dealing with an athlete, you recognise there are some needs required to improve performance, but you feel that to introduce the subject to him or her would clutter up their minds. So you decide not to tell them and try changing things around by reshaping their behaviour. The trick is to impose on the athlete, persuade them to achieve certain aspects of training and mental exercises without them realising they're doing it. It hasn't to be a prescriptive thing, otherwise all they would have to do is look up the information in a manual, adopt the principles and hope there would be a positive result at the end. All an athlete really wants is improved performance. Too much information can confuse and distract from that goal. Given each individual is different, with completely different needs, coaching should rise above the simplistic and lazy level. It must be said the real difficulties arise when one of my athletes moves to another club and another coach cuts across my decision by introducing all of the areas I chose not to discuss. That is incredibly frustrating, because neither athlete nor coach realise I've already taken everything they are now considering into the equation. It can be destructive and confusing for the athlete.

Dealing with management is a different ball game. More political. I try to establish where every individual is coming from, their interests and passions, and then attempt to make them all compatible. Generally, most people in the game are thinking along very similar lines and often don't realise their own personality or ego deficiencies. So it's necessary to tell them white lies in order to bring them together, and I have no qualms about doing it. The complexities of my role are without boundaries, but I hope some of my explanations give a flavour of my attitude and actions when embarking on this rugby adventure.

A revolution was taking place in a sport previously steeped in amateur ethos. Sir John Hall, one of the mainsprings of this transition, had bought the club and renamed it Newcastle Falcons to make it a wing of his European sporting club vision. He'd already had a major effect upon Newcastle United and was buying up ice hockey and basketball, so the city was buzzing.

At the time of Rob's approach, I was actually already on board as Gosforth's first professional coach working with an amateur club. They paid me relatively well and I saw it as a real challenge. I was a football man through and through. It was Charles Buchanan who had introduced me to rugby at Gosforth and I quickly learned that coaching, whether it be football or any other sport, is much the same. People make the mistake of coaching sports instead of people, so my transition to rugby was relatively easy.

Make no mistake, there is a difference between football and rugby players. The latter are tougher, more intelligent and more capable of being empowered. However, there are signs that it might not stay that way as the money and high profile the new generation of rugby players is receiving could have a negative effect on their attitude. I sincerely hope not, but as we all know, money and adulation brings with it a heavy price. Footballers have a high opinion of themselves and have the potential to be better athletes. However, they are less liable to taste success in their careers, and accept that fact. Rugby players can be manipulated towards success for it appears more tangible to them. Obviously in football there are many special players, such as David Beckham and Alan Shearer, but by and large I stand by my view from a general coaching perspective.

Sir John's foresight in bringing Rob in as director of rugby was a masterstroke. His aim was to make Newcastle Falcons the most successful club in Britain. To be perfectly blunt, there was absolutely no chance of that ever happening with the existing set-up at Gosforth. The lads were canny, but as a team this era was a far cry from their glorious past. In simple terms, you'd have done a fabulous job if you could get them to be competitive in a game – motivating them to win was almost a miracle. There were some solid players – Paul Van Zanfleet ('Tank'), Arnie (Richard Arnold), Ross Williams, Neil Franklin, Steve Douglas, all good material – but we weren't going to win anything with them alone.

The best trainer and friend I have ever met. Without his help and encouragement, I wouldn't have been in the Falcons . . . but most important of all his influence on me as a human being has been even greater, and for that I will always be in his debt.
    Richard Arnold – Newcastle Falcons

It was also heartening to witness how the original Gosforth players responded and increased their game when alongside the top signings. Richard Arnold (Arnie) is a case in point. The Arnie who came over from New Zealand is certainly not the same man today. He arrived in Britain as a raw-boned youth, with a rough and ready manner, who called a spade a shovel. He didn't care a bugger for anyone or anything and his play on the field demonstrates that raw quality, but off it he has now become a sophisticated man with responsibilities – a wife, Helen, and daughter, Esme – and a lovely personality.

There is a responsibility, however, when trying to change people. The line has to be a fine one and honed to the positive.

Rob's standing in the rugby world was unique – his credentials impeccable and credibility without question – so he was able to draw in top-class players. However, he was regarded as an unknown quantity in the area of management and there was a feeling of resentment among some locals who felt that the director of rugby job should have gone to someone from Gosforth, and perhaps with some justification. It soon became apparent that Rob not only had management and business acumen, but a core of steel as he began building a formidable squad starting with Dean Ryan and Steve Bates, colleagues from Wasps. Remarkably, public perception was that these three were very close mates, but whilst they were good friends, they never lived in each other's pockets. In fact it was their time at Newcastle that actually brought them closer as pals. Steve had to finish at the school where he was contracted so initially it began with myself and Dean working together. It can't be stressed too strongly just how much influence Dean had on the team. His army background brought superb leadership, and there is no doubt that, as Rob was still on the field of combat, the two of them controlled the games completely. It was marvellous to watch them in action and very soon the excitement they generated began to spread throughout the club, and then into the public domain.

I first met Steve in 1995 when I arrived in Newcastle as coach to Newcastle Falcons Rugby Club and have enjoyed a close relationship with him ever since. His warmth, enthusiasm and friendship have been a massive influence on my development as a coach. I believe I have had the privilege of learning team preparation from one of the best, if not the best, in Britain today.

When I first experienced his methods I wasn't sure about their validity and, like many players, was surprised and sceptical about his slightly unorthodox style; but when you have the opportunity to talk about his philosophy, it is quickly apparent that he has a fantastic knowledge of physiological and psychological preparation, and possesses massive experience in professional sport. There is not much in the fitness industry that he has not considered and either adapted or discarded, and the evidence of his ability is the success that his teams have enjoyed throughout his career.

He is totally focused on the individual and his improvement. As a result, you very quickly learn to trust him implicitly and the results for those that do are usually spectacular: the development and progress of England's greatest fly-half ever, Jonny Wilkinson, is a fine example of his work. Blackie is unique and there are many players who owe him immense gratitude for the way they have been developed and nurtured while in his hands.

It is rare in professional sport to meet men of integrity and loyalty, but Steve is the exception to that hard-nosed individual. He is very tough and determined, but lurking just below the surface is a caring and compassionate man. In times of great stress and disappointment, he has always been the rock on which I have steadied myself and regained my confidence and strength. I consider myself to be fortunate to have been given the chance to work alongside him and I hope that opportunity will present itself again in the future. We have had some great days with the Falcons. Winning the League in 1998 and the Tetley Bitter Cup in 2000 are memories I will treasure, but the best memories will be the times I have spent with Blackie, discussing, evaluating and planning with a great friend.

He once said to me that we were on the same wavelength and each knew instinctively what the other was going to do next, particularly on the training field. Compliments don't come much higher than that. It is impossible to put into words the extent of his influence on my career and on its development up to now. All I know is that I am hugely grateful that he took an interest in me and will always be indebted to him for it.

Steve Bates – former Newcastle Falcons coach

I was to learn that Rob Andrew is a terrifically strong character, and he would need to be as events changed for the worse a couple of years later when the club was in crisis. On the surface a little skinny kid who loves all sport and is incredibly competitive, he refuses to be beaten. To the casual observer a lovely person, but a horrible little sod when it looks like he's going to lose. He will do anything, absolutely anything, to win – the traditional English bulldog. I've never had a player who both knew how to, and wanted to, win as much as him. His more cerebral understanding of how to win took him to levels in the game that very few have achieved and often his tactical and gritty determination won games that he had no right to win. A rare talent. He loved playing the game in a certain way, though if he had to change it to another style that he didn't enjoy as much, but it meant winning, he would employ it. Ultimately, what he likes more than anything is winning. For my money, what he achieved at the Falcons will never be equalled. It was amazing to bring a team from nothing to winning both the League and Cup, and that was down to him. He cares deeply for his players and team, and his passion is unquestioned.

There was resistance to me from some of the old guard, which was two-fold. Some said I was a golden boy making a fortune, which sort of gets in the way, and feared there was going to be a management hatchet job to get rid of them. So it wasn't very positive from them and the environment became a struggle, especially the politics between old and new. As normal I took a step back and tried to concentrate on the players. There was also a feeling of negativity among others that, because I hadn't played the game, it was impossible for me to understand the culture. Rubbish! As I said before, it was people I was conditioning to be the best. It seemed, and I may be wrong here, that the old guard didn't have the courage to embrace success, while the new kids on the block looked at me a little sideways when at an early squad meeting I pronounced we were the right people at the right place at the right time. Up to that point, everyone had been talking about achievements in the next year, but I felt this was negative and said if anybody wasn't prepared to do it now they should walk away.

Other coaching staff were upset and felt I was putting too much pressure on the team, but I argued if such a simple message was too much for them they shouldn't be there. Using a simple analogy, if my mother was lined up in the Olympic 100 metres final and felt the pressure, she shouldn't be there. If we were having a dinner party and I had to do the cooking, I'd run a mile . . . there's no way I should be there. These were professional sportsmen, highly paid to take the responsibility that came with it. I had total belief in both my own ability and those I was working with. They were talented and had proved themselves, so why wait for tomorrow? Obviously it is necessary for everyone to pull together and in the same direction, but by the same token if everybody is thinking the same, somebody isn't thinking. There has to be space for some original thought, otherwise colouring numbers in a standard manual could simply achieve success.

So I predicted we'd get promoted . . . we got promoted. I said we'd win the League and Cup . . . we won the League and Cup, and my detractors had said it wasn't possible because I had never played rugby before. I rest my case. But the important thing was Rob and the players judged me on my results, which I'm proud to say worked out for the best. However, taking people on the ride with you can be dangerous if your belief isn't matched equally with the responsibility that brings.

Of course, even now there are those who said it was lucky. There always are! I always refer to the story about the guy who wanted to set up an airline route from New York to Seattle. Experts estimated it would take 124 days, putting everything into place from conception to application. He did it in 9! Know why? Because he didn't know it should have taken 124. All that means is that people are limited by their own imagination and the imagination of those around them. We keep going back to tradition, but I make no excuse for repeating that it can only take you so far, because techniques and understanding have moved on light years. Yes, I was definitely lucky; lucky my introduction to the Falcons allowed me time and space to implement what may have seemed radical at Newcastle United.

There is only one single regret I have about meeting Blackie – I wish it had been sooner. Sure I would have been a better, fitter rugby player; but more than that, I would be a better person. 'If you help enough people to get what they want, you can have everything you want.'
  Zig Ziglar – motivational speaker

Blackie, I don't know what your goals are, but I know they will become a reality. You deserve that and more.
  Tony Underwood – British Lions, England, Falcons

Other first-class players were recruited – Gary Armstrong, Gareth Archer, Tony Underwood, Doddie Weir, Pat Lam and Inga Tuigamala. A real good mix of different personalities, every one a pedigree athlete, but that wasn't the be-all and end-all to success. Gary, a tough-as-old-boots Scot and natural leader by example, was one of the most interesting because it was felt perhaps he was coming to the end of his career and maybe we could get another year out of him. But five years later, he was still playing some of the best rugby of his life. He has only recently retired at the age of 39.

All we did was change his training – a bit of weights, a few days off, concentrate on his skills and tailor his output in such a way that his effort was kept for the park on match days. Gary is a dogged individual with a heart as big as a lion and courage by the sackload, and I learned a lot about the human condition from him. So the learning process was not a one-way street. Then there were others, like John Bentley, the international league winger, and as 'off the wall' and dynamic a character as you could chance to meet, and Nick Popplewell, regarded as one of the finest Irish forwards of the past 25 years, who gave the team 'biff', and very soon, even though some of these players were in the autumn of their careers, they brought about a massive change.

Pat Lam was also a terrific signing, an absolutely stunning player in his leadership qualities and physical skills, but getting the best from him was difficult, because he didn't really like training. I had to kid him that he was training well and reward him when he wasn't working at it, almost embarrassing him into training hard.

I clearly remember the first time I met Blackie. I had arrived in Newcastle the day before, after a 30-hour journey, to begin my new contract, so jet lag had already kicked in. Dean Ryan picked me up from my hotel and said we'd go for a little session at the gym with the 'trainer' and Richard Arnold, our fellow back-rower. This would be our training group for the season. As we walked into the gym I recognised Arnie from back in New Zealand, but when I met Blackie I must admit he took me by surprise. First, he didn't look like I expected him to, and second, he gave me an enormous hug, which I would only expect in the islands of Samoa.

That first day in the gym with Blackie set the tone for our relationship as professionals and mates. I have never been one for lifting big weights and training in the gym, and so I hate being compared to fellow players on the amount of weight they lifted in the gym. Well, all three of us had a go on the seated bench press, full stack. Arnie went first and did 22 reps, then Dean 23 reps just to annoy Arnie, then me 3 reps, possibly 4 if he was generous. I could feel the reddening of my face and that wasn't from pushing, then Blackie came close to me and said, 'Fantastic effort,' in his loveable Geordie accent and proceeded to praise me and tell me how much he looked forward to working with me. I had never come away from a weight session feeling so good, and my first impressions of the finest Geordie person I had ever met made me realise that I had made the right decision to come to the North-east.

A lot has been said about what the team achieved during those Championship-winning years, but we as players knew that none of it was possible without Steve Black. For me personally, I have never been as fit, strong, fast or powerful as I was working with Blackie, and I must say on record that before the season was over I beat both Arnie and Dean on the bike, the treadmill, the stepper and occasionally in the weights, which was a long way from our first session. I know they won't like it, but check with Blackie, my mate!

Blackie, thank you for everything. I wish you and your family the very best and hopefully will see you down here one day. Take care, God bless and I love you.

Pat Lam – Auckland head coach and forwards adviser to the All Blacks

Inga Tuigamala was a revelation as a player. His physical strength, speed, change of pace and ball handling were second to none, and all wrapped up in pure charisma – a real crowd pleaser and the first million-pound superstar in this new rugby world. I was with Rob Andrew in a hotel room the night he did the deal to sign Inga. It was a huge step for rugby union and a huge step for the Newcastle Falcons, and Rob and Sir John embraced the circumstance with their usual aplomb. A new era was born.

With players of the calibre of Inga Tuigamala, Pat Lam, Gary Armstrong, Nick Popplewell et al., the dressing-room became a marvellous place of research for the management voyeur. Jimmy Greaves once said the best team talk he ever had was a manager looking into the dressing-room and saying, 'Best of luck, lads.' Everyone's needs are different. Some want to be shouted at, others such as George Graham and Richard Arnold demand a smack across the face. Then there is the quiet one who needs a cuddle or another who demands to be totally ignored.

The odd insecure one needs bulling up in front of his mates. Others have to be taken down a peg or two.

The first time you see Blackie, you're greeted with the sight of a very broad man with a thick beard and a Geordie accent. At first sight you think, 'What does this man know about fitness?' but, as with most things, looks are deceiving as I found out to my cost at St James' Park, where he managed to push me beyond what I thought was my limit. Over the years, my limits changed every time he pushed me harder. In my time at Newcastle Falcons I managed to play for Scotland 25 times and, although it was quite a lot to do with playing in a good team, in my eyes Blackie had a huge part to play in that, something I will never ever forget or be able to repay.

For me, the thing about Blackie that makes him stand out as a fitness adviser, and I use that in a broad term because he's much more than that, is that every time he takes a session he asks you how you are. If you feel good he trains you hard, and if you don't he will train you as hard as he thinks necessary, which could be anything from ten minutes to one hour. For me, after playing for 22 years, that is the best thing a player can hear before he starts training. He's much more than a fitness man, he's the best motivator I've ever encountered and he'll draw the deepest emotions out of you so as to make you play the best you can. He also has the finest sense of humour a man can have. For anybody who buys his book, if you have any aspirations of reaching the highest level, you wouldn't go far wrong in employing the services of one Steve Black.

Blackie . . . I owe you everything.

George Graham – Scotland, Borders

The trick to a dressing-room wind-up is to have it all decided with the individuals beforehand . . . completely choreographed, never spontaneous. For instance, Tony Underwood would come to me prior to the match and say he needed me to give him a hard time to get him going. If he was training and said, 'I think I've done enough,' he didn't want you to agree with him. He wanted someone to say, 'Like fuck you've done enough. Now get out there and I'll tell you when you've done enough.' And whilst it was against my natural attitude, I went along with it and it worked for him.

Dressing-room motivation is probably one of the most interesting aspects of my job – knowing just what buttons to press. The psychology is far bigger than most people realise, and makes the difference between winners and losers. Get it wrong with one of them and the whole balance of confidence can be tilted. A lot is often made of the great preparation before the match, but in reality clever game plans mean nothing, for once they step onto the pitch and the whistle blows they have to fight for the right to play the opposition. Do it to them, before they do it to us! Or as Carwyn James (coach of the British Lions, 1971) famously said, 'Get your retaliation in first, boys.'

The fitness side is easy; any conditioning coach with a modicum of experience can do it, because it involves basic cardiovascular and strength training. But in realistic terms that only represents about 15 per cent of the whole. Once again we have to go into the toolbox to select the correct spanners. For example, too much aerobic work will have a slowing effect. Anybody, whatever shape or size, provided they are tough enough, can complete an aerobic course. But anaerobic work is a whole different ball game and requires toughness of the mind in direct correlation to desire and will to succeed. It is in this area that the champion is fashioned.

Then comes the real secret: visualisation. Take the scrum. Eight players have to merge together as one to destroy the opposition. You tell them to lie down and imagine the whole process. 'Get down, bind tight, got your distance and your breathing's just right. You're feeling powerful, strong, supported and in the best possible place. You're hitting the opposition with great ferocity and intensity. The hardness and all the power of that scrum is coming through and you're pushing them all over and you can do what you like with them. They can't make any inroads into you, and they're weakening by the second. You're getting stronger by the second.'

Visualisation is one of the most underrated forces for success. Your mind controls your body and when you're imagining going by people, sprinting, and nobody's getting to you . . . the power and exhilaration of touching the ball down . . . you've done it! And if you think it enough . . . it happens. Of course, the reverse is also true. Think negatively and it will come to pass. Everything is won in the mind and you will only be as effective as you want to be.

The really difficult aspect in coaching requires one of the great human traits: courage. Able coaches often lack the courage to carry through that thing called rest, which is far more important than training. It takes bottle and knowledge to implement, and I try my best to inculcate how vital it is to rest both players and staff colleagues.

Initially, I saw Rob's appointment as a figurehead, much like that of Kevin Keegan at the Magpies, only with more substance. The difference was Rob was still playing, and his most impressive aspects were his commanding presence on the field in controlling matches and that incredible will to win. Any concerns I harboured as to whether those skills would transfer off the pitch after he retired were totally unfounded. His management and tactical brain give him an insight into players and tactics which was a joy to observe.

Signing million-pound Inga was without doubt his biggest test, a massive responsibility for such a young man to make. As I've said, I remember being in the hotel room talking to him about it and heard myself totally out of order saying, 'Hey, you're a pathfinder, not a follower. You're a leader.'

Bearing in mind Rob was still playing himself, Inga's signing was a major decision in rugby history. This was ground-breaking in a sport in which people had played for nothing or a couple of pints in the clubhouse afterwards. The significance of signing the mesmeric Samoan was a watershed for the whole of rugby and clearly signalled our intentions.

There is no doubt Rob Andrew is a special person, both as a player and an observer of rugby potential. In fact I'm sure his ability to spot players' qualities such as their desire to win and awareness both on and off the ball is more important than the recognition that they are good players. I was privileged to be there at the start of the rugby revolution, witnessing a stream of wonderful talents blossoming into the game. Of those, probably the greatest of them all was young Jonny Wilkinson and it's amazing that, even after all of his spectacular success in the North-east, only after his

World Cup exploits has the world come to terms with the fact that we have one of the greatest sportsmen for decades. Again, it is exciting to reflect that I saw him from day one.

A fine young man, multi-talented and physically far stronger and bigger than he appears, Jonny's appearance belies his true stature. To put him into perspective, he is light years ahead of Barry John at his peak. As a personality, he's not just a nice lad, but totally honest and never flowery. He'll tell you exactly what he thinks, and he lives and breathes rugby. Hell-bent on success, nothing will stand in his way to become the best player in the world. Although he has above average intelligence, he was never interested in academic life. All he thought about was kicking, passing, tackling, working out strategy. It is his life. He's a total one-off who will go down in rugby history as one of the true heroes. I was captivated by his singular approach and professionalism, even at 18, and his constant search for perfection is an example to anyone who aspires to success. He's a wonderful role model for any young lad coming into the game.

In February 2004, it was fantastic sitting in a star-filled audience at the Newcastle Civic Centre to see Jonny being presented with the Freedom of Newcastle upon Tyne. That is the highest award a Geordie can get, but the finest award we could give him is to call him a Geordie. To have been there right at the beginning of his career and witness what he's become is absolutely marvellous. He's adopted the North-east as his home and, more than that, the North-east has totally taken him to their hearts as a son.

Sitting there as he accepted the honour so humbly took me back to when he first came to the North-east. The man to thank for that is Steve Bates, who had taught him at Lord Wandsworth School in Hampshire. Steve, who has a critical eye for talent, spotted him very early on and when he came to Newcastle Falcons as a coach began extolling to Rob what a terrific prospect this young lad was. He said that he was confident that Jonny had all the attributes to be a successful rugby player in the professional game. How astute that judgement proved to be. Steve Bates not only did the North-east a favour, but was instrumental in helping to create a legend.

When I first clapped eyes on this young lad, I tried to get to know him and build up a portfolio in all respects. What struck me immediately was his excellent work ethic and attitude. Extremely enthusiastic, he obviously loved what he did and after a quick once-over he most certainly appeared to have talent. As it worked out, he had more than a little bit. With most people in life, if you encourage them it tends to bring out the best in their enthusiasm. With Jonny that wasn't necessary because he was already off-scale. We have a video of him at 12 where he is saying his aim was to be the best player in the world, and at 25 not only has he achieved that, but his intention is to be the best and most influential player of all time. Even taking that into account he doesn't sit back and bask in the limelight, but constantly strives to take every area of his game and training onto a different level, which gives an indication of his self-belief, motivation and attitude.

Jonny has an extremely engaging personality, and whilst appearing reserved and a little shy in public, once you get to know him privately his sense of humour is completely off the wall and this I completely relate to. Very Reeves and Mortimer-esque. We have a lot in common, really. He likes music and movies and all aspects of entertainment. He is a total fan and loves American football, basketball and every area involving physical and mental skill in sports. What I realised very quickly was his great hobby in life was also his chosen profession. When these came together, it brought out the best in his personality and made him completely happy in his environment.

From day one he made an impression on everyone who worked with him or saw him playing and it can't be emphasised just how big that impression was. People forget this, but by the end of our Championship season in 1997 he was actually first-choice centre and partnered by either Inga Tuigamala or Alan Tait. Make no mistake, great as those two players were, Jonny's name was first on the team sheet. At 18 years of age, that was incredible and showed just what his potential was.

Through the years he has worked diligently and without complaint on all aspects of his game and over that time has changed his emphasis ever so slightly. He still has a terrific work ethic, but he now does what is effective, not just covering everything. He now has the confidence to do effective work which is in the process of taking him onto a new dimension altogether. Remember, at 25 he's captained England, has over 50 caps, been world player of the year twice, a World Cup winner and also has Grand Slam, Six Nations and domestic League and Cup medals. So if anybody was destined for success, it was Jonny. His only real fault was that his work ethic was so high and he worked so hard, had it been allowed to continue it could eventually have been detrimental. All that energy had to be channelled and, thankfully, it became a big step forward and worked well for him.

People will often say about players that their strong points can also be their weakness. This is particularly apt about Jonny because his strongest point is a work ethic that gives him strength of character, mental toughness, integrity and total professionalism. But it can also be counter-productive, if not harnessed. He's now beginning to make major roads into that because he's said, 'Right, I need to do that, that and that to be better, and if I'm told to rest, I've got to.' It's only natural to move towards the things in training you like doing and are good at. Unfortunately Jonny is a unique character because the little bugger lies and is good at everything, and my quest is to find out exactly what he's bad at because that's the area that will take him even further.

As a trainer, he is phenomenal. There is simply no stopping him and one of my goals is to make use of that ethic at the Falcons because unfortunately some of the players just come in, do their bit and go away. I can't understand that mindset, and whilst most people do respond to Jonny, I sometimes wonder if he is simply a one-off. His dedication in the pursuit of excellence is generally associated with scientists or artists with a passion and intensity that is off-scale. He is so focused people don't fully realise just how much. They will talk about it on television and in newspapers, but working alongside him is way beyond any other comprehension. I have said this for some time now, but we don't realise what a phenomenon we have on our hands. When he arrives for training the spirit is jumping out of him in anticipation of work, but I have to keep telling him that, at 25, he has a long way to go and, God willing his health is retained, he will not be at his best until he reaches 32 or 33. The responsibility of keeping him right to get him to that level is enormous, but a pleasure and a mouth-watering prospect for his future development as potentially the finest player the world has ever seen.

What amazes me is that Blackie exhausts himself every week to ensure everyone has the opportunity to go out there and do their best, and that is a fantastic skill. But he has become, along with my family and my close friends, the driving force behind my goals and ambitions, and without watering anything down he is a part of every single day in my life. If I don't train with him, I will be talking to him about what we intend doing the next day, or how to spend my time off. So I meet and talk to him every day, even if it's not about training, and it's a huge factor, because much of my confidence and self-belief comes from my respect and belief in him.

I go to Blackie with my goals written down on a piece of paper and tell him this is what I want. With his experience he will absorb and amend what he thinks needs amending, but never in the goals sense because I know that I have confidence in what I can achieve and he has the confidence in what he can help me achieve, but I am willing, by giving him my goals, to put that other side completely into his hands. I'm actually almost giving him the sheet of paper and saying, 'Right, that's yours now, I've written it, I've got my copy and that's yours.' I don't write down how many shuttle runs, so many passes or X amount of weights. All I say is, 'I want to be in the best physical shape, fitter than anybody else, stronger, more powerful and explosive for my size,' and when it comes to how am I going to do this, all I write down is, 'This is to be undertaken by Steve Black.' I don't need to explain to him, all I know is I want to improve and develop to those levels and I have the confidence in him to know he's the best in the world at what he does and if anyone can get me there . . . he will!

My commitment then, to achieving that, is to turn up every day, be there to see him, be right on time, right on target and ready to go. Then I just let him do whatever. I have never questioned anything we do on the training side of things. Sometimes we do some crazy things, other times less crazy, but never a question of doing a few more of these or those. If he tells me to go home after ten minutes, I go home. That's the relationship we have. I've given that part of my life to him because I have complete faith in him, and as a close friend I want to win as much for him, because I know how important it is for him to be part of a winning side . . . and know he wants me to achieve my goals also.

To be honest, I can't understand why more players who have him at their disposal in a professional sense don't accept the fact that there is so much the guy can do for them. If you want to be 10 lb heavier and 30 per cent fitter, 20 per cent faster and achieve seemingly impossible goals . . . Blackie can do it for you. All you have to do is work on what he advises and all he asks from you is your personal pride and integrity to be in place every time you're there. Give exactly what you've got in every training session, in every game mentally and physically, and not to play-act being more tired than you are, not to be mentally weak enough to give in before you have to . . . and then training and playing rugby is so simple. And with so much faith and confidence in the guy, all you have to do is go out there and give everything you've got and just know that he will take care of everything else.

That is so good for me and also the fact that my brother and I just like training with him because it is so much fun. It's fun, because in between training, when we are having a little break, he talks absolute rubbish, because it's funny what he says and because his humour is just another example of his professionalism. He is there totally for you and knows exactly what you want, and has total confidence and faith in what he does and the way he does it. He is the best at what he does and I know that to be exactly true. No one is able to follow him, because no one has what he has. It's not written on a piece of paper . . . it's in his feelings, his knowledge of you as a person, a special something that is able to get the best out of you as a person.

He gets to know every one of the players as a personal decision, as a commitment to every one of them in a remarkable way. To get to know that player, how he operates as a person, as a friend, knowing their limits and therefore being able to push those limits back when the player doesn't think he is capable of any more. And that's something you don't get nowadays . . . that important area between coach and player . . . developing their relationship.

Everyone knows the professional game is a cut-throat business and that players will have to leave. Some will be told to go, others of their own accord, so if you're not good enough, you're not good enough! But even if leaving is on the cards, in any training session while you're part of the squad, Blackie is there to be your friend to help you through it. He gets to know you well enough to know when you're at your best or when you need a rest. Often, when I turn up, he will take one look at me and say, 'Get in the pool, you're not looking well enough,' and that's just the great thing about him, because you know you're with someone who has your interests totally at heart.

Blackie will get the best out of you, but will only do it the right way because he knows how to do it properly. He certainly lets you know how he feels, but always starts his sessions with a hug greeting and this builds up the bond, creating exactly the right atmosphere. Sometimes I get frustrated, as does he, in wanting to achieve what I do, and I can't quite see sometimes what I'm doing, and get kind of lost. For example, I'd been ill for a week and a half and didn't realise how weak I'd become when I returned to training. It was very tough and I was failing on exercises I'd never failed before. I had come back and tried to show him that I could still do it, but because I was so tired, I couldn't get over this barrier I figured was my limit at that time. So I was screaming and shouting and he was telling me I'd done well, and I was telling him in not so nice words that it wasn't good, that I'd let myself down, and was poor and weak. His response was quite an angry one which suddenly gave me a shock. A bit like when you're driving and you kind of nearly have an accident and it wakes you up and you think . . . well, maybe he's right.

I get frustrated when I can't achieve what I want, but I have learned you just have to go with it, for if Blackie says something he actually means it 100 per cent. Some of the things he says to the team and individuals, in the manner he does, are very harsh, but they're said in a very honest way and you need to know that everything he does is for your benefit. If you're slacking or not pulling your weight and letting people down and it gets told to you by Blackie, well, that's as good an indication of it being true as there is and I've seen people respond to that brilliantly.

There is also a slight air of mystery about Blackie and it is something you just don't want to find out. Like putting your hand into a cold, dark pool.

What I must say about him is very important. He is the most unselfish person I know and, as I have got to know him over the years, day in day out, I know he often isn't feeling well. Quite a lot of the time if anyone asks him how he's doing, his answer is always 'top of the world' or whatever, because he knows that being positive is the infectious thing to do, and then people are able to feed off that. There is never any complaint or moaning, even if what he is going through must be absolute hell. He's always marked with pure positivity and that is what people need and this shows his tremendous strength of

LEFT: With Allan Bateman (centre) on corporate duty for Life Fitness. (© Regency House Studios)

TOP RIGHT: Peter Beardsley, his son Drew and I celebrating our Twickenham Cup win.

ABOVE LEFT: How did Glen McCrory and Gosforth's John Curry ever have this strength? (© Newcastle Chronicle and Journal Limited)

ABOVE RIGHT: Former Fulham manager Paul Bracewell on the way to recovery. Paul is one of the best professionals I have ever met. (© Newcastle Chronicle and Journal Limited)

TOP LEFT: Jonny and I sharing a laugh!

TOP RIGHT: Richard Arnold and I celebrate
the 2002 Tetley's Bitter Cup win.

ABOVE: A Falcons frenzy! The 2004 Powergen Cup win.
(© Newcastle Chronicle and Journal Limited)

TOP LEFT: Top judo player and my good friend
Geoff Oughton in an unfamiliar pose.

TOP RIGHT: The bairns! Mark, Emma and Stephen.

ABOVE: Four just men (clockwise from top left): Pop Robson,
Lennie Heppell, Malcolm Allison and I.

TOP LEFT: Feet of Flames – Jason Robinson in
Brisbane after the historic First Test Lions victory.

TOP RIGHT: One of the great characters –
John Bentley and I at Mam's for breakfast.

ABOVE: A familiar pose over the last 30 years.

TOP: Somebody up there likes me! That night they didn't.

ABOVE LEFT: Mam and Dad in a confectionery shop.

ABOVE RIGHT: My family – Mam, Julie, Nana, Stephen, Mark and Emma – yes, Julie's pregnant.

TOP LEFT: Blackie at 20 . . . nearly 30 years and a few stone ago.

TOP RIGHT: Welsh dream team – (clockwise from top left) Trevor James, Graham Henry, Lyn Howells, David Pickering and Alun Lewis.

ABOVE: Uncle Billy, Julie and Mam with me at our wedding.

TOP: The bairns – early on! Stephen, Emma and Mark.

ABOVE LEFT: Julie, Emma and I in family pose.

ABOVE RIGHT: With my good friend Bryn Pringle in party mode.

TOP LEFT: Lar Fawcett and I on the way to training.

TOP RIGHT: Young Blackie – I didn't always have a beard!

ABOVE LEFT: My nana as I remember her.

ABOVE RIGHT: My sister Roz with
a young Stephen and Mark.

character. Having got to know him well enough, he will now let me in on when he isn't well, which adds to our relationship and helps me understand him better. Despite what he's going through, there's never any desire to be negative, which must be incredibly tough and I have learned a lot from that fantastic attitude, because I now realise there is a time and place to talk about problems, otherwise always be positive and try to make everyone else positive. That is what Blackie does . . . he always makes everyone else feel better, no matter how bad he feels. He is an exceptional human being, I am privileged to have met him and will always treasure his friendship.

Jonny Wilkinson – Newcastle Falcons, England, British Lions

Fitness is an all-embracing term actually meaning little in relation to professional sportspeople because they should be in good condition as a prerequisite. You often hear someone comment about a specific player saying, 'He tried hard.' Well, isn't that what he was supposed to do in the first place? Should he get a special tick for trying hard? I don't think so. As a coach, I need to know more about someone. For instance, did he excel at this or was he outstanding at that? When 'new rugby' broke, everyone went berserk on general fitness, and to a certain degree they were right, but that should have only been the starting point. To be professional it had to be several notches above that norm in specific fitness. For example, in athletic terms, a runner like John Regis, one of our finest sprinters at 200 metres, looks terrific, as if he could take on the world, but anything from 800 metres up might be a different matter.

So fitness and looking good is only cosmetic. Training and conditioning, both physical and mental, must be specific to event and ability, and even that can be broken down. Take two players of equal ability in the gym on strength, speed, agility and balance, but one of them is called Joe Bloggs and the other Gareth Edwards. Joe Bloggs will always be fit and look good, but Gareth Edwards was one of the greatest rugby players ever to wear a Welsh shirt. Many of the clubs lost the plot by concentrating solely on fitness, and given a scale of one to ten they would all probably come out at eight, nine or ten, including all of the international squads. So it comes down to who has the best players, which in turn means the wider the choice, the better.

New Zealand and their Super 12 clubs display fast and entertaining rugby, but they are suspect physically when up against a committed England or France. Rugby is still a religion in New Zealand, so the All Blacks will always be prominent, maybe not world dominant, but always prominent and a team to beat. I'll be very surprised if they ever come back to be the force they once were. Australia are different: they have big hearts and you must never write them off, but that's about as good as you'll get with them because they haven't a great deal of people to choose from. So their pool is too small for perennial success. They've probably had their day, but again will always be a formidable team to overcome. England, on the other hand, are a completely different ball game – stacks to choose from, nine years into the professional game, these are the boys for the future. Wales? Far too small. Ireland and Scotland, the same. They produce some magnificent players, but in the final analysis there is realistically only one team in it – England. The only way the others would be able to compete with England is by each of them staying together as an international team and being run as a club team to develop solid teamwork. Getting them together a few days every so often is doomed to failure, because the Unions that control them will only perpetuate the problems. They will produce the odd flashes of brilliance, but usually more of the same.

I recognised very early on that, whilst the Falcons were extremely fit and we had some terrific players, it was not the best team. I had to work hard on them psychologically, because the mind game was far more important, keeping everyone's confidence and hunger to succeed on the up even when, at times, I was kidding them. It was my job to remind them of their strengths, convince them they were the best, so their weaknesses went unnoticed. Had I trained them conventionally, we would have done all right, but there was no chance they would have become champions. Like the comment earlier about trying hard . . . it had to go further than that. I told them, in order to win, I expected them to come off the field more knackered than the other team. If next day the papers said the Falcons won a hard-fought game but the other team came off the park the stronger, I was delighted. I expected the team, to a man, to come off the field shattered.

There's a fallacy that we have to entertain the punters and in many respects that's right. But if that sort of conversation took place at meetings, I would simply get up and walk away because it is negative. My job was getting them up to win. Winning builds in entertainment, but that comes afterwards. Leeds United used to batter out results and, once they won, used that confidence to display flair and belief to produce entertaining football.

Another important aspect of my role was to stay completely separate from politics within the club and sport in general. Whilst accepting politics is a fact of life, had I become involved with any one group, my credibility and objectivity would be undermined. As a single-minded maverick this may be considered a weakness, but I am proud of it and know in any company or situation I stand head high. Whenever failure is examined in any organisation, it's a knocking bet politics and not the performers pulled it down. Why are these people involved – apart from paying wages and sorting administration? Answers on a postcard!

A cheek-by-jowl account of matches is not really necessary as the record books speak for themselves, but in that first year (1995–96) we had to consolidate as a team, otherwise we were going down. Once we got hearts and minds together and it started pulling round there was never any danger we wouldn't stay up, and we did! In 1996–97 we were promoted to the Premiership, and in 1997–98 we won the League and Sanyo Cup in an unprecedented season. I doubt whether this could ever be achieved again. It was a unique situation; we had very good players, a very good side, but not the most talented. It was a roller-coaster season and we didn't seem capable of being beaten, but it is the defeats that stick in your mind, not the victories. For instance, we went down to Bedford and were done by a more highly motivated side. Frank Warren, their owner, may have played a master card when he went into their dressing-room and allegedly offered an unplanned cash incentive to beat us. True or not, the story illuminates which way rugby was going. From that point on, despite all our wins, the season became very tight because other teams realised we were beatable. It created a marvellous atmosphere for the run-in and we had some fantastic results. Winning at

Leicester was wonderful, then taking Bath at Gateshead and losing at Saracens in the last seconds by a drop goal in front of a 20,000-strong crowd were magnificent days. But we had self-belief and managed to grind out a result to win the League.

What we had put together was remarkable and the common belief is we had bought success, but nothing was further from the truth. As many clubs have learned to their cost, buying good players is not always the answer. There is evidence on a daily basis, where transfers for millions here and there have had no effect on team results whatsoever. A most important factor for our success was good players, yes, but the process of gelling them together as an effective team was the critical element. It's understandable how the public thought the former, though, because the media portrayed the image that Sir John had come into the club with all guns blazing, much as he did at Newcastle United.

It is a matter of record that when Sir John Hall brought Kevin Keegan to Newcastle United he encouraged terrific, exciting, passionate football, the club was saved from relegation and it is regarded as a very successful period . . . I certainly think of it that way and feel so privileged to have been a part of it. However stimulating that period was, historical analysis may send a different message. We didn't actually win anything, but fans always refer back to those Keegan days with great affection. However, if Manchester United had had the same run as us, it may not have been acceptable. So it is important to put Sir John's imput into perspective. He was a very successful businessman who passionately believed that the North-east could add trophies to its accepted status as a hotbed of soccer. He took the football club so close and the journey was exciting for all concerned: player, coach, manager, spectator alike.

Fortunately, at the Falcons, we were able to give him that success in sport he craved and the fact that we won the Premiership at our first attempt was undoubtedly down to the recruitment of Rob Andrew, Dean Ryan, Steve Bates and myself as the driving forces behind his Geordie rugby initiative.

On a personal level, I always found Sir John an enthusiastic supporter whose intentions were always for the best, but because he was driven I suspect he needed more from his involvement. On many occasions he and I had heated discussions, but I think we probably both benefited from them. I knew him from my days at Newcastle United and one particular situation from then springs to mind, when he called me into the office for a chat and a cup of tea. At that time I was a little sensitive: the honeymoon period was over and he asked what was the matter. My contractual agreement at the club was woolly, to say the least, so I asked when I was going to get a proper contract.

I was more than frustrated and told him if it wasn't rectified, I would walk away from them, and outrageously said if I did it, would be a huge loss to Newcastle United. I went even further to say it would also be a huge loss to me as I'd had a love affair with the club since childhood. Looking back, in my excitement I was more than a little forthright, but I take my hat off to the man for taking time out to listen to me and I think it was that situation that maybe unified our relationship.

It seems as though I've known Blackie for a lifetime: from the early years at St James' Park, where he became the guru of the dressing-room, until he followed me to Newcastle Gosforth Rugby Club to be part of the rugby union revolution.

A man of many talents, especially in people motivation, he is someone who should always be part of your team.

Sir John Hall – chairman, Newcastle United FC and Newcastle Falcons RFC

A couple of years later, I was at Jedburgh with Sir John for a Falcons match and he collared me just before I left to join the Welsh international rugby team. He took me for a walk round the field and came straight out with a question about Newcastle United. 'What's going on at this football club? You know all the lads.'

As per normal, I batted it back and said it wasn't my job to tell the tale.

'Why don't you ask them?' I said.

'I'm asking you . . . it's in a mess. Who are we going to get in as manager?'

An interesting question, so I answered it directly. 'There's no doubt who you should get. You've got to go for Bobby Robson. He's a North-east person who I suspect has been black and white all his life. He has great experience and charisma, and the fans would love him. On top of that, the players will respect him for what he's achieved in the game.'

'We can't get him.'

'Have you tried?'

'We can't, so who else is there . . . who's the best of the others?'

'There's nobody.'

'What about Gullit?'

'Suspect . . . magician as a player . . . as a manager, we can't be sure. At Chelsea, Graham Rix ran the show. Gullit was only a figure-head, and when he joined in on the training field, he, himself, was brilliant. However, as I say, the feedback on him as a coach and manager isn't universally positive.'

Sir John then changed tack. 'So what about here then . . . it [the rugby] hasn't got the same buzz?'

'No.'

'Why?'

'A problem over the bonus for winning the League last season might have something to do with it.'

Sir John then said that nothing had been clearly agreed, so he felt the club had let no one down. I told him that there'd obviously been a pretty serious breakdown in communication because, whatever the truth of the situation, the lads, en masse, expected to receive an extra reward for their success. Sir John took my comments on board and I never did find out what came of it as I left the club soon after to take up my position in Wales.

There were other occasions, like in Perpignan, where the Falcons battled hard in the European Shield. Sir John had motored across to see us and we were beaten, though we had already qualified for the quarter-final. It was an incredibly hostile game. The crowd pelted us with everything but the kitchen sink, spat on us and even hoisted our replica shirts up onto a pole and set fire to them. The French are like that, their passion for the game is uncontrollable. Yet, having subjected us to disgraceful behaviour, as hosts they couldn't have been more gracious. Anyway, I got a message that Sir John was going ballistic and on his way to the dressing-room to give the team a piece of his mind. Knowing our dressing-room atmosphere could ignite, I headed him off in the tunnel. Looking back, I can understand his passion and reasons, which he perhaps thought were valid, but the lads had played their hearts out, been battered, kicked, gouged and had stud marks raked across their backs. They'd have torn back at him. Knight of the Realm or not, our confrontation was heated, but I was intent on preventing him confronting the lads, even at the risk of being sacked. Once again, he listened to me and wasn't a happy man, but he didn't go in. To be perfectly frank, it was in his best interests because the lads all liked him and if he'd continued with his intended course of action, he may have lost a little respect from them and both parties didn't need that.

In the next European Shield match against Agen, we were narrowly beaten 12–9. They were one of the best teams in Europe on their home patch and we did ourselves proud, being most unlucky not to take it. Again the message came to me, 'He's on his way.' Again it was the same performance and I had to prevent him entering the dressing-room to confront the boys, who again had given their all. He intimated that a less than committed performance was behind the loss. Sir John is a passionate man, but he's only human and sometimes that manifests itself in emotional outbursts. Again, I was fully prepared to stand my ground for the lads, pointing out that he was letting his emotions get the better of him. He stopped and then said, 'Right, it's now down to you to make sure they don't take advantage of the hospitality and get on that plane as soon as possible,' and stormed off.

I smiled to myself because I realised he'd gone way over the top and there was nothing further to say on the matter. Needless to say, the lads represented the club at the after-match function before heading off for the flight home.

The atmosphere was a bit chilly after that and at the next match he beat me to the dressing-room, where he was praising the boys for their efforts, giving nothing but positive input. I admired him for that and it was probably his way of redressing the balance between us. I would like to think we had an honest, man-to-man relationship.

In many ways it's a shame that, after the finance and effort he put into rugby, he didn't remain to see it through and reap the rewards. What was interesting about him and his relationship with sport is that his ability to start great things isn't in question, for without his energy and money the

Falcons wouldn't exist today, so he deserves enormous praise for that. It is also a huge irony that Sir John pulling out of the club nearly killed what he had started. Fortunately, resilience on the part of some very committed people concerned with the club's welfare at that time saved the day.

As regards the players who came in, many were sensational – the top of their profession – but still needed careful handling as each one was different. Deano was a fanatical trainer who loved this professional environment but his focus was on hard work rather than any structured goals. His attitude had been honed during his army background. He was very tough physically and mentally, with an uncompromising nature both on the field and in the gym. We've all got strong points and we've all got weaknesses . . . I hope that my professional relationship with Dean helped bring out his strengths and helped him improve his ongoing chance of success. I like Dean enormously. He's my type of guy. What you see is what you get with Dean. He passionately believes that the road he takes is the right one. I'm glad to say that his efforts seem to have been rewarded in that hotbed of rugby down in Gloucester to follow on from the great impact he made here at the Newcastle Falcons.

I clearly saw him as a grafter of the highest order and, being a bit of a romantic, thought that Rob, Deano, Batesy and I could grow together as a group. I spoke to Ken Nottage, the chief executive, about it. Without going into the gory details, it involved finance, and Steve Bates and I were so keen to keep Deano we offered to compromise our own salaries in order to retain Dean's skills and presence within the club. I tried to explain the relationship, our roles and potential, in order that any negotiations we had were amicable and fair, but it became a nightmare. We felt if we stuck together, success would come and then we could sort out a longer contract, which would even itself out. I pleaded with Ken to understand, telling him that unless it was resolved amicably it would cause a rift in the club, which could have disastrous consequences. He wouldn't or couldn't have it and the situation became critical when Deano and I left the club in 1998, he to go to Bristol, me to Wales: a break-up of a winning team that should never have been permitted.

Here was a group of highly talented, strong-minded players who were not always pulling in the same direction. People always rebel and George Hallas, coach to the Chicago Bears, had the best quote ever when he said that anyone you ever meet, find out what they like to do, pander to that, then change them. Very clever philosophy and it has always stood me in great stead as a coach.

I learned a lot in those three seasons and the biggest impression I got was the level of indiscipline which prevailed on the field of combat. Not having played the game, I was disadvantaged in some respects, but totally objective in my assessment. I admit that, had I been playing, I would have been disgraceful, because there were so many cheap shots. I would have nothing against a bloke giving me a punch on the nose, so what? That's a man-to-man thing. But I have witnessed some diabolical cowardly behaviour – coming in from behind, stamping on heads – and serious injuries which were totally out of order. Deano had a point when he said if he witnessed something like that being done to one of his teammates, he would ensure retribution was exacted. Professionally, I sometimes had to throw my hat away, but I still pointed out it was silly to retaliate because you would always disadvantage the team and give penalties away. The game is so tight now that possession is everything, especially when we know the damage a kicker like Jonny Wilkinson, Rob Andrew or Neil Jenkins can exact. Discipline is vital.

That team of Rob, Dean, Steve and myself was top-class. We worked very well together, all had a similar work ethic and the different things we brought to the table complemented one another. I've written extensively about Rob elsewhere in the book and the last few paragraphs have highlighted my admiration for Dean, but I would like also to pay a tribute to Steve Bates. Steve's a top man whose niceness hasn't stopped him progressing and making a contribution at the elite level of his chosen profession. He has a good mind and heart, and we work very well together. Batesy has left the club now and I was delighted to hear of his appointment as head coach of the recently formed Borders team in the Celtic League. He has our old pal George Graham as his assistant and forwards coach, and I'm sure those two wily characters will get the job done right up there in Scotland.

BLACKIE

So, even though I was well established at the Falcons, I knew that nothing ever stays the same and that the success we had gained in such a short period was beginning to subside. Little did I know, however, that the frustration that was beginning to build within me for further success was going to propel me into a whole different stratosphere of challenges – challenges that were going to change my life and career path once again.

Chapter Seven

THE RUN – THE WELSH EXPERIENCE

Blackie is the most positive man in the world. The glass is always half-full, never half-empty . . . and I love him to death . . . in that man-to-man way, you understand. He's a joy to be with.

Graham Henry

I was sitting watching TV at home in Westmoor, Newcastle, one evening in 1998 with Julie and the kids. The telephone rang and when I answered, the person on the other end introduced himself as Graham Henry. He said 'You probably haven't heard of me, but I'm the former Auckland Blues coach from New Zealand and I have just been given the job of coaching and lifting the fortunes of the Welsh national rugby union team.' I told Graham that yes, I had heard of him and yes, I would look forward to meeting him to discuss rugby preparation. He said that Inga Tuigamala, Pat Lam and Ross Nesdale, three wonderful players we had both coached, had told him that my methods were different but enjoyable and very effective . . . and he wanted to know more. We arranged to meet at a hotel close to Bristol Airport for this chat.

I looked forward to meeting Graham and swapping ideas concerning how to prepare for playing and winning in professional sport. In the interim period between the phone call and the meeting, I received another call to let me know that Graham would be bringing along his boss at the Welsh Rugby Union, Terry Cobner, actually the former Welsh captain and a legend within the rugby fraternity in the Principality, and Jim Blair, former Auckland and All Blacks fitness coach who had recently taken up a post at Bath RFC. This further whetted my appetite.

I spent my first three weeks in Newcastle without understanding a word Blackie said. The broad Geordie accent was difficult enough, but when you add to that his tendency to either mumble in a monotone or sing Pavarotti-like, I was completely lost and had to revert to nodding whenever he said anything to me. It didn't take long, however, before I realised how lucky we were to have him in our camp.

It was a special time in the mid- to late' 90s when it all started at Newcastle Rugby Club. The team was laden with internationals and driven by two of the biggest names in today's English game [Dean and Rob]. However, one of the telling differences between Newcastle and the other teams trying to make the most of professional rugby was our man Blackie. I'm sure we were the only rugby team in the world with an overweight playwright as a fitness coach, but Blackie was no ordinary fitness coach. Of course he knew his stuff when it came to sports physiology and physical fitness, however, it was his ability as a mentor and sports psychologist, and comedian, and storyteller, and actor, and singer, and movie buff, and all-round good bloke, that made him such an asset to the team.

Ross Nesdale – Ireland, Falcons and All Blacks lineout coach

I got down there late morning and the first to arrive was Jim Blair. We introduced ourselves and chatted as if we had known each other for years. The subculture of our language was reciprocally understandable, maybe a factor in that being that, for both of us, the first sport we had been active in was soccer, not rugby. Jim had played soccer to a professional level in Scotland before he had gone on his travels, ended up in New Zealand, and been given the chance to get rugby players fit. I'd also been brought up in the soccer world but, first during my association with my old pal and boss Charles Buchanan and then with the former England great Alan Old, I'd been given the opportunity to train the then Newcastle Gosforth rugby team. We'd both taken soccer drills and adapted them, and we'd both had success with the players and teams who'd used these bastardised regimes, although it must be said that at that time Jim had experienced so much success at the elite rugby level that I felt it a privilege to have this opportunity to discuss our methods one to one.

Graham and Terry arrived after a relatively short period and our discussions began. It seemed obvious to me that here were three dyed-in-the-wool sportspeople who had that passion not normally associated with ordinary working life, or not often anyway. There were many things we fundamentally agreed upon: sessions should be carried out high-tempo and the content of those sessions and the skills taught should be readily transferable to the field of performance. Probably the only area where we differed in practical terms was in the level of trust we placed in players. They were all aware of, and came from, an environment where the physical testing of players was an inbuilt accountability, where there was an ongoing appraisal by the technical coaches as to whether or not a player or players were fit enough to play the game at the level they were operating in. All very rational and objective, and up to first-team level I feel hugely influential in constantly reinforcing the necessity of being generally fit to play the game. But at an elite level, I hold the belief it's both a cop-out and an unnecessary justification of the coaches' and players' work on a weekly basis.

I've found that because it's human nature to want to be respected as a valuable member of a group of competitive people that the player and coach each lose sight of their real focus, which is to win the games. Many coaches and players become obsessed with getting better test results, and having everyone know that, in order to safeguard their professional positions. I've been told by so many other coaches that Mr X has improved his 5- and 15-metre acceleration time; broken his bench-press and squat records, and completed the team agility drill in record time. That's marvellous, I've always said, quickly followed by the question, 'Hand on heart, has he improved as a player during this time of physical improvement?' A response to this question is invariably, 'It's hard to qualify' (Yes, but in this instance it generally means no!) or 'Not really noticeably.' I then expound the value of getting players specifically and individually fit to play the game at the level they aspire to. If suitably motivated, it's a wonderful and trusting build-up to game play.

Other people who have assumed positions at the top of their chosen profession are definitely not, in my experience, enamoured with having to take ongoing tests to justify their being in the ballpark for selection in their chosen employment. In fact, at that level, they wouldn't do it and rightly so. If you are selected to do a job, you should be allowed to do it. If the selection process is right, then you'll probably do the job well. If you don't, then those that selected you can get rid of you. That's the way it should work. But if you select a person/player, give them every possible chance to succeed. Don't put them under so much pressure that they enter the game and waste so much energy justifying their presence that they haven't got enough energy or enthusiasm to actually do the job to the level they would otherwise be capable of. Trust and support them! You'll get rewarded for it. Be optimistic. If you treat people fairly and with common decency, showing your trust for them, in most cases you'll get a result, believe me. I believe in the good nature of people and that their intrinsic desire is to please and therefore do a good job.

I once read that individuals are influenced by the books they read and the people they meet. Steve Black, affectionately and universally known as 'Blackie', certainly fulfils the second category in my life. I have never met a more positive person. During my association with him on the Welsh international scene, his influence was integral and invaluable in the success of Wales during that victorious run in 1998–99. He was the energy of the side.

Blackie is a huge person – huge in personality, huge in commitment and huge in humour. He is a giant – I would like to refer to him as a 'sleeping giant' but sleeping is a habit he has not cottoned on to!

I enjoy Blackie's company. I enjoy speaking to Blackie. He is unique; a one-off.

I value the friendship of such a caring and sincere person.

Alun Lewis – Celtic Warriors backs coach and former backs coach for Newport and Welsh Rugby Union

The meeting went well. When Terry Cobner and Jim Blair left, Graham and I continued to chat. He informed me that both he and Terry would love me to come on board and be part of the coaching/management team which they hoped would bring back the former successes of Welsh rugby. Whilst he said I'd excited them, I admit I saw a great opportunity to further put to the test my coaching philosophy at a higher level.

It didn't take me long to buy into this unique opportunity, certainly not from a professional standpoint. It was more difficult from an emotional standpoint because of my love of Newcastle and the people I was working with. I'll cover this decision in more depth elsewhere in this book, so I'll concentrate on the fact that I'd made this decision and how I set about realising a goal I deeply believed was possible: that was Wales as an ongoing top-three team in the world! No, I hadn't lost my mind, and yes, I did know their unfortunate run of results over the previous few years, and yes, I was aware that the media thought they had no players capable of resurrecting the onfield success of the great '70s teams of Edwards, John, Davies, Quinnell, Cobner, Bennett, Bevan, etc. But I disagreed, I really did. I knew they had some good players who, after having done my homework, I deeply suspected could be very good if supported in the right way and allowed to flourish collectively in the right environment.

Wales had, and has, good rugby players. Wales had, and has, some excellent rugby coaches. What Wales didn't have was a confidence that reflected their ability or a culture that was intent on building that confidence. The media, in certain sections, seemed to gloat when the team hadn't done well and was influencing large sections of the public in their daily support and belief in the rugby team.

I knew Graham was positive. His record suggested his competence! The more I enquired about this person with whom I'd decided to throw in my Geordie hat, the more positive I was about our impending union. The only slightly negative feedback I got from any source during these investigations was that his thirst for victory and success had sometimes led to him not giving as much attention to the individuals involved in a team quest as he was giving to the immediate team cause. Whilst this was only the opinion of a small number of people who'd been associated with his coaching career in New Zealand up until this point, I decided that if it did indeed have any truth to it, I could certainly balance that effect with my coaching style. So a potential marriage made in heaven was to ensue. Did it turn out that way? Up until the World Cup quarter-final exit, we'd made unbelievable progress.

Our first Test together was against the world champions, South Africa, at Wembley, our home pitch whilst the new national Millennium Stadium was being built in Cardiff. A couple of months before, Wales had lost by almost 100 points against this great South African team and the prospect of playing a return game at what was basically a neutral venue was daunting, to say the least. How could Graham and I instil some believable confidence into a team so low at that time that they didn't like walking around shopping or socialising for fear of a derogatory comment from a passer-by? I needed an impact, a big impact, and I needed it quickly.

My role, as it has been at the Newcastle Falcons and the other teams of athletes I have trained through the years, is not what the public would generally think a fitness coach to be . . . although that's an integral and hugely important part of what I do. I also assume a responsibility for the emotional and psychological areas of preparation associated with coaching a team at this elite level.

The first few weeks had led me to believe that not only did the players feel under pressure from the media and public, they also felt under pressure during their training because they were being subjected to ongoing fitness tests. The result of these tests, or the regime that was employed to give them better fitness, was not being rewarded during their games because, well, basically, they were getting beaten just about all the time. So how could they get confidence from the way they were being prepared?

I gathered the squad together and told them that I was abolishing fitness testing and that my only concern was to help make them better rugby players. In the course of them becoming better rugby players, I told them I expected them to become fitter both mentally and physically, but I'd let our results be an indicator as to whether I was right to trust their application to the prescribed regime or not. I actually always keep a record of how fast they are running, how long they can operate at high intensity, how strong they are, how long they are capable of being strong for at game intensity and specific game-related activity, and how well their skills held out under pressure of game intensity. My scrutiny of the specifics behind their conditioning was, I know, ahead of what the conventional tests could show because it was more personal and didn't incur the stresses that conventional fitness tests have, because the players didn't know I was monitoring them.

Why didn't I tell the media about this testing approach? Maybe it would have defeated the reasons behind doing it, don't you think? Oh, ye of little faith! Taking conventional testing off the agenda had a huge effect. I also changed some of the training immediately because it takes time for new exercises to have any effect. No matter what some people try to claim, you can have an immediate effect by increasing or decreasing the volume of training and/or the intensity of training. I changed the volume (lowered it) and the intensity (increased it). I knew this would give the players more energy going into the game and would allow them to compete at a similar speed to the world champions, because their legs wouldn't be as heavy from doing too much training. Obviously, along with Graham's tactical acumen and confident demeanour (which was immense at that time, by the way), this worked a treat. We put on a super performance and I sincerely believe, had our concentration not been broken by a South African streaker when the score was 20–20, we could, and on the day should, have won it. I think some of our players, who had given everything and had grown and grown in confidence as the game went on, had a brief moment to reflect on the position and the score, and basically froze. The word 'froze' is maybe a bit strong, but it's the only one I can use to get across the effect that stoppage had.

Still, it was looked upon by everyone as a moral victory and, given the circumstances, it was. I think probably only Graham and I were deeply upset that we hadn't won because we really expected to. We were the only ones who were used to regularly winning with all our teams at that time. We viewed a loss as a negative! Believe me, it always is. You can salvage many lessons that are positive from a loss. As professional coaches, that's what we are supposed to do, isn't it? But to accept or celebrate defeat is a cop-out. A game has a winner or loser and you've got to win to be successful. As sport is an entertainment at this professional level, commercially, if not spiritually, eventually I think you need to do it with a bit of style or your supporters will vote with their feet and stop coming to your 'performances'. But if it's a choice between consistently losing in style, or just winning whatever way, the second option is the definite starting route to take.

We were aware of both approaches. We needed to win to lift the players' confidence, their self-esteem and that of the Welsh nation in general, but we were also aware that the Welsh nation had been used to the superb style of the great '70s team and that's what they would respond to over time and that's what would place the current team perennially higher in their affections than if we'd won playing a drab brand of rugby. I actually could relate to that from my Geordie homeland. Our 1950s football team which won the FA Cup three times was an entertainment legend within the sporting world. 'Wor' Jackie Milburn, Bobby Mitchell and the Robledo brothers were revered for their dynamically skilful play, and Kevin Keegan has attained equal status in Geordie hearts because our team during Kevin's era played with flair, poise and put a smile on the face of everyone who watched them.

When Blackie came to Wales everyone quickly recognised that this guy was something special. He immediately made an impact and all of a sudden we began to believe in ourselves again. He totally changed my approach to training, both physically and mentally. Even though I had a lot of international experience, he gave me so much confidence in my own ability. There isn't a negative bone in his body and his sense of humour is wonderful, always a smile or a hug. He lit the place up as soon as he arrived.

He made fitness training meaningful and specific, but more importantly he brought to it a rare commodity which doesn't normally go with training. He made it enjoyable and very quickly Welsh rugby began to reach levels it had only dreamed about before.

Blackie would do anything for you and was always there if you had a problem, no matter what time of the day or night it was. He gave everything for Wales and the players responded to a man. They all loved him.

On a personal level, he extended my international career and I will always be indebted to the support and friendship he gave me. Wales is a lot poorer for his

leaving, and allowing him to leave was the biggest mistake they ever made and we're paying for it now.
   David Young – Wales, Cardiff

Our style against South Africa was undoubtedly exciting. The next game, against Argentina, down at Stradey Park, Llanelli, actually showed our marvellous running talent, but also highlighted our set-piece and defensive weaknesses. We won the game before a packed Stradey crowd and scored some great tries, but were awful defensively, especially from a scrummage standpoint, and we knew we had plenty to work on. The build-up and aftermath to this game was overshadowed for me by the death of my father-in-law, Harry, and I left as soon as the game finished to go back home to help support Julie and her family. My son Mark had travelled down from Newcastle to accompany me on the journey back. I remember being hugely thankful that he had and that he was there with me. These family situations, as everyone knows if they've experienced them, are difficult and deeply upsetting for all involved, but being far away from home is increasingly frustrating and not being able to console Julie, Stephen, Mark and Emma face-to-face immediately was upsetting.

This game was before Christmas and we didn't meet up again before the build-up to the first Five Nations tournament this coaching team would have the opportunity of experiencing. During that time my family moved down to Wales with me. I was delighted they did so and my only concern and worry was for my son, Stephen, who stayed in Newcastle to study law. Of course, my mam and Julie's mam, Ann, were still in the North-east, so we had no shortage of support or places for him to eat and get his washing done! Needless to say, he was OK and visited us regularly over the next 18 months in Wales. Mark and Emma came to live in Wales with Julie and me. Emma went to Rougemont School in Newport and loved it. Her headmaster, Ian Brown, was a super guy who made her very welcome at the school. Mark went to the University of Glamorgan to study law.

The build-up to the Scotland game was a bit cerebral and I felt not intensive or aggressive enough. I should have been more vocal about my concerns but thought that we had a better team than Scotland and would beat them anyway, in spite of our preparation not because of it. By winning the game we'd further build the team's confidence and in that positive environment I'd be able to shift the style of preparation to what I considered to be our best chance of ongoing victories. The dressing-room before the game was not what I was used to. It felt like we were getting ready to play a game of chess rather than take on Braveheart (Gary Armstrong) and his men at Murrayfield!

My worst fears were realised when Scotland scored after a minute or so. We rallied late in the game, but not enough to bring back the deficit we'd incurred and, for me, a lesson was learned. I voiced my concern in the dressing-room after the game (too late for this one, I accept, but not for the next) and Scott Gibbs, a warrior if ever there was one, agreed. Later, Graham said he'd underestimated the intensity of the Five Nations and the fierce pride associated with the competition.

Next up was Ireland and I was hell-bent on ensuring we'd be up for that 'home' game at Wembley. Our general build-up was a little faster and definitely more aggressive. My before-game team talk was unbelievably animated and over-the-top theatrically aggressive. That's the way I'd planned and rehearsed it and that's the way I played it.

I really wound them up and was probably at my most aggressive in the dressing-room. As I spoke the words, you could hear a pin drop.

'Get out there and streetfight those bastards! Don't let them have a fucking inch. Hit them hard, hit them often, destroy their resistance. Hammer them down, then hammer them again and again. If you're really tough, really, really tough, you'll do it with discipline and within the rules of the game. If you're real men, and I haven't seen it yet from any of you, you'll take this game by the scruff of the neck and drag it and push it to wherever you need it to go. You fucking show me it, 'cos I've heard all about this Welsh passion. Where is it? This is fucking Geordie passion and when it's firing like this, I'm fucking unbeatable . . . absolutely unbeatable. Come with me, lads, we only have winners here. I believe you can do it. They want to have a go at you, they want to embarrass you. They want to chin you. Well, I'll tell you what I'd do. I'd get the first one on . . . I'd chin them first, then keep chinning them right through the game . . . then shake their hands and apologise at the end of the game, and if they get aggressive again . . . chin them again.'

I needed to know just how much these guys would give if you stoked their fires and gave them a licence to bring out the Welsh Dragon spirit. I got the answer I wanted and needed. They didn't just give it a crack . . . they gave it everything. Our collective discipline was very poor, but our desire to win and beat the Irish was massive. We gave away penalty after penalty, won just about all the physical confrontations and were penalised for them all – not ideal, I grant you, but you need to be competitive and if it's one of your strong points, you've got to get used to using it, obviously within the laws of the game and effectively, but use it you must. By half-time we were well behind, and went to something like 23–6 before staging an unbelievable comeback, totally fuelled by the collective and aggressive desire to win as a team. We eventually lost 29–23, but I can't remember ever being happy like this after a defeat at any time in my career. The reason was I knew we had a team! I'd seen an all-round exciting performance against South Africa, some exhilarating skill against Argentina and now some great grit and determination against Ireland. If we could only put all three together, someone was going to get a hiding.

That happened in our next game against Italy in Treviso. We really did play and prepare well, and put over 60 points on the Italians, who generally can be very competitive on home soil. It was a super victory and Graham told me he was especially proud of the way we played and the attitude we'd shown. I was delighted. So, having prepared and played well, we celebrated well and had a memorable evening on a boat we'd hired for the team to party along the canals in Venice. The memory of walking around St Mark's Square at 1 a.m. with many of the team and coaches is special.

I must say, by that time, our managerial team had started to forge an excellent relationship based on respect, increasing trust and, I feel, a genuine affection for one another. Lynn Howells, Alun Lewis, David Pickering, Trevor James, Alun Carter and Mark Davies were all super colleagues and incredibly supportive of Graham and me. Doctors Evans and Williams were excellent characters, and were committed and skilful practitioners who also helped make the environment special. I knew we had started something unique. I remember telling Claire (our PA) one day that I really felt we could win the World Cup if we could channel all the positive energy that had started to be generated by this group of people. We were starting to feel like a club side and I suppose we were. There was a unique situation in Wales whereby Cardiff and Swansea, probably the two strongest teams at that time, after having tried to get into the English League and failed, were in limbo competitionwise and were only playing friendlies. As a consequence, I had access to all our international squad on an almost daily basis. As we got closer and closer as a group, we got fitter, more specifically mentally and physically, to deal with whatever opposition came our way.

The next game was against France in Paris, and what a game it was. Graham asked what I did each night before an international as I didn't have a meal with the rest of the management and coaching staff. 'Well, I go to church, Graham,' I told him. 'I just sit in church, say a little prayer hoping that the team can represent its abilities well and do itself justice. I go through what I'm going to say in my team talk during warm-up and generally feel really energised by the whole experience.' Graham asked if he could come with me and the next day Graham, Lynn, Alun, David, Trevor and I all called into the church I'd been to the night before and said our respective prayers before we left for the game at the Stade de France. Graham and I did this for all our games after this, accompanied by all or some of the others. The first time we didn't go to church together before a game was against Samoa, our group game at the 1999 World Cup. Strangely, it was the first game we'd lost in 12.

We really played well and won a super game of running rugby against the masters of running rugby at a stadium that months previously had held the final of the soccer World Cup. Unbelievably, we'd a bigger crowd for our game than they had for the World Cup final! I saw both games and the crowd got it right! When Thomas Castaignède missed a penalty at the very end of the game and we won 34–33, it was no more than we deserved. I remember running onto the pitch and going to Ben Evans, who was playing his first game for his country since the death of his mother. Ben had dedicated his performance that day to his mam and she would have been rightly proud of him. It was a moving moment. Craig and Scott

Quinnell, two super guys and two players for whom I have great respect and affection, almost squeezed the life out of me. I must say that whilst Scott is acknowledged the world over as a truly wonderful international player (and rightly so), Craig hasn't really got the recognition he should have. Craig always trained very hard for me and gave some sterling performances during our 11-game winning run for the Welsh team, probably none more dynamic than that afternoon in Paris. Shane Howarth, Scott Gibbs, Garin Jenkins, Peter Rogers, Colin Charvis and Neil Jenkins were all superb, although it's unfair to pick them out of an excellent team on the day.

If anyone in rugby is special, it has to be Blackie. Just to hear his name brings a smile to my face. He's an inspiration both on and off the pitch, and the reason I went to Cardiff was to train with Steve Black. I took a hell of a lot of flak because of my fitness, but Blackie stuck with me through thick and thin, and was always there for me. He didn't falter once. I have some incredible memories of him and in particular when we were in Argentina for three weeks it was Blackie who kept our spirits up. One day he took about ten of us to the cinema and we had no money. 'No problem, lads, just get in there and I'll sort it.' We all went in, got popcorn and drinks and he was at the back. We all thought he had the money but he didn't, and told us not to worry about it. When we were all in he suddenly fell to the ground and pretended to have a fit and the cinema were so worried about him we were never asked for the money. When he 'recovered', he came in smiling and said, 'Sorted.'

Blackie took me from one level to another, both physically and mentally, and put the fun back into Welsh rugby along with self-belief. It wasn't just a physical thing with him, it was the psychology, always smiling, always up for it, no matter how bad he was feeling. He worked me hard and gave me a new lease of life.

I was out of the sport for a season with a broken back and Stephen kept in touch and supported me through difficult times even though he had gone back to Newcastle. When I did get back into the national squad, it was the same twenty-two players apart from one or two new faces, but the atmosphere was different and when I had a laugh and joke I was given short shrift off the manager who thought I was too flippant. I realised then that the fun had gone out of Welsh

rugby the day Blackie left and that indeed was a very black day for us. Blackie is out of this world and a great friend.
  Craig Quinnell – British Lions, Wales

Next up? The English at Wembley in London in a home game for us! Incredible . . . couldn't possibly win . . . well, we did. A great day and the most dramatic finish. The last ever Five Nations game of the century – could the game live up to that sort of billing? Playingwise, maybe not, but dramawise, a big 'Yes!' After being behind to a superior England team whose lack of discipline allowed Neil Jenkins to keep us in the game by kicking everything from everywhere, we scored a fabulous and memorable try from Scott Gibbs as he danced around English defenders to score to the right of the posts. Graham Henry talks of looking up to the gods in the final seconds and saying, 'Well, if you're going to do something for us – now is the time.' Yes! So our pre-match visits to church seemed to have borne fruit. But the game wasn't won. It was still 31–30 to England, but we had Maestro Jenkins to take that kick for us to win the game. With Jenkins, you never considered the prospect of a miss because he just didn't do that! Over the conversion went, taking the score to 32–31 and a great, unforgettable victory which allowed Scotland to win the Five Nations. Gary Armstrong, my old Newcastle scrum-half and Scotland's captain, left a message of congratulations and thanks for our victory. Third win in a row.

My team talk for the England Wembley game went like this: 'We are going to be as effective as we decide to be. That means that if we decide to win, we will. We know it's not going to be easy, everything in the ballpark is close. We're every bit as good players as they are. We're as good men as them. Some people who don't know you like we do actually think they're a better team than you. How misguided can some people be? The goal we have is worthwhile. It's for a country of around four million to get the better in a contest off scratch against a country of fifty million. Our desire to do that must underwrite all our efforts. You had a big say in how we're going to play the game, a huge say, and we trust you enormously.'

After that on the agenda was an end of season trip to Argentina, one of the toughest rugby environments in the world (no northern hemisphere team had ever won a series of Tests there). Thirty-seven players were selected for the tour and, with only thirty places available for the World Cup squad, there was more than enough to play for. Thirty-seven players went and were all available for selection for both Tests and two wins. Professionally, you can't get much better. I had a classic coaching moment on that tour. Some things and times stay with you as special memories and that First Test certainly has.

I hadn't been that happy during the build-up and I felt that we'd done too much in the way of time on the training field in our preparations. I was worried because I knew the Argentinian team were strong, powerful and quick, and although I also knew that they'd a big stamina problem, if you let them get a head of steam, and a few points up, then that momentum can take some stopping. I did know that, all things being even, we were 30 points better than them. Doing too much before games doesn't affect your stamina; it affects your reaction time, sharpness and your ability to win and use the ball effectively. Just before half-time, as I'd suspected, they were too quick and powerful for us, and we went 23 points down.

At half-time, I sat everyone down and passionately told them why we'd gone down by so many points and that there had been nothing they could have done about it – the physiology of the situation was against them. But now that had passed and the second half held no advantage for the now tiring and less rampaging Argies. I knew that, because we were 30 points better than they were, we could pull that deficit back. If we believed and if we stayed patient but alert and assertive in all we did, then we'd win. We played as we should have in the second half and went from 23–0 at one stage to 36–26 winners, the greatest and biggest comeback in international rugby union history. The game had gone exactly as I knew it would.

Although the Second Test was less dramatic, we won it to take the series 2–0. On the day of the Test our 'police guide' motorbike led us to the stadium on the longest route imaginable, got us there 40 minutes before kick-off, changed the arranged warm-up venue and then put us in a different venue that was in the glare of the very debilitating sun. We didn't argue or make a big thing of it. We just got on with the preparation, focused our intentions on playing and beat them. Great! As we flew home, we were excited and were collectively looking forward to playing the world champions in nine days' time.

Wales had never beaten South Africa and so the size of the task ahead was enormous, but one which we had all started to believe was achievable. We'd now won five international games in a row, and when a team has been going through such a prolonged period of defeat, that winning sequence becomes hugely significant. I thought that a win against the then current world champions could give us the impetus to go on and win the World Cup. We'd now become competitive . . . game by game. We were in the midst of getting the winning habit. The third phase of any team's development, winning competitions, couldn't be put to the test until the World Cup. Winning our games up to the World Cup and ensuring that we were in the best mental and physical shape for the tournament was our only pathway to success. Significantly, we had a few days off after getting back from Argentina. We got together briefly before the game . . . very little time for physical work, almost nothing. I couldn't have been happier.

It was an exciting time in Wales. We'd started to win, the World Cup was but months away and our national stadium was nearing completion. This South African Test was to be the first game in the new stadium, but the crowd size was to be limited to 29,000 instead of a finished stadium crowd capacity of over 70,000. Saying that, on the day, that 29,000 sounded like 70,000 and they provided inspirational support for growing heroes. The game was tough (they all are at this level), but less of a problem to win than I'd anticipated. Because winning is such a marvellously effective medicine and a tonic for all involved, I knew that if we kept up our current progress, and we met South Africa at any stage in the World Cup tournament, this Wales team would win. I could sense they had that personality make-up. We played reasonably well, with great confidence and increasing belief, and won the Test. Another record! First Welsh team to win in Paris for over 20 years; first northern hemisphere team to win a Test series in Argentina; now, first Welsh team to beat South Africa. We needed to believe that we could be the first Welsh team to win the World Cup. I knew the strength of the opposition at the time and I also knew we were capable of beating any team on any given day – I needed all the management, coaches and players to believe that. After that opening victory at the Millennium Stadium, I felt, for the first time, all involved thought we'd become genuine contenders for the title.

We then had a break to recharge our batteries and to spend some time with our families. We regrouped a month later and began our World Cup preparations up in Brecon. We took over an entire small country hotel about six miles from Brecon town centre and trained at the public school in the town centre. Buying houses is supposed to be best guided by the term 'location, location, location' – well, so was the start of our World Cup preparation. The hotel was very clean, comfortable, welcoming and emotionally warm. Oh, and very discreet and relaxing – exactly what I wanted and the team needed. The squad and management team really were great together then. There was a spirit forged on overcoming an expected adversity and stringing together six wins in a row against live opposition. In France, England and South Africa, we'd beaten three of the top teams in world rugby, including the current world champions. In sport, a run like that makes you not only feel good, but also makes you believe in yourself. Those results had given credibility to my personal philosophical and trusting approach, not just from the players but from the coaches who worked with and close to the national squad. I knew that if we could have played the World Cup tournament then we were definite semi-finalists and, in my mind, having got that far, probable victors. I also knew that we had to ensure the pressure from the public expectation didn't begin to have a negative impact. It certainly hadn't so far, although the winning run was starting to have a very strong effect on the public's expectation of their national team's achievement . . . or potential achievement.

I felt it was necessary to bring out of the closet the rest of my eccentricity to not only further support their well-being physically in the build-up to the World Cup, but to help deflect their focus on this public expectation and associated stress. We trained six times a day for around ten to twelve minutes at a time at a bright, high intensity, mostly using a variety of games as the main stimulus. We played touch rugby and as many derivatives as we could think of, with decision-making, leadership qualities and collective reward and celebration for drills/exercises or games well executed. We played with rugby balls, American footballs, basketballs, netballs, handballs, medicine balls and 'pretend' balls! Our skill work and our handling during the 'pretend' ball phase was quite simply phenomenal – no passes astray or dropped. Remarkable. We continually reinforced the 'shape' of the pass and praised players for getting it right. Our small-group teams were each coached by one of the management team. After following my orientation guidelines, where we got rid of all the young boy giggles concerning pretending to play and score against live opposition, we played a series of imaginary games in our build-up to the week's focus of beating our opposition. These games went very well and it was lovely to hear Graham getting excited about coaching his team in this real competition consisting of imaginary opposition! In fact, when I called all the teams together to ask for their appreciation and judgement based on the quality necessary to win a World Cup, their feedback was great. I asked Graham how his side had done in the game so far. 'Bloody great, mate! We've scored five tries and put fifty points on the All Blacks and it's not even half-time. Great performance!' This was a great time for this team. Everybody got on well together and we could feel the whole of Wales behind us. We finished the week up in Brecon by playing an imaginary World Cup final, winning it, of course, and celebrating our triumph together.

We moved our training camp down to Cardiff, across to Pembrokeshire and then up to North Wales, where we were treated incredibly well and were received so warmly by the locals. The local authority up there had catered for our every whim and really did us proud. They'd shipped in the finest training equipment and ensured that our social support was second-to-none. Actually, this book gives me a chance to formally, and personally, thank for their help all the people who supported our World Cup build-up. Good on yer! We then headed for our camp in the sun in Portugal where we did some good organisational work and, on reflection, probably spent too long on the training field. Nonetheless, we finished the week definitely ready to rumble.

We were peaking a little early and my diary entries suggested that, although we had fun together that week, a tetchiness had descended over the camp and lots of little, inconsequential niggles had started to appear.

Let's face it, for a team who had spent the last few years as no-hopers and whipping boys to emerge with a genuine chance of victory whilst the competition was being held in their own backyard, the pressure was on! It would have been unrealistic to expect anything else, so the slight unrest was understandable but not unacceptable as we believed (I know I did with all my heart) that we were going to win the World Cup.

Our build-up games against USA, Canada and France had extended our winning run and, although we hadn't played particularly well, we still had that air of a side that had begun to expect to win. To show how far we'd come, the French game was approached with little trepidation or perceived threat and, to be fair, the team emerged as winners.

Opening games at World Cups are not classics, nor should they be. You've got a job to do and that is qualifying for the next round. The team needs to get through the opening stages injury-free, relatively unscathed emotionally and take the field in the quarter-finals ready to do themselves justice in a one-off confrontation. Whilst I wasn't ecstatic with the way we were playing, I was pleased with the way we'd evolved and the first round delivered what was expected, i.e. we qualified for the next stages without too much trauma. Argentina were competitive without ever threatening to beat us; Japan gave us a chance to run the ball around and open our legs a bit; and Samoa, with my two pals Pat Lam and Inga Tuigamala in tow, 'mugged' us at the Millennium. The statistics from that game would tell you that Samoa couldn't possibly have won – well, they would be wrong, as win Samoa did! Fortunately, it didn't affect the team's progress and we looked forward to welcoming the very effective Australian side in Cardiff.

My health had been the only thing to suffer during the opening stages and I'd collapsed just after half-time of the opening game against Argentina. But, after a six-unit blood transfusion in Cardiff, I joked that I was more Welsh than ever and felt ready to take on all-comers by the time our quarter-final came about. This was one bout of an ongoing series against that cunning adversary, ulcerative colitis. I think I'm ahead in our contests, but to be fair the condition seems to have remarkable stamina and keeps coming back for another shot at the title!

BLACKIE

Steve always put his family, friends and athletes before himself, even to the detriment of his health. This was seen in the build-up to and in the World Cup where he wasn't very well, but still had time to meet and alleviate most of the Welsh management and players' anxieties. Whoever came in contact with him was better for the experience. He is a very loyal friend and long may he be so.

Lynn Howells – head coach, Celtic Warriors, and former head coach to Welsh Rugby Union

We could have won that Australian game. We really could. Yes, I know they were the better team on the day, and yes, statistically they had territorial advantage, although we had far more possession than them, and yes, although we had the stronger physical scrummaging pack, they were more streetwise and definitely played the referee better than we did but, taking all that into consideration, I've been involved in sport long enough to know that the better team doesn't always win and, at 10–9 down with 11 minutes to go and Jinksy on the pitch, capable of dropping a goal or kicking any penalty that would come our way, we were still in it. It wasn't to be and all credit to an Australian team who believed it could win . . . and did.

So the journey had ended with a quarter-final loss to the eventual winners and world champions. I was hugely disappointed because I thought we'd win the bloody thing, but I was nonetheless pleased with the progress the team had made over the last year. Now was the time to consolidate that improvement; to keep going the way we were. Wales had (and still has) many good players; we'd won 11 games in a row; beaten England, France, then world champs South Africa and Argentina in their backyard. What we needed was patience and a bit of belief. We actually got neither.

The players went back to their clubs and we didn't see them until just before the start of the Six Nations. When we did see them get together, it was for some trial situation, followed by a 'panel of mentors' discussion before the squad was announced for the Six Nations. Let's put the record straight. Trial games are cop-outs. They may work at school level but if you've got to have a trial game where players are expected to perform with complete strangers against another team of strangers, with a set of tactics thrown together on the night . . . and you want to make a professional judgement as to whether that player should be in your international squad or not, if you really believe that's the most effective and professional way to handle the situation, you should be sacked! Lee Davies had been the best centre in Wales all season leading up to the Six Nations in 2000. Either pick him because he's a good player, or don't, if he isn't. I heard people say that he hadn't really 'shown up on the night'. Of course he hadn't – it would have been a bloody miracle if he had. He was playing with players he hadn't played with in a team that had never played together against another hotchpotch team! How can you shine in that setting, other than being completely selfish any time you get the ball and doing a bit of show boating? The team had gone back to be as poor as when we took the reins. Tragic. We should have had the belief and patience to keep building the nation's rugby confidence. Winning games, working hard, enjoying it; bringing young players through in that winning environment so that when they pulled a Welsh shirt on, they expected to win.

At any rate, the momentum achieved by the Welsh squad was now being sacrificed. The 'club' feel that we had nurtured in the national side was being dissipated. It was time for me to move on . . . of which, more later.

Sitting in a warm Atlanta flat sometime in June of 1999 I rang home to find out the latest score in the First Test between Wales and Argentina played at Buenos Aires. To my dismay, I was told that Wales were losing by 20-odd points at half-time. Time to take a dip in the pool and relax in the hot Georgia sun. Yet again Wales had suffered another 'false dawn', this time under Graham Henry and some bearded eccentric Geordie called 'Blackie'. If you think English football has had 30 years of hurt, you should try being a Welsh rugby fan.

Fast-forward 16 months and I am sitting in the North Stand of Wales' Millennium Stadium watching the only good Welsh team, certainly of my generation, being motivated, inspired and, more importantly, playing for that same bearded Geordie.

I believe in order to understand Steve Black as a conditioning coach, you have to totally take him out of our sporting context. He does not belong in Britain, this country of ours that glorifies gallant losers and shoots down winners as being too 'arrogant'. Blackie is a Yank athlete, an Aussie cricketer and an Eastern

European weightlifter rolled into one. By which I mean he has a winning mentality and strives for excellence. After I spent a few years in the USA experiencing first hand their sporting culture, which is 25 years ahead of the rest of the world, it was sobering and disheartening to return to Wales where 'sporting excellence' is an oxymoron. Enter Steve Black. This guy reminded me of the innovative and classy coaches I had seen working in the States, and placing him to direct the then current Wales rugby team was tantamount to putting Kiri Te Kanawa in the Spice Girls.

Wales is a country that embraces progress reluctantly, but Steve managed to jump into the deep end of this cynical rugby culture in the most visible place – the national team – and change it positively rather than let it change him. After dealing with a lot of players post-World Cup I know for a fact that the Wales team in '99 sincerely believed or even knew they would win that competition. Now you must believe me that this just 'does not appear anywhere' in the Welsh mentality. It is no coincidence that during his tenure Wales took on and beat the best in the world, and since his departure that same group of players experienced a freefall Franz Klammer would be proud of. Most of his theories and ideas really do fly in the face of current conventions, but hey, so did The Beatles.

I feel privileged that I know him and his family.

Trystan Bevan – conditioning coach, Newport RFC

The Welsh team can be great again, but only if they start enjoying the whole scene again. Don't let people tell you you've not got enough good players or that the coaching is rubbish or that you let your emotions get in the way of progress. If you believe all that, you can't ever win. It's not about just playing a certain way; there's not just one way to be successful – use what you've got at your disposal, play to your strengths, then you really will have a chance – you always have. Try to be somebody else and you've got no chance! You may get to the stage where you can impersonate them for long stretches in many games, but not long enough to win them and not against meaningful opposition. Playing well for periods of the game, but still getting beat game after game against reasonable opposition surely isn't acceptable for one of rugby's great nations. It's insulting to coaches, players and fans alike. Use the Welsh personality to pull together and overcome anything any opponents throw at you. If the Welsh team don't cultivate and celebrate the unique personality characteristics that are Welsh, and take that great national pride into their game, they'll not achieve.

You can't be successful copying others who are playing to their national strengths. Results show it doesn't work. There are some great rugby people in Wales, support and encourage them for Pete's sake, don't take away their self-esteem. I met and had the privilege of working with some super people whilst in the Principality. Lynn Howells was the forwards coach throughout my time in Wales and we got on like a house on fire. Lynn and Dennis John were doing a smashing job at my adopted Welsh club Pontypridd, and I always enjoyed going along, standing on the terraces and supporting their fine team. Neil Jenkins, Daffyd James, Geraint Lewis and Kevin Morgan were just four of the many fine players they had at that time. The camaraderie that was on show each time I visited either their training sessions or on a match day reminded me so much of my Newcastle Championship-winning team. I saw most of their home games and they took some beating in Pontypridd. At the time of writing, I hear that Lynn has gone to coach in Italy after his Celtic Warriors team were disbanded by the WRU. You must believe me when I tell you that Welsh rugby can't afford to lose coaches of the calibre of Lynn Howells and his partner at the Warriors, former Newport and Welsh national coach Alun Lewis. Having worked extremely closely with these two guys, I know how much they care for and put into Welsh rugby. Alun, Lynn, Dai Pickering, Trevor James, my good pal Alun Carter and the legend that is 'Carcas', aka Mark Davies, were as good an international management team as you'll find anywhere in the world, and our results showed that. My only criticism of that group of people that Graham Henry and I had the privilege to work with was that they didn't know how good they were or how close we were to becoming a perennial world top-three side.

Steve Black is a professional of the highest standard, a man of integrity, dedicated and fully committed. Also he is a bloody nice bloke who cared for those around him and made them all feel a part of something special. The effect he has had on this group of Welsh rugby players and management team will stay with them forever. It is a pity that some people out there did not know the full story, they could learn a great deal from him and his professional attitude.

Alun Carter – project systems analyst for Welsh Rugby Union

Chapter Eight

FULHAM – THE AL FAYED EXPERIENCE

Every man has his own destiny; the only imperative is
to follow it, to accept it, no matter where it leads him.
Henry Miller

Having left Wales on a low, Julie and the kids still living there and me being
without a job wasn't an experience I would recommend, but I did have an
iron in the fire to take me back into football. The press had blown out of
all proportion my helping Paul Bracewell, the manager of Fulham, but
when he found out what had happened, he asked me to go there and help
him out officially. I had known Paul for many years, having coached him as
a player with Newcastle and Sunderland, and I respected him immensely.
It was a terrific gesture to offer me this lifeline, but it wasn't just an old pals
act. He knew and appreciated my methods because he thought along the
same lines himself. I was excited and relished the thought of getting back
into my first love, and with a team that looked as if it meant business. As
usual, Julie and the family backed me to the hilt.

Kevin Keegan had not long left Fulham and Paul asked me to go there
on a part-time basis to do some fitness and motivational work with the
players. It meant commuting from Wales, but I was more than happy to do
it and, more importantly, it provided security for us in a very uncertain

business. I had been getting great feedback from the players that the club was on the verge of exciting times. Kevin Keegan had done his usual job of signing quality players and I knew several of them personally. Chris Coleman had played for Wales, and Lee Clark, Kevin Ball, Andy Melrose, Andy Neilson and I had been extremely close in the North-east, so my transition was smooth and pleasurable. I had worked with many of them, could relate to them and this all added to the comfort zone. Coaches Peter Bonetti, Viv Busby and Frank Sibley, who'd been at West Ham all his life, were stimulating to work with. This was an ambitious club and Mohamed Al Fayed was the type of guy who not only craved success, but demanded it. Nothing was short of acceptable, so I was well motivated and knew that, if we were successful Al Fayed would be there with the financial support. He had injected a huge amount of cash, Kevin had spent wisely and it was exciting to think I could be a part of something special. I slotted in perfectly. It was a good set-up. The captain, Chris Coleman, headed up a fine squad and the players were up for it, training hard, and my relationship with Paul was spot on. Commuting, whilst tiring, at least gave me time and space to settle my mind. After a couple of weeks, Paul said Al Fayed had agreed for me to work there full time. I looked forward to this situation with great anticipation. The atmosphere seemed to be right, so I entered into negotiation with the club to secure a formal contract.

A meeting was set up in November 1999 with two of Al Fayed's executives in a hotel in Barnsley, well away from Fulham; it appeared they wanted a low-profile location. I didn't know quite what to expect, except I was convinced they would wish to suss me out properly and I prepared my answers to any possible questions with care. After short introductions, one of them came straight to the point and said, 'Well, Blackie, what do you want?'

This took me by surprise as I had expected finance to come way down the list after all the other necessaries about training methods, attitude, etc., but I just gave him a figure that I felt was a reasonable compensation for my coming on board. But, to be honest, I fully expected them to bargain it down. The reaction was surprising, but refreshing as he just said, 'Yes, fine,' then gave a huge sigh of relief. 'Is that it?'

I said, 'Yes, I think so,' with the speed of the negotiations dazzling.

We shook hands on it and, as he was leaving, he turned and said, 'The chairman told me to give you anything you wanted,' before smiling and leaving the room a happy man. There is no doubt he meant it and if I'd known what was coming I could have asked for whatever I wanted and it probably wouldn't have been a problem. Such is the way Al Fayed does business.

I began settling into the full-time routine. The buzz around Fulham certainly gave the impression they were going somewhere, but Al Fayed was impatient for glory and demanded it moved faster, even though the team were doing a good job, progressing steadily and setting up a good solid squad. Then after telling everyone at the club, manager, coaches and all the staff that Paul Bracewell was doing a magnificent job, he unceremoniously sacked him, right out of the blue. It was bizarre. I turned up at the training ground one morning when Al Fayed landed in his helicopter and out he came with his entourage, including minders and doctors. All very dramatic, as everything he does seems to be. Everyone was addressed and he came straight to the point, 'We've sacked Paul Bracewell. A lovely man, we really appreciate him, and the work he's done, but we don't think he's high-profile enough for this club at this time. We wish him every success in the future.'

It really was quite shocking and I felt for Paul, but it just shows how ruthless and cold the business side of the game is. I was angry and frustrated, and I know Al Fayed is an unusual character, but he, or those advising him, hadn't recognised the top-quality person Paul Bracewell was. Up to that moment he had taken the club on an unbeaten run of 17 games, which was a measure of his expertise, but Paul wasn't a big enough name with glinting media charisma and I found that sad. Paul gets things done; his intention is always to do things the right way and given the opportunity he will go on to be a top manager/coach in the great sports cauldron that is soccer.

Of course, the chairman was paying the money and he could do what he wanted, but dropping the bombshell in this way wasn't brilliant man management. Fulham have gone on to the Premiership, but the groundwork done by Kevin Keegan and Paul Bracewell should never be underestimated in that success. As an insight into Al Fayed's personality, the following episode stands as a good example. He strode into the meeting area on that same day Paul's sacking was announced and gave us a talk. At the end he looked round the room and said, 'Does anybody want to say anything?'

Kevin Ball had put a speech together and eloquently delivered it for a few minutes. It was straight talking and I felt he had put some excellent points to the chairman as to how we all felt. After he had finished, Al Fayed looked round the room and said, 'Does anybody want to say anything?'

It was as if Kevin Ball didn't exist. After Paul left, I was then offered the post of assistant manager to Karl-Heinz Riedle, a most lucrative offer and, at any other time, tempting. However, I couldn't even consider taking up the position as Paul Bracewell was my friend. My loyalty to him had to come first. So, after five months of doing something I really wanted in football and a top job now landing in my lap, it wasn't to be. I am certain that, on a whim, I would have been chopped at a second's notice. Had Paul remained there, I would have stuck with him and enjoyed the job immensely, for that is where my sporting heart lies. To be present in a dressing-room after your team has beaten Manchester United or Liverpool is a wonderful experience and something to be cherished. To date, I have never matched that feeling in any other sport, but that is the goal I strive to achieve in rugby, and it won't be for the lack of trying.

Al Fayed was an interesting and complex character, but you can't take it away from him that he breathed new life into Fulham Football Club. One day I was taking the warm-up prior to the game against Stockport when one of the lads said, 'Blackie, here's your mate coming.'

I turned round and there was the man himself, full of bounce. 'Are we going to win today?'

My reply was, 'I'm disappointed and can't believe you've even asked me that question. Of course we're going to win."

And we did, 4–1. I can still see him coming into the dressing-room and offering the first-team squad £1 million each if they won promotion, which was quite an incentive. Clarkie, in his rich Geordie way, was laughing and said, 'Is he joking?' And I had to tell everyone the man was very serious. However, I often wonder if that promise was fulfilled when they did make the Premiership.

Al Fayed was and is a larger-than-life character in every respect. His presence was huge and he's a very likeable person. He's done absolutely brilliantly in backing Chris Coleman as manager and they are now a team to be reckoned with in the Premiership. When I reflect on that period, there may be some regret from a career standpoint, but I don't regret my decision as my loyalty to and friendship with Paul was far more important than furthering my career at that time, or any other, for that matter.

I was now unemployed once more, stranded in Wales with my family. But not for long. The North-east was calling, and I couldn't wait to get back!

I first met Steve many years ago in a professional capacity when I was in rehabilitation. His hands-on, caring approach inspired my confidence and motivated me to come through an extremely difficult period in my life. We subsequently became good friends with a mutual respect, and despite our careers putting distance between us, have always kept in touch. When I was manager at Fulham, Steve came on board as fitness coach when he left the Welsh rugby squad and I was delighted to be working with him.

It was then I realised the depth of his integrity and how close a friend he was, because when I was sacked, Stephen also left the club on principle instead of capitalising on the situation, which he could easily have done.

Words can't really explain how I feel about him, but I have total admiration for him as a professional and genuine human being. He's a special guy, never satisfied, and always prepared to experiment with new methods in order to better his knowledge for improvement of those around him. Steve doesn't take defeat lightly and endeavours to succeed, always unselfishly putting others first despite his own problems.

I am proud to call him a mate.

Paul Bracewell – England coaching staff

Chapter Nine

BACK TO THE FALCONS

I'd rather be a lamp-post in Newcastle than a millionaire in any other city

Étienne Lenoir

Should you ever go back? Is anything like it was? Well, going back to the Falcons was certainly a good test for that theory. When Dave Thompson first approached me about returing to the North-east, things in Wales were not going as I had wanted them to professionally, or indeed positively. We'd not really had the players together as a team since the World Cup and I was getting a sneaking suspicion that, because the World Cup hadn't been won, there was a mode of thought that was pushing to 'start over'. Throwing the baby out with the bath water just wasn't the way forward. There was so much we were doing right. We just needed to show courage, keep our cool, keep our belief and our focus on winning games. You can't reinvent the wheel and this was proving to be our biggest problem. To change things as radically as people were suggesting would take two or three generations and, you must believe me, players, coaches, managers, administrators and most of all the public will not wait that long as nobody is guaranteed tomorrow. How long were you going to have to wait for a victory? It's a big cop-out to say that changing the entire structure of the game would be better for a country whose love and passion for the game of rugby union had evolved out of the best national intentions over a century. The truth of the matter is, and this is an Englishman speaking, there are good players in Wales, there are good coaches in Wales, there are good clubs in Wales and the country is full of excellent rugby people. I know that, and as soon as the people of Wales accept that, they can start progressing again.

Anyway, I'll cover that elsewhere and I had no intention of resigning or even considering a return to Newcastle. Yes, I felt homesick, and when Rob Andrew's secretary, Sharon Talbot, asked me if I would like to be the main speaker at a tribute dinner for him at Kingston Park to celebrate his retirement from rugby, I jumped at the opportunity. It was an honour to be asked, but it was also an opportunity to go home and see my old mates.

The 'do' was terrific, and totally fitting for Rob, who deserved the plaudits from his peers, the sporting community and beyond. It was a privilege to be part of his celebration. I was on good form and enjoyed the night, but it did underpin that feeling of being comfortable in my own backyard. After I'd said my bit, Dave Thompson, the Falcons' new owner, approached me. Dave is a rough-and-ready guy who doesn't suffer fools gladly, a dyed-in-the-wool rugby fanatic who'd taken over the club with a burning desire to make it great. He must have a heart like a lion, because when Sir John Hall left morale was at rock bottom, but as a former player and successful businessman, Dave knew what was needed from the inside as well as the outside. I'd met him on a couple of occasions socially at rugby matches, but wasn't at all close to him, so when he said out of the blue, 'You're coming back. You do know that?' it was a complete shock.

'What are you on about?' I said.

He just gave one of his wry smiles and said, 'I want you back here.'

'Just a minute,' I said. 'You shouldn't be talking like this, it's unsettling.'

And it was, especially under the circumstances, when he had me on my home soil with the people I loved.

I left it at that, but the seeds had well and truly been placed. It was no secret in rugby circles, there were real problems within Wales, and I was the focus of intense media attention as I was telling anyone who would listen to me that the problem wasn't with the opposition (we'd proved we could handle them), it was the Welsh media-promoted lack of self-esteem within the rugby environment. I now knew, if everything went wrong, at least I had a home and security to go back to. I did think about it a lot, and talked it over with Julie, and as time went on, the more things were poisoned in Wales, the more the idea appealed. Since I'd got to Wales, I'd worked day and night in my adopted homeland to bring the glory days back to the Principality. Statistics would back up my empirical feeling of ongoing achievement. When the people and players around me were as confident as I was in their ability, we were a match for anyone. When we were winning all those games and beating world champions, nobody was suggesting Welsh rugby needed a complete overhaul. But after the World Cup, when the national team's preparation changed focus, and with the Welsh clubs reclaiming their players for the domestic game, the strength of that winning team was lost. The result was a poor Six Nations performance. The media turned against us. The media and, I've got to say, some of the hierarchy within the rugby fraternity of Wales started to suggest that I knew it was time to go and that opinion was too misguided to be able to be talked around.

However, all thoughts of a prospective return to the Falcons were pushed to the back of my mind when the Fulham offer came along, and when eventually those events turned out pear-shaped, I contacted Rob Andrew to see if the offer was still open. If that wasn't to be the case, American football beckoned, as did a couple of prospective opportunities with southern hemisphere rugby teams.

I met Rob Andrew and Dave Thompson at Heathrow Airport prior to taking my mam to New York for a holiday. Our meeting was very relaxed and I felt relatively comfortable with the terms on offer. I didn't have a job title and jokingly called myself a chief purveyor of enthusiasm. My contract was agreed on a handshake, nothing on paper. Incredibly, that has been sustained right to the present time, based entirely on professional integrity and trust. As a freelance fitness and motivation adviser, I have my own company, which subcontracts me to work for the Falcons. This is my first priority, but means that, given the time and opportunity, I can pursue my speaking engagements and take on individual athletes from other sports in an advisory capacity. This keeps me fresh professionally and expands my knowledge, both practical and theoretical, which is to the Newcastle Falcons' benefit.

On meeting the team I immediately saw there had been many changes, and not for the better. It was a shock to my system because the team I had left was full of enthusiasm and confidence, and what I saw was a disillusioned bunch of formerly fine sportsmen who had forgotten about winning or success. And because the team's core was now so young and immature, all strategy seemed to be based on damage limitation. I realised the challenge was going to be even greater and that one fact fired me up. By and large the squad were young kids, and whilst they had obvious talent, they were raw and inexperienced in the ways of rugby. I remember well one of the very first games in France, when Steve Bates was emotionally upset for the lads because he thought he was in some way letting them down by allowing them on the field to be beaten up by grown men – 32-year-old Frenchmen who had played all their lives at the top European level against 19-year-old kids who were feisty but getting blown away. So I decided to inculcate a different mindset. 'Hard lines' and 'Good effort' were replaced with 'We're going to get over the gain line every time,' and 'We're going to out-passion everyone.' I told the squad the same message that Vince Lombardi had given to his 1959 Green Bay Packers, 'If a team wins because they are better than you then so be it. But you should never ever, ever, ever lose a game because the opposition want to win it more.' This mindset was the foundation stone of our rebuilding process.

This process began day by day, individual by individual; where anyone from the outside looking in would say, 'He's a loony, that bloke. Nobody can possibly be that up and positive every day talking all that nonsense.' It was fine me coming back with dreams of success, but I had to rise to a challenge way above my expectations, and I knew if I let the squad carry on as it had, there was no chance of achieving anything. Despite my experiences at the end of my tenure at Wales, at no time did I lose any confidence in my ability to achieve or communicate my vision, as I knew that, if my advice had been followed, Wales would have continued to do well. So, my inner belief has never wavered even under the most difficult of circumstances and I knew at each and every 'bad patch' that this self-belief would carry me through. At times, I question other people's commitment and agendas, but I never question my own.

I had been presented with a young team who were going to have to learn how to play a man's game. Of course we still had stalwarts like Inga Tuigamala, Gary Armstrong, Doddie Weir, George Graham and a smattering of other older members as the core of the team to show these young guns how. But as they were in the final phases of their careers we couldn't always rely on them being fit enough to do it on a game-by-game basis, great players though they still were. And as they were looking towards retirement I knew I had to concentrate on the young players. The older guys had reached that stage in their careers where ambitions ranged from just surviving to maybe pulling on the coaching tracksuit. It appeared that their sole *raison d'être* wasn't to win games for Newcastle Falcons but to hang on by their fingernails to a career in professional rugby. This didn't show a particularly good example to the youngsters who undoubtedly looked up to them.

I was shocked by the negative attitude of the team as a whole and their lack of ambition. It was as if they had chucked it mentally. After all the hype and attention during the Sir John Hall period, it looked as if they had had such a kick in the nuts, they'd almost given up. Our results were poor and we were in grave danger of being relegated. Something had to be done to raise their spirits. My decision was to put everyone through an accelerated professionalism course in one year, when normally it would have taken three. For example, I addressed all the common questions: 'Why shouldn't I go on the drink tonight?' 'Why should I train hard?' 'Why shouldn't I go to parties? I'm only young once.' Well, everything has a price and these questions are always answered by performance both on and off the field. I constantly drilled quotes into them, such as from Joe Louis: 'Everyone wants to go to heaven, but nobody wants to die.' I kept telling them that if they trained and lived diligently, they would get their rewards. Their perception of themselves wasn't very high, so we needed to build each player's self-esteem, set them a series of goals in training that they would safely be able to accomplish, reward them for that and then slightly raise the bar again. It was of paramount importance that the players were not allowed to fail any of these tasks during this process of spiritual rehabilitation.

As the squad's spirits grew, it became increasingly clear that the problem certainly wasn't talent, as there were enormous amounts of it on hand. We just hadn't developed an environment that would allow that talent to flourish and to accelerate the experience process on the training field. We'd just started to feel a bit sorry for ourselves and we needed to change that mindset as soon as possible. Attitude is something which you can change and it can be done pretty quickly if the stronger characters at the club subscribe and use their influence to pull many of the others off that fence they sit on for comfort's sake. You only need three or four of them in reality to change the face of the club, but they've got to be the right three or four. As we progressed toward the possibility of a cup final appearance, many of the older players, maybe seeing a cup-winner's medal as a marvellous end to their careers, started to step forward and drive the quality. They upped their own input, but also that of the youngsters who could have the deciding role as to whether the club would win that cup or not. I constantly drummed into them that they should be competitive every week, then get the habit of winning, then learn how to win competitions. Preparation of their minds as well as their bodies was paramount.

We weren't brilliant, but spirits did lift. Steve Bates and Martin Brewer were doing a marvellous job at this time and we were starting to refocus Rob Andrew's attentions away from the political front and back to the field of play. We began to work very well together with a squad limited by confidence, belief and ability at that time. We got the rub of the green (the club needed it) and won the Tetley's Bitter Cup at Twickenham in 2002. It was a marvellous day not only for the club but for the North-east in general. After two wonderful Cup final tries from Tom May we rode our luck and nicked it with a disputed try in injury time from Dave Walder. This was probably a fitting testimony to the open playing style much favoured by Steve Bates, an innovative and at times visionary coach. It was a great confidence booster, and small flashes of individual and team brilliance were beginning to show. And we also managed to avoid the drop, which would have possibly destroyed the club forever, because I couldn't see Dave Thompson forking out money in that situation.

The youth of our team was now being talked about nationally. In particular Jonny Wilkinson, Tom May, Jamie Noon, Micky Ward and Michael Stephenson were all impressing me with their ability and professionalism, and stood as examples to the rest of the team. I managed to persuade Liam Botham, whom I worked with in Wales, to come to the Falcons. I knew him to be a diligent and potent player, and, possessing the genes of his father, Ian Botham, there was no doubting his talent. Liam's dedication meant that his influence on the training paddock was just as important as his performances in games. He matured into a very important club man and popular figure in the North-east along with the other members of the Rat Pack! But, as is the way in this game of ours, Liam has subsequently moved on and even changed sports to rugby league where he has made a good impression for Leeds Rhinos in the Super League. I'm not surprised.

On the home front, Julie was still in Wales with the kids, and the twins, Mark and Stephen, were preparing for their final year at university. I had the added pressures of finding a home. Having been a townie all my life, I made one of my best decisions and decided to move into the beautiful Northumbrian village of Whalton. The family joined me and my life was coming back together as abnormal as ever and then suddenly, along came what was the greatest honour and opportunity of my sporting life, the British and Irish Lions.

Chapter Ten

THE LIONS RAW

It is fatal to enter any war without the will to win it.
General Douglas MacArthur

I started this book with brief details of my outburst at the British and Irish Lions players and coaches at Coff's Harbour. In the chronology of the events of my life it is as well that I return to the British Lions' 2001 tour of Australia in this chapter. It was a tour that should have been the pinnacle of my career but became one of the most frustrating and depressing periods in my sporting life.

'Beware of what you dream lest you should get it' is a wise old saying, and nothing could be more apt regarding my selection and build-up to the 2001 Lions tour. From the announcement that Graham Henry was taking over as coach, and knowing the relationship we had, without sounding conceited, I had a strong feeling I would get a call. Graham knew what I was capable of and many others at that level thought the Lions job would suit me because I wouldn't attempt to impose any new conditioning regimes and would have the confidence to support the squad in their given environment. At the same time, I would have an acknowledged ability to supplement any of their existing regimes, should they need it.

The biggest hurdle I have to jump daily concerns my health, which hadn't been good for a long time and continues not to be too good. I have a strong spirit, though, and my single-minded approach to work keeps me focused. I suffer from obstructive sleep apnoea, a most distressing and dangerous condition which dictates my life completely. The last time I went into a clinic for observations, apparently I woke up close to 600 times a night and I was told I was an extremely severe case. Basically, you fall asleep, then hold your breath and when you can no longer hold it, you wake up. Added to this I have ulcerative colitis, which means I lose a lot of blood, making me so tired I sometimes have to nip in for a transfusion. I am on constant medication, the side effects of which have resulted in my weight soaring. Quite simply, I am seen as fat and, having been an active athlete, this is highly embarrassing. I used to think all overweight people were subject to a self-induced condition. I now know better. So I live with constant tiredness, pain and lack of self-esteem because of my appearance. When I was attached to the Welsh national squad, there was a spell when the tabloids made jibes at my size, which hurt deeply because they didn't know the facts. The point of all this is that I felt all these factors might prevent me taking up a Lions post, if it ever came my way – to such an extent that I told Rob Andrew, 'Rob, even if I am asked, I am not going to go, because I am not well enough.'

Now, that statement may have been spurred by two possibilities – one, my not being well, and the other, my not being selected. As it turned out, Graham Henry told me of my selection and went as far as to say there was nobody else that could be considered. He said that the decision hadn't come from him but from the Lions board in Ireland. So, from a professional and an ego standpoint, I was very pleased. But then I had to sit down and address the situation – what was I going to tell Rob? As far as I was concerned, my change of mind was based upon the fact that I would only live once and that no one knows what lies around the corner, so when the opportunity presents itself, I should grasp it with both hands. I am always telling others never to procrastinate, so it would have been hypocritical not to heed my own advice. Here was a once-in-a-lifetime opportunity that I would have been crazy to turn down. Not only was it a huge personal honour, it was also a feather in the cap for Newcastle Falcons and the North-east of England.

Reaction at the club wasn't exactly as I expected. The Falcons' hierarchy thought it might pull me off track in relation to what I was attempting to achieve with the team. It was felt that I wouldn't be able to give up my time because there would be nobody with the players in my absence and they would suffer for it. Later, when I came to consider that response in the unemotional light of day, it was a perfectly rational and reasonable train of thought. What upset me at the time, however, was that Newcastle Falcons could even question my commitment to them. Up to departure with the Lions, and while I was away on the tour, I would have put in place solid conditioning regimes. The Newcastle Falcons were of paramount importance to me and there was no way I would have allowed anything to interfere with that professional commitment. The depth of my relationship with the players was intense and every one of them knew I would run through brick walls for them if I had to.

My prevailing belief was that my selection for the Lions would reflect well on the club. Added to that, it meant I would be there first hand to look after the Falcons' prize asset, Jonny Wilkinson, and professionally and personally that meant an enormous amount to me, being part of the coaching team and affording me the opportunity to protect him on tour. My influence could and did save him from over-training, something which I feel allowed him to make such a significant impact on the Third Test when he almost won the series for us. Of course, he suffered a nasty injury but he returned from the tour well and without suffering from burn-out. He is a sensible lad and looks after himself, but I would like to think I had an influence there.

In blind innocence I thought they would have been as excited as I was, but I have to recognise that they were looking at the bigger picture because they were paying my wages to enhance Newcastle Falcons. It's the recurring dilemma surrounding club commitments and representative honours, and I can certainly see both sides of the argument. However, I felt my professionalism was in question and it certainly put a dampener on what should have been a special moment and something to rejoice. Added to that, I didn't go with the Lions until they actually left. So I missed out on getting to know how the coaches really ticked. I agreed with the Falcons that this should happen, but if a similar situation occurred again, I would insist on going – any breakdown with the coaches on the tour therefore lies partially at my door.

My response to the opinions of the hierarchy at Newcastle Falcons was to harden psychologically my resolve to double my efforts at the club and leave no room for future complaints that the Lions tour had jaded me. I actually now realise that all my thoughts and anxieties were too personal. In the cold light of day, from a business point of view, I now understand what disruption can occur when an important member of the staff is away on other people's business. I had been judging the Falcons management without really considering their position. Whether this was selfish on my part, or poor communication on both sides, is debatable, but I have found that, over the past two seasons, when Jonny Wilkinson has been away from the club, his absence has caused a major problem. At the end of the day we have to win games and anything possible to enhance that situation has to be done. Preparation is important and the person who sets that preparation has their part to play. My feelings became quite emotional, but I now recognise that the Falcons' management were a little bit more insightful than I understood them to be. As a learning experience it was invaluable and I now appreciate that while personal honour is fine I am part of a business team.

Despite all the negatives I was excited about the mountain to be climbed. British Lions is romantic, *Boy's Own* stuff. You look up as you come out of the tunnel on the other side of the world and see 25,000 travelling fans. You know millions around the world are watching every move. The hairs stick up on the back of your neck and your heart pounds like a drum.

My first priority lay in becoming familiar with the management structure. I saw it as part of my job to make the components of that structure gel. All in all, they appeared solid, experienced and motivated.

Donal Lenihan, overall team manager, was a good guy in every respect. He was a very emotional and sound person with solid principles. An excellent player in his time, he had represented the Lions, so he knew what the honour meant and what it was all about. He was extremely well regarded in Ireland and respected throughout the international rugby world. Donal was amiable and great company, a smashing bloke. I liked him a lot. He was certainly the best man for the job and the second best singer on the tour.

Graham Henry, as head of coaching, was the key figure and ultimately took the flak coming with that responsibility. Graham is a first-class coach and a first-class man, and was fully deserving of the position. I have nothing but total admiration for him. He is now in the role he was born for – as the All Blacks coach.

Andy Robinson, Graham's deputy, had a similar commitment to his coaching role. He was a nice bloke and a good player in his time, and together with Graham, they made a solid team.

Phil Larder, the defensive coach, was very much more egotistical than the rest and initially a bit more effective than the others. I believe he is the cornerstone behind the success experienced by the current England team. With the players we had available on the Lions tour, and given more time, I think he could have made our defence impregnable.

David Aldred, the kicking coach, was constant in whatever situation he found himself. He was single-minded, biomechanically superb and as good as anyone in the world in his chosen sphere of the game. His successes with the likes of Rob Andrew, Jonny Wilkinson, Matt Burke, et al. have all been well chronicled and rightly so, but I always get the impression that David is not that happy just focusing on the kicking aspect. I think he is a frustrated head coach!

Alun Carter, the analyst, was superb. He was one hell of a worker and always had everyone's best interests at heart. He was a complete professional and great company for me.

Dr James Robinson had been on two previous Lions tours and knew his game inside out. He was a good man with a young family he often spoke about. I liked him as a person and could relate to his home situation, which showed his vulnerability at times – and I like that in a person.

Mark Davies, the physio, was a good mate. He was a former Welsh international flanker and a great lad with previous Lions tour experience, a laconic sense of humour and terrific personality. There was always plenty of fun and laughs when he was around. I can't speak too highly of him. Mark has a way of never letting the pressure have a negative effect on him.

On the face of it, then, we had a top-class Lions management and coaching team. However, something that appears to have been forgotten is that management and coaches are no different to players. They have great days and not so good days. Great players don't always play well, and coaches and management can perform just the same. I could spend a fortune going to Real Madrid to watch Zidane play and, on the day, come away extremely disappointed because that is human nature. So whilst a lot of our coaching and management was top drawer, much of it wasn't in practice. That's life. We were only together for a few weeks and, as it has been said on so many occasions, the only people who can be at their best every day are mediocre. Athletes only peak for specific events and it was totally unrealistic to expect our squad to peak for eight weeks. Once again, that applies to coaching and management.

Make no mistake about it. Graham Henry had, and has, huge ticks for him as a manager of renown with major success, certainly in Auckland, where he twice won the Super 12 championships. But there is no way he should have been made senior coach for the Lions tour. No question, he was, and still is, an excellent coach who knew inside out the southern hemisphere way of playing and all the top players. That put him right in the frame and he had adjusted, with Wales, commendably to the British way. His Welsh record was special, but he needed more than that. This was a British and Irish Lions team. His early success with Wales was in decline and the media were after his head.

People have to understand that coaching is about being effective, making players and teams play better with only one objective – winning! I have enormous respect for Graham and his work ethic. There is no doubt he gave that job 100 per cent in effort. But no matter how hard he worked or whatever he attempted to put into place, it was never going to be good enough. In any given team you have to pick the right players at the right time in the right positions. Well, you have to do the same with the coaches.

So, for the British Lions, while Graham was certainly an understandable and very good choice from an ability standpoint, Clive Woodward was the natural choice because he had a team that was winning on a regular basis and the Lions were predominantly English. But he had been sidelined and that one decision by the selection gurus proved to be a disaster. Woodward had fashioned a wonderful winning team which formed the majority of the

Lions squad, but their loyalty lay firmly with him. Be under no illusion, all great teams are run by the players and that England team was no exception, with Martin Johnson very much to the fore. They were an extremely tight group of players and Johnson's actions later showed just how that force could be mobilised for good or ill. This came to fruition when Dawson and Healey were under possible threat of being sent home for their ill-timed newspaper articles criticising the day-to-day regime. I felt at the time if the management had made the decision to send them home, then Johnson would have left with them. I didn't say it then but my gut reaction was confirmed when his book came out and he actually said he would have gone with them. That was the true power base for this Lions tour and a significant factor in why we failed.

The big problem with Graham's selection as coach was that there was a real history between the Welsh and English players and a history between Graham and the English players. When I say history, I mean a negative one. It started when a letter was sent to the Welsh Rugby Union for the attention of Graham Henry and his management team during the Five Nations of 1999. A doctor had been travelling on a train and allegedly sitting in the same carriage as the English team management. He couldn't help but pick up the loud tones coming from this group and wrote of their apparent racism. Having been married to a foreign lady who had suffered racism, he felt personally aggrieved by what he was hearing this group of guys saying, how much they disliked and disrespected the Welsh, and that when the game came it wouldn't be a problem. Players' names were bandied about and bad-mouthed. The letter writer couldn't believe how arrogant the English players were and it struck such a chord that he sat down and wrote this personal letter, something he had never done before. I saw the letter and at the end of it he wrote, 'and I wish you all the very best in the game and hope that you beat this team of bigots'. The letter seemed to be authentic and was subsequently investigated by a member of the administrative staff at the WRU to verify its content.

Maybe it could have been ignored and thrown in the bin but it was used, and used as a stimulant for that current Welsh team – not that they needed much to play the English. We said to them in the wind-up before the match at Wembley, 'When you are tired, just remember how much they disrespect you, just remember they don't rate you in any form or fashion and how they are going to walk over you and manipulate the situation and that you are so weak psychologically that you are going to go with their manipulation – and they are better players than you anyhow.'

Added to that, an English player came over to me before the game and one of the English management said to him, 'I know you know him, but stay away from him before the game. He'll break your concentration.'

I was surprised by this because these players were very close to me – it was a ludicrous situation. Anyway, as the end of the game came, with five minutes to go, Clive Woodward walked down the steps to talk to one of the ground staff and he said in loud tones, within hearing of the Welsh management and coaching contingent sitting on the sidelines three or four yards away, 'Where do the winning team have to go to pick up the cup and be presented? I don't know what to do here at Wembley.'

There was almost a physical fight between Dr Roger Evans and Clive Woodward. Dr Evans, a highly respected consultant from Wales, was dreadfully upset and extremely emotional. He wanted to physically confront Woodward, who pushed him out of the way.

Then, incredibly, Scott Gibbs scored a fabulous try which was converted at the last second by Jinks (Jenkins) and, lo and behold, it turned out to be one of the most dramatic finishes ever in the last Five Nations. Wales won the match. To say Wales as a nation were happy is an understatement. We were very, very proud and rubbed it in a little bit as well because even when we were thrashed in the Six Nations a year later, that win was still being celebrated.

Graham Henry was quoted in the newspapers and on television interviews highlighting the arrogance of the English. So these were the same people we now had to pull together and persuade to die for him. It was never going to happen – there was no genuine respect from either side. I knew Graham could have put it behind him, but I don't think influential members of the England party could. But even now, as I re-watch the documentary, *The Henry Files*, I actually don't think Graham did put it behind him and he was terribly biased against that 'English thing'. He tried ridiculously hard to balance it out by being more on their side and overcompensating to show how fair he was with the Lions. I believe he overcompensated so much that we lost the series.

The history, then, was well documented and created a camp atmosphere between the English and the other players in the Lions squad. An 'us and them' attitude prevailed right from the start – England versus the rest. It wasn't a happy camp. To say otherwise would be simply looking the other way and fooling myself, because it was patently obvious that certain of the English players didn't want Graham Henry there at all. While Woodward couldn't be accused of sulking, he certainly made no attempt to help Graham, who I believe tried to mend fences to no avail. Woodward could possibly have been thinking, 'Who is this kiwi to get this job? The bulk of the team is English, he's got all my coaches and I have set up the whole thing but I am not in.'

Frankly, he had a valid point. Graham Henry's allegations of 'arrogance' obviously riled, so the antipathy wasn't all one-sided. Graham also decided to use England coaches – another big mistake. Not that they weren't up to it but he should have taken on board people who would have backed him 100 per cent and were more prepared to merge in with the team. The problem was they had not worked together and Graham's coaches should have come from the group he had successfully worked with in Wales. The loyalty of the English coaches was naturally towards Woodward, because the last time England played Wales they hammered them, so maybe their mind was set and they were saying, 'What's this bloke doing telling us what to do?' There could have been a little bit of that in the background. I certainly think Andy Robinson was 100 per cent behind Graham. The others I am not so sure about. It was heavily rumoured that Woodward would have been a happy man had his coaches not taken up the offer.

A fact which stands out in my memory, indicative of Woodward's attitude, was that whilst in Australia commentating for the media, not once did he come to our camp for a friendly chat or to wish us well, yet it was rumoured he was regularly in the Australian camp. Why? Media duties? I can't answer that one but I do know if he had popped in to say, 'Well done' or 'Good luck, lads', it would have been a terrific boost for everyone. It seems, on the evidence, maybe, just maybe, he didn't want us to win. It would have been far better for him to have accepted the situation as it was and then positively given us his absolute support. I spoke to him once on the touchline and asked how my Newcastle lads had done on the recent England tour and he said I should be extremely proud of them. I was enormously pleased at this and had he repeated his sentiments on one of the Lions' training days it would have boosted their morale no end.

But, I repeat, in my opinion he was the right man for the job and by the same yardstick there is no way I should have been picked as the conditioning coach. A specialist conditioning consultant and adviser? Yes, but not the main trainer's role for that group of people. If the coaching staff had been predominantly Celtic then I was an obvious choice, but since the core strength of the squad was English, the job should have gone to Dave Reddin, who would have looked after the English lads and done an excellent job. I suppose my selection was strongly influenced by the work I had done and the success I had had with Graham Henry and Jonny Wilkinson, and whilst I was confident in my ability, there is no way I could have forged the relationship Dave already had with the core of the team in such a short space of time. In this regard, I observed and offered unconditional support and advice where I felt it was needed, but I didn't impose my thoughts on anyone other than my coaching colleagues. To have done otherwise would have been disastrous. Dave telephoned to congratulate my selection and that made a huge difference, showing what a true sportsman he is.

The choice of Martin Johnson as captain of the Lions of Great Britain and Ireland was also questionable, to my mind. I found Martin different from the person I had expected – a little bit of 'tales of the unexpected' – because I hadn't been with the man in a team environment before. Phil Larder told me Johnson was the most inspirational man you could ever meet. As the tour progressed, it became more apparent that he could be seen that way because of his influence on the players who had worked with him over a long period of time. But those who hadn't were still left with a feeling of mystique as to his effectiveness. Probably by the end of the tour the big guy's commitment and passion to playing would have won many people over. His playing career goes without question and he has tough, uncompromising qualities, but in my opinion he wasn't the right leader for this particular tour, with this particular management team. Had Clive Woodward been coach, he would have been exactly the right person.

At team talks Martin would sit silently for long periods with little verbal input, although it must be said the physical effect of his presence was always significant. When he did say a few choice words, they were duly noted by the players and coaches who knew him really well and knew what made him tick. But for those who didn't, he wasn't particularly inspirational. On the field there was no doubting his unbelievable confidence and his leadership by example, but off the field I didn't have the impression he was the most inspirational person for this group of players.

I honestly believe making him captain added to the philosophic weakness of the tour squad. I can only refer back to the passage in his book where he says that if Dawson had been sent home, he would have jumped on the plane with him. Support for a player is one thing, but that attitude is not one of strong objective captaincy, especially when the reputation of the Lions was at stake. It doesn't make sense. Had he carried out this threat, it would have been an absolute disaster. Dawson was out of order, apologised and was fined, and to his credit he got back on board and did everything he could to contribute to the Lions' victories during the tour. I might be wrong, of course, but for my money the man who could have led us to victory was Keith Wood, whose leadership qualities were traditionally inspirational, probably more than anyone else by a country mile. An interesting postscript to this issue is that Martin, in his take on the tour, also suggested that Keith Wood would have been a better choice to captain the Lions.

Another superb player who could have thrown his hat in the ring for the captaincy and who was very good socially with all the other players was Lawrence Dallaglio, but he was out of the frame through injury. So, for me, Wood was the natural captain for this tour and at times certainly stepped forward and did just that. If he had been captain, he could have been backed up by the respective leaders of Scotland, England and Wales, each playing his part to help gel the collective responsibility of the team.

Having said all this, Martin has had, and continues to have, a fabulous rugby career, and the more you get to know him, he is a very likeable person. I can understand 100 per cent how he came to be such a successful England captain. I personally enjoyed his company and the one-to-one sessions we did on the tour.

It may seem that my comments about Martin and his suitability to be the captain on this tour are harsh, but they only apply to that particular tour. Subsequently, if we have to assess his leadership style, it would be by example rather than words. So, as he has got better in his playing career, this has reflected in his role as captain. The two are inextricably linked. He puts his body on the line and inspires, and this affects the other players and that is a rare quality, but in my opinion this is also something which has improved with maturity and experience. I think his experience in the 2001 Lions tour was part of the evolutionary process which has increasingly helped him to cope with the immense pressure associated with his role within the game. I can honestly say that I have never seen him have a bad game, but once in a while, due to his highly competitive and uncompromising nature, he might give the odd penalty away. When he does, it is not necessarily a bad thing, because, as it showed in the build-up to England's World Cup win, the message to the opposition and his teammates was that he would not stand any nonsense and that he would do anything to succeed. So the total package Martin portrays is giving the right vibes. He is saying, 'You are taking on a hard-nosed Brit and I am taking no shit from you.' Martin is not about silky skills, great practitioner though he is; he is more of a British bulldog who is going to be first over the trenches. Winning the World Cup has obviously been the pinnacle of his career and leading the Lions to victory in South Africa was a marvellous victory for that tour party's team spirit, while their play probably didn't deserve it. Martin has grown even more in stature as leader as his performances have proved, so by the time the World Cup came along he was exactly the right man in the right place for the right job.

In the final analysis everything would be laid at Graham Henry's door, but the real story began long before, when the seeds of failure were built in prior to team or management being selected. Graham gave everything to the squad, he couldn't have given any more, and it was shocking the way he was treated. But that's Graham's story and he has already told it. This is mine!

For me, being selected for the Lions was the greatest accolade you could receive in coaching. I personally think it is equal to, if not slightly more prestigious than, the Olympics because of its focus, with the collective group of people all pulling together to display and use the best of Irish and British qualities. It's that bulldog spirit, winning wars together. Remember, we don't play any Lions Tests at home. They are all away, so we go into their backyard and find the best in the world to win the war. When you are picked to be part of that, you are so proud it's beyond belief. So the passion is there to start with. Then you look around at the people you are with. Although I had nothing to do with picking any of those players, if I had, I would have had one other kid and that would have been a fellow called Gary Armstrong. He would definitely have been there. There is no doubt in my mind, even at that stage in his career when he was playing for Newcastle Falcons, his indomitable spirit was what we needed in Lions Tests situations. But he wasn't there and the squad was the poorer for that.

Near to our departure we had a squad week at Tindley Hall in Hampshire, which wasn't bad but was nothing special. Those who ran the place itself were good people and that was fine but there was very little concentration on rugby and it was basically a holiday, with so-called bonding games and some fitness training thrown in. The professional team which had delivered the week's event did a very good job and I congratulated them for their focus and passion. Unfortunately, I am not a big lover of these types of events and I questioned the longevity of whatever effect they have. Concentration was on social aspects and how we were expected to behave, instead of videos and solid classroom discussion on tactics. By no means did we have any strategy sorted out before we left for Australia.

My feeling in general was that preparation was pretty poor. We should have been consolidating it over 12 months in order that coaches and players got to know one another properly. The philosophy of what we had to achieve could have been absorbed with regular squad get togethers. That didn't happen and it made the job difficult right from the outset because, basically, we had to gel people who were foreign to one another. Most of the newspapers were scathing about the number of Welsh players in the squad, and the Scots also came in for a hard time. The Irish got off lightly. It was obvious that the England squad were favourites and they did take advantage of that. It was evident that many of the players were signed up on deals with newspapers to write columns, so Lions' selection was going to be extremely lucrative. Some players made vast sums of cash whilst others did very well but just received a basic. To my mind, all the cash coming in should have been pooled for the benefit of all. British Lions is still a tremendous cachet, but this has transferred into big bucks and I have to wonder if some of the players' concentration was being diverted slightly by the opportunity of financial gain.

Early on the players set up tour guidelines as a code of behaviour and attitude in order to move us on as one unit. This was written down and understood by everyone at the meeting. 'What is said here, stays here. Do you all agree to that?'

'Yes,' they were unanimous, fists in the air. It was almost straight from the scene in the movie *Pearl Harbor*, when Alec Baldwin, as commanding officer, tells his recruits, 'Everybody take a step forward and we are going into battle, boys, but 75 per cent of you won't come back. Are you still with us?'

'Yes!'

Those guidelines included all the clichés about loyalty, professionalism, teamwork and solidarity, and on paper it looked flawless as a battle strategy, but critics such as Eddie Butler of *The Observer* and other newspaper warriors can say what the hell they like, because when it came down to it, many of the squad weren't together – they broke the code.

As the tour went on, commitment to that old adage of 'what's said here, stays here' would undoubtedly be tested, even though in those early days it was generally felt that the honour and integrity of the Lions tradition would ensure that any personal grievances would be broached and settled in-house. Unfortunately, that level of personal commitment to the team cause was not found to be universal and the law of silence was broken. Players were to complain of too much physical stress and the reality would be that they would have a point. However, the revelations would bring enormous psychological stress to the environment. My frustration was that both these stresses could have been avoided had they been handled more professionally by all concerned. The major problem nobody seemed to pick up on was that two wrongs don't make a right and the effect of one complaint certainly didn't balance out against the other. It just had a double negative effect. The outcome of the series suggests we could have negotiated the effect of either the physical or mental impact of these unprofessional inputs, but not both.

This attitude was to impact on everyone and shouldn't have happened. Certain members decided, in their wisdom and inflated egos, to break the rules they had set up. It was sad and shocking, and I knew once that happened we were going to struggle to retain unity. It was a minority, of course, but it is the way of the world that a disruptive minority always makes life difficult for everyone else. The protagonists, strangely enough, already had a winning Lions tour behind them – maybe this was a factor which stopped them going that extra mile for the sake of the tour party and keeping their mouths shut to the outside world. Their actions certainly didn't help our cause and definitely helped the struggling Australian set-up by giving them something to hang their hats on. Andrew Blades, a World Cup winner himself in 1999 and my coaching partner at Newcastle Falcons in 2002–03, was a member of the Aussie coaching team for that tour and he was to tell me that the apparent break in the Lions camp was a godsend to their spirits.

On the night prior to our departure for Australia we had a huge dinner in a large marquee in London and there was an air of excitement and anticipation. The place was packed with television people, ex-Lions, sponsors, selectors and celebrities. The kit we were given was vast – sets of training gear, video cameras, you name it, there must have been at least £10,000 to £15,000 worth of gear each, shoes, shirts, everything. But because of my strange shape, none of it fit me. When I asked Eden Park, our clothing suppliers, if they could find something suitable for me they replied that if they did they would sack the tailor! In addition to all this, if we had won the series, each person would have received £27,000, as well as the private deals on top. Let's not forget, the players were paid by their home clubs also. This is big money and for a couple of months' work, top players could earn more than triple what the average wage-earner could in a year – not soccer, but not bad!

So, flushed with excitement and humour, we boarded the plane, full of high expectations. After a long and tiring flight, we arrived in Australia and lodged in Freemantle, about an hour from Perth. Now, the players had had a long, hard season, what we had to do was give them some guidance. We had to marshal the troops, give them the best gear, guns and food, and mobilise that unit in someone else's backyard to be victorious. There is no reason why we shouldn't have done just that. The main reason we didn't is because our preparation had become much too influenced by the proprietary regime from Down Under. We were trying to be southern hemisphere people but we weren't. The incredible thing is that the attitude wasn't coming from Graham Henry, but from the other coaches. The influence on the squad's preparation for this tour had undoubtedly come from the southern hemisphere, as had been the case with the English squad over quite a period of time. In the mists of the full battery of analyses, flow charts, videos and meetings, coaches appeared to have forgotten all about effectiveness.

We didn't seem to have the courage to say, 'Let's rest.' All we needed was organisation, enormous energy on the day and to work hard. On the day of the game, we needed to go in with a full tank. We could not improve our skills significantly now, if at all, in those few weeks, with the age of people we had there. We couldn't possibly do that. We couldn't improve our tackling but we could improve our organisation, and we could achieve that if the coaching was more succinct and our energy levels were sufficiently high in order to stay enthused.

Instead, despite the jet lag from the flight to Australia, we hit the ground running and were excited at the buzz. We landed about 1 a.m. and began training about 7.30 a.m. This was silly. Even the doctors couldn't get through to the management who 'took note' of what we were saying but dismissed it in a foolish course of action. We had troubles, for there was a gruelling series of matches and travelling ahead: apart from the three crucial Test matches, we had another seven warm-up games. Even with a squad of 37 (which became 44 after a run of injuries), it was critical we made a good account of ourselves in all games. That decision to work the lads like dogs right from the off was a major contribution to our failure to win what was clearly a winnable series. Everybody and every player was affected by it and many came to me daily saying how tired they were, never having done so much training in their lives. This obviously wasn't true as training wasn't that bad, but after a long season it could be perceived as such. I made my feelings clear to the other coaches which put me in a difficult position as condition coach and dictated how I approached the politics in the forthcoming weeks because I realised there were several agendas involved here – there were those who wanted to look good and others who wanted to do well.

Astonishingly, I felt we were playing the game on the training field when our opponents weren't there. All we were doing was beating ourselves up, amassing injuries and tiring the lads out. In contrast, the Australians had their wives and families and were partying. Our management were smug: 'Oh, yes, but we are more focused than them.' Well, we weren't more focused. We were doing it differently and that doesn't make it better or worse, just different.

I constantly looked at the managerial side of the tour, and our interaction with the players, and explored different ways in which we could strengthen the environment, in particular where I thought there was a personality clash in the offing, or someone with a personal problem for whatever reason within the squad. I made every attempt to befriend everyone, get them on board.

In order for you to get a feel for the role I was expected to perform, there follows a diary of our first match day during the tour, which began with a clash against Western Australia.

As explained, I normally get by with around two or three hours' sleep a night, so on waking there was so much preparation to do. I'd complete writing notes to every one of the players, plus the substitutes and other squad members. These would be handwritten and delivered to each room personally. They might contain comments about the forthcoming match or his previous day's training. They might point out how well he is doing or just small personal observations to help. Sometimes I'd tell them how important they were, even though they weren't playing. I tried to learn as much as possible about each player, their birthdays, families and such details, because this gave me an important personal approach. My passion and enthusiasm for the job underpinned every decision I made. It had to go like that otherwise it would have been impossible to fulfil my role. I saw my main function as setting an environment for everyone, players and management, to allow them to flourish and pull the whole thing together, ensuring they all arrived at games in top form mentally. I also needed to ensure the coaches weren't working too hard but I seem to have fallen down on that. The schedule would go something like this.

7 a.m. The first players start waking for breakfast between 7 a.m. and 9 a.m. I have no hard and fast rules about when a player should go to bed before a match or when they get up, but I will find out what makes them happy. I am more worried about establishing what puts them in a good frame of mind so I try to find out what they do at home under normal circumstances. Do they read a book? Watch a film? That sort of thing. About 10 per cent of the team are early risers so it is important I am around then. Breakfast is simple – cereal, toast, honey – but what they have eaten three to four days previously is what built up their story.

9 a.m. The bulk of the team rise between now and 11 a.m. on match days. Players may get out of their normal rhythm before a game. So, mindful of this, I remind them that they should only eat what they eat at home.

2 p.m. Players start warming up for the match. We work on a few lineouts, confirming calls, that sort of thing. I take this chance to begin reinforcing their roles in the game. Words now need to be specific and detailed, because they know I am taking every interest in them. You need to know them well enough to ensure your words are not contrived, or you will lose credibility. I try to give them triggers as the day goes on.

4 p.m. We organise a pre-match meal around three or four hours prior to kick-off. Some like pasta, others soup and sandwiches. You must be able to cater for everyone. You could advise them as best you can but if a player in his 30s likes a particular thing, and he is a super player and has been eating the same thing for years, you don't stress him by saying he shouldn't have something. Having worked with Jonny Wilkinson since he was 15, I have helped educate him to eat the right things and he enjoys eating them – a real professional long before many others. Although I attempt to eat properly, if we are going to have a little treat, we might have it together, particularly after a hard training session or a

match. We might get back to the hotel and have a couple of bowls of chips or a toasted steak sandwich. You don't want the players to think they are being deprived all the time.

5 p.m. Graham Henry takes the team meeting in our hotel. He has the starting 15 in a semicircle around him and behind them are the bench replacements and coaching staff. Before this commences I might have dropped Graham a little note or bought him a book with a special inscription or even dug out some quotes that fit the occasion. For him, I say I hope they will be of some use, and he appreciates it. I tell him I am looking forward to hearing him speak and remind him of some great speeches he has given the players in the past. Graham speaks superbly to the players and is inspirational in this, our first game. The talk lasts about seven minutes. He talks to the group as a whole, but as he goes round the team, he stops at particular players to make points. In this first meeting, Donal Lenihan presents the players with their shirts. A lot of thought and preparation has gone into this gathering. The tone has to be right and come from the heart – it does.

5.30 p.m. We all hop on the bus to travel to the game. It is extremely quiet. Every member of the 37-man squad and all the coaches are there, and it is important we are united as one. Closer to the game I might sense a player needs his own space. I try to watch body language rather than what they say to work this out.

6 p.m. Arrive at the ground. I leave the players alone for the first 15 minutes to let them get used to their surroundings. Some will be quiet, others talkative and others listening to their headphones. Before going out for the warm-up I gather them together for my team talk and start feeding in trigger points.

7 p.m. As we move back to the dressing-room, I may pick out one player who I think will have the key role in the match. In the first game it is Scott Quinnell and I explain to him how important I think he will be. We go over his role again. Back in the dressing-room, after a warm-up, I may give the team talk in a huddle, but on that first night I sense that Keith Wood, who is leading the side, would rather talk to them. I take a back seat, although I stay at the side. Keith delivers a great speech and I am only there in support.

7.30 p.m. Kick-off. I remain near the substitutes but get more animated and move around more as the tour goes on. I am still learning my role. Being in radio contact with the other coaches, I may offer some advice and vice versa. It is an important two-way dialogue.

8.15 p.m. Half-time. We are cruising. I have seen dressing-rooms where they may have a small Mars bar or banana for the players in the interval, but I favour only liquid and on this tour an isotonic drink from Lucozade is supplied.

9.15 p.m. Full-time. Even if we had lost by 50 points I wouldn't be going into the changing-room and telling them what they did wrong, especially on a tour like this. We have another game to look to and have to be careful about any negative thoughts. But as it happens we won by more than 100 points and broke the Lions' scoring record. It is time for me to go round the dressing-room congratulating everyone, making sure the boys are OK and don't need anything else.

10 p.m. Once I make sure the players are fine, I start to switch off. Rarely do I go to the after-match function. I am usually so physically and mentally shattered and will probably go into the stand or out onto the pitch for a reflective period. After we have travelled back to the hotel it is like I am shutting down for the day and someone has unplugged me. I may have a bath and switch off as the day comes to a close. I will make some notes, write a report of the day and perhaps something for the captain, thanking him for all his hard work.

The pride of the Lions is very much at stake in every game. I immediately began assessing everyone and introduced my own system of taking players on one-to-one sessions. Very quickly we established our territory. Of course, Sod's law kicked in when Neil Jenkins suffered a head injury requiring ten stitches when he clashed with Jeremy Davidson in training. Phil Greening then damaged his knee and other players aggravated knocks and niggles they had been carrying from our long British season. The training was taking its toll long before the Test games and it should have given coaches and management the gypsy's warning. These injuries created a storm in the press, who accused us of working the players too hard and, of course, they were right!

At any rate, the tour was now well under way after that first run-out against Western Australia in Perth, which turned out to be basically a training session, with the Lions destroying what are only part-timers by 116–10. Some said it was a waste of time, but I felt it was good for the team to get a taste of the country and a feel for the ball in competition. It was also important to adjust to travelling and different playing environments.

Our next game against a Queensland President's XV at the Dairy Farmer Stadium, Townsville, four days later was much the same – a run-out and familiarisation. Then on to Brisbane four days after that to face the Queensland Reds at Ballymore Stadium. They were a tough proposition but we finally dominated them and went on to win 42–8. It was an uneventful game, but we were beginning to play as a team and came through it with our heads held high. Graham Henry was particularly pleased but told us to keep our feet on the ground and be ready for the next encounter against an Australian 'A' at North Power Stadium, Gosford. We all knew this was going to be a real test of our fitness and ability as a team, because it was obvious the Aussies were intent on roughing us up.

The press had been winding us up with the likes of Bob Dwyer setting us up as cheats in the scrums and lineouts. It was all niggly stuff and it turned into an all-out brawl between the two teams with further injuries to Dallaglio, Back and Greenwood, which was worrying. Beaten 28–25, we showed the world we could be intimidated. Worst of all, we had been softened up for the First Test, and it showed the ugly side of rugby. McCrae cynically made a premeditated and unprovoked cowardly attack on Ronan O'Gara, for which he should have been dealt with through the courts instead of the paltry seven-week ban handed out to him.

Devastated by this turn of events, we needed a lift. Then Graham made a cardinal mistake by honestly revealing his mindset concerning Test-team selection. He called a press conference and announced that 'we are now going to have to concentrate on the Test team', which immediately alienated some of our lads, bringing out into the open many of the issues that had been festering.

From then on – if not before – the way the second team was treated was insensitive and showed an ignorance that shouldn't be in evidence at this level. Here we were, world-class international players being treated like second-class citizens. Initially they were all top players, all pushing for a Test place, then it became increasingly clear that the second team knew they didn't have a chance. What they wanted from management was to be able to knock on their doors and say, 'Have I got any chance? I am proud to be here but you know my dreams for being here weren't for carrying the water.'

Many of them were devastated because they knew they were now just along to make up numbers. They should all have been seen individually before final selection at home and told in no uncertain terms what their role in the squad would be. The players' response would probably be 'Will I get a game?' At that point they should have been told that, unless serious injuries occurred, their role would probably be that of squad member.

Then, to show fairness and integrity, I would have given each player time to consider and if the player declined or accepted he would then know exactly what part he was to play before we ever get on a plane. There could have been no negatives if this had been done, and getting into the Test team would have been a bonus. Without that understanding, there was little point in telling them that we are all in this together because it simply wasn't true. That's what happened to our squad, and it wasn't right.

A classic case in point was that of Colin Charvis, whose situation was an example of the broader issue, because he was completely confused by the selection system. Management were upset at him when he made noises about being left out, but they shouldn't have been because it was they who had confused him. Colin had done everything expected of him, and more, and only wanted to know what he had to do to secure a better grading for selection. He was frustrated and a little forthright in his approach, but the management didn't really understand what he was about and put it down to 'bad attitude'. It wasn't any such thing – they didn't want him, full stop, and whatever level he achieved, he would never have been selected. That's the bottom line. Many others were in the same predicament, which didn't augur well for team spirit. I have no problem whatsoever when non-selection is on merit, if a tight choice and difficult decision has to be made, but to have players working their socks off in training, getting trampled on, whacking into the bag and pulling their pluck out, there has to be some repayment.

To ignore and almost dismiss Colin was wrong and the selection committee could have played it much better. He and others in the same situation should have been given the big picture. A full and frank explanation of the complexities and difficulties in selection, owing to the quality and merit of all the players, should have been laid out. By putting it that way players not selected would be prepared for disappointment, but at the same time it would keep them on board. You can't have them working their balls off for you, then just walk away and ignore them. The odd arm around the shoulders, a little explanation and care, giving sensible and understandable reasons, would have gone a long way. If I had been a player in that situation, I would have been distraught at being sidelined. As a direct result of this policy Colin and the rest of the second team were used as training aids, giving them minimal contact, so they didn't prepare 100 per cent to play. It was wrong. It created a huge rift between first and second teams, and added to their criticism.

Saying and meaning all of that, the build-up to the First Test at the Gabba, Brisbane, was terrific, despite press comments, internal unrest and the fact we were picking up injuries. The emotion and tension prior to the match evaporated as soon as Jason Robinson scored his awesome try. Jason had come into the team with a big question mark over his head, having transferred from rugby league, but his blistering pace set the standard and psychologically we had the edge. At half-time we were still up 12–3, but there was complete confidence in our ability to break down their defence. Jonny Wilkinson was kicking well, and then only 40 seconds into the second half Brian O'Driscoll jinked and created a wonder try, lifting everyone's adrenalin even higher. Everyone knew we would win it, but the Wallabies fought hard right to the end. Our spirit and determination saw us through and in the end the victory was ours by 29–13. It was one of the greatest Lions performances in recent history.

We were euphoric, and perhaps one or two were beginning to think it was in the bag – big mistake. The Aussies had fight on their side and there was no doubt we now had an even bigger battle on our hands. In beating the Wallabies in their backyard so decisively, we had wounded the animal, and there is nothing more dangerous. Even though success was uplifting, we had made mistakes. The lads had been worked too hard and there was a question mark as to whether they had enough left in the tank. The Dawson press episode, of which more shortly, then gave us a real downer, Colin Charvis was cited and looking at a ban, and Matt Perry was injured. It was a crazy period of activity and not all of us focused on the next Test which was only a week away at the Colonial Stadium in Melbourne.

After celebrating we should have done nothing except turn up for games and rely on the fact that we had the most professional and best players from Britain and Ireland who desperately wanted to win the Tests. The meetings should have been discussing organisation only. These guys had been playing top-class rugby for years. Unfortunately, the damage had been done already and the only possible way of winning those two Tests was to do nothing and go in with a full tank.

Our squad had only been together six weeks, while the world champions had been together for years and grown in strength together – yet we still hammered them. But instead of doing nothing we did a little bit more, and a little bit more, and the cumulative fatigue, coming on top of the amount of work we had done building up to the First Test, made us a spent force – even though the workload up to that Test was good. Having a good time together could still have been as important as the work ethic, but it wasn't. In all honesty the best of that Lions tour was the week leading up to and including the First Test. After that, it was all downhill.

Our job was to beat the Aussies and I was proud to be part of it all, yet in the end we seemed to be constantly fighting the press. But no one could have foreseen the fatal publication of two infamous pieces from within our own party which severely holed us below the water line.

Matt Dawson's sensational newspaper article put the boot in first. In the shape of a personal diary, he indiscreetly said we were being trained too hard, team unity was breaking up and some players were planning to return home. He accused Graham Henry of treating the players like children, forcing mindless training on them and not being inspirational. We were all devastated by this lack of discretion and loyalty, and it created tension within the squad. I have to ask the question: why didn't everyone on the tour go to the newspapers and start beating their gums? Why didn't everyone say that Graham Henry was a load of crap and, more to the point, why did Jonny Wilkinson, rated the best player in the world, say Graham was inspirational and great for his career?

Then, to compound matters, and knowing the effect this article had on team morale, Austin Healey decided to vent his spleen in a piece in *The Guardian*, ghost written by Eddie Butler. To make the situation even more devastating, he levelled a personal attack on Justin Harrison, the Australian player, describing him as a plod, a plank and an ape, and this just before the final Test. I am sure Butler did his best to raise the temperature by using dramatic licence, but if the Aussies wanted a little extra motivation, Healey had provided them with it on a silver plate. What Dawson and Healey did was wrong. It poisoned everything and was instrumental in partially wrecking what should have been the most successful Lions squad in recent history. The knock-on effect was catastrophic because, instead of us talking about what a good team we were and doing the job properly, now every conversation revolved around those articles. We had taken our eye off the ball and the media had a field day. Comment has been made that management allowed players to write columns, but that was agreed under the understanding that players would naturally use their common sense and self-discipline. Perhaps it would have been better if we really had been a boot camp, as was also hyped up by the press.

It has to be said, however, that a tribunal held later in Dublin over this affair decided, in as close to legal conditions as possible, that Healey hadn't written the article and it was all the work of Eddie Butler, so great plaudits to Butler, who had a marvellous, positive influence on that tour. Well done, what a great patriot! This was all coming from somebody who was, is and can be a very good journalist. For me, the articles lacked integrity. If there is blame to apportion, we have to ask at whose door it lay. The article had Healey's name on it, yet the tribunal said it was Butler's words. I suppose we will never know what really happened and as Healey was exonerated, which is fine by me.

While researching the personalities of the Lions players pre-tour, I was approached by a senior, respected international and former Lion who told me in no uncertain terms I would have bother with Dawson and Healey. The expression used was that they were 'well up themselves'. Dawson I found to be more cerebral, but Healey always gives off his laughing, joking character. If that were true he, would have been a terrific asset. But his laughing is always at the expense of someone else. A lot of it can be very humorous, even when directed at yourself, but in reality it engenders a cumulative sensitivity and doesn't augur well for togetherness. That was a pity, because he can be a great player when he puts his mind to it.

Given that information, in my even-handed way, I tried to take both of those players – and the rest – as I found them. Putting the comments to the back of my mind, I went out of my way to try to get on with them, as I did with everybody. While Dawson wasn't everyone's cup of tea, after a few sessions in the first week I warmed to the lad and quite liked him. His vulnerability made him a real human being. As a professional he was somewhat calculated, as if he had studied a little handbook entitled 'Teach Yourself to Become a Professional'. His skills as a player were there to admire and he gave of his best on the field, no argument with that. Upon reflection, I honestly believe he regretted his action. He apologised and was disciplined, but it is also good to remember that we can all make mistakes.

Healey was always hyperactive and did raise a smile, but after the 45th time a niggle ceases to be funny, so he became like a piece of grit in your eye. A solid, quality player, capable of moments of magic, but like many extroverts he is always trying to be the centre of attention and at times that can become a little tedious. He likes to be regarded as a 'character' but unfortunately his contribution on this tour didn't reflect the talented package that is Austin, and the silly article with his name on it was totally counterproductive. On a personal level, he actually said many nice things about me in his book but he certainly didn't understand why I was with the Lions. He couldn't understand that I wasn't there to do fitness coaching. I should have sat him down and said, 'For God's sake, sit and listen! You are an intelligent lad. Look, I can take anyone and subject him or her to a fitness regime and get them racing fit but that's not what I am about in this instance, setting or time. What you have to understand is you have been training for 20-odd years. I've got you for 6 weeks. By your own admission, you have played 51 games this season. It's nonsense that I should be giving you fitness training. By your own admission, you are doing too much, so why are you writing and saying such things about my role when you don't understand that maybe the approach is more subtle than you think?'

But I doubt if that ever crossed his mind. Maybe the impetuosity that contributed so well to his on-field performances stopped him from thinking before making decisions off it! By rights, Dawson and Healey should have been put on the next flight home – of course they should have – but at that stage that particular disruption couldn't have been negotiated by the team and still leave us with a realistic chance of defeating the world champions, so it was the right decision to keep them on board and support them for the rest of the tour.

The press situation was quite ridiculous. I know and understand they are looking for a dramatic headline, but you have to wonder where their minds are really at. One thing is for certain, they don't listen to what they are told. To illustrate this point, I took the whole press conference one day. It was packed with journalists waiting to pounce on every word. One of them shouted, 'Blackie, what does Graham Henry think of the press?'

I said, 'Well, I think he has quite a lot of admiration for . . .' and before I could finish, shouting and laughter began. You would think I was in parliament being heckled from the backbenches. I let them go and when it died down I continued, 'And I am sure that he has a lot of admiration for some of you, but maybe not as much for others.'

That was exactly what they were like and, to be honest, I knew that the management didn't really want to speak to them too much because they were concentrating on getting a team together. Apart from that, you don't need a lot of time with the press because they all ask the same bloody questions and it wastes a hell of a lot of time.

The media were also well out of order in accusing us of running a 'boot camp', because nothing was further from the truth. I do believe we were training too much but it wasn't a boot camp by any stretch of the imagination. Poor quality of reporting of this type is mischievous and doesn't help anyone's cause, other than I suppose the sale of the newspapers concerned.

Because of my sleep apnoea, I would often be in the reception area of the hotel at 5 a.m., still working, when some of the squad would trail in after a night on the razz. I knew what was going on but never became a spy for the management. Instead, I told those involved individually, in no uncertain terms, that they had to produce on the field. Again, it was just the minority, because the bulk of the lads were spot on, but strangely enough, the guys who 'went over the side' did perform well, which makes me wonder about coaching methods and the actual effectiveness of the preparatory techniques.

Training had become a major issue – the players were feeling tired and jaded, and, despite telling the coaches repeatedly, they weren't taking heed. That is the truth. So, while I led the way in voicing my concerns over the length of our sessions, it wasn't a boot camp.

It seemed that right from the start the coaches were out to impress one another, and there was also an arrogance in the air that we were going to win anyway. It got to the stage where I said to Don Lenihan, 'Should I just fuck off? Because I don't need all of this. This is a fantastic honour here coaching the Lions, but now that the honour thing is out of the way, I want to bloody win this series . . . and I know we can and should win. But to do that we need to go into the Test games with a full tank and as fresh as we possibly can be at this stage in our playing year. If we don't, we're knackered – their well-honed teamwork will defeat our stronger and more talented and tired side. I'm telling you straight, they're tired and their cries for help are being ignored. Look at the evidence. We've got Matt Dawson, Jason Leonard, Dave Young, Rob Howley and other senior members of the squad telling us, and more importantly each other, that they are doing too much.'

Donal agreed with me and while I know he must have made representations, it didn't register with the management. The coaches came back at my nagging and said that the players weren't doing this, that or the other, more or less accusing them of not just getting on with it. My response was, 'But you're not playing the bloody games and doing the training, and you don't know what it's like. It's a long time since any of you did any physical exercise, so if the players say they're tired, they must be. If you're saying they shouldn't be, that's not the point, because whatever the reasons, psychological or physical, you must listen to them.'

I was asked for my solution and suggested the squad should be going into the gym more, because that gives a feel-good factor. They argued it would tire them out even more and I pointed out it would do nothing of the sort. The gym had pleasant distracting influences – they could have a bit of a chat and relax. It wasn't just by chance that when I took them into the gym I let them get away with doing nothing. It was for a specific reason – they needed rest and relaxation. You'd think I was talking to myself and hence I blew up as illustrated at the beginning of this book.

The Second Test was upon us before we could breathe, and the possibility that we could beat them again was a mouth-watering prospect. The Colonial Stadium, Melbourne, was packed and pre-match hype had 60,000 fans in a state of electric anticipation. As the players ran out for the game, the hair was standing up on the back of my neck, and I could see the emotion and pride welling up in everyone's eyes. I don't know how they got there, but we had massive support and this gave us a magnificent boost. Many of our supporters must have gone into hock for the trip and it made me realise just how big this Test was. We owed it to them and everyone back home to give it our best shots.

We began solidly and for a good period of the game kept them out magnificently. Mistakes were being made but we got away with them and Jonny Wilkinson was on target with his kicking. Then suddenly the game took a nasty twist when Nathan Gray hit Richard Hill in the face with a shocking flying tackle, putting him right out of the game. Considering Colin Charvis had been banned for a far less serious infringement, it was a disgrace that Gray wasn't even sin-binned. Even though we went in at half-time five points ahead, that decision was a defining moment. We went back out pumped up and confident, but unfortunately the rub of the green didn't favour us. Disaster struck. We hadn't taken the points on offer in the first half and were punished for it. Just after half-time, Joe Roff intercepted, scored and that was it. Their tails were up, they scored again very quickly and our shape went completely. Their tactics were superior in every department and we were slaughtered 35–14. To make matters worse, Jonny was stretchered off with a leg injury and Rob Howley had a nasty bash in the ribs. Truthfully, we deserved to lose and it underpinned just how resilient the Aussies were. So it was one-each now, with the final Test in Sydney, a real battle, while we were starting to suffer badly.

Significant factors were now beginning to bite into the squad. Their desire and ability to win the final Test was not in question, but the cumulative effect of an eleven-month-long season and the incredible pressure brought to bear in the run-up were noticeable. We were patching players together to get them out on the park. Having said that, they were a tough bunch emotionally. We had a lot of big-game players who had been there before and when it came to the wire their character was not an issue. Also, for all different reasons, they wanted to win – ego, the whole world watching them – they all had a different motivation, as it is in life. But it was a difficult week and probably due to the condition of the players there was less work done by them in the build-up. Of course, it was too late and in the circumstances it probably wasn't far from being as good as it could be for that moment in time. It was judged just about right, apart from coaches not having the courage and confidence to do nothing at all, and this showed in that Third Test because we were a vastly superior team, but were knackered. Nonetheless, it went right to the wire in a very close, good game of rugby. We lost a nail-biter!

What came back to haunt me were the words of Rob Andrew, who came to see me in my hotel room after the First Test at about one o'clock in the morning. He said, 'You've got to win next week because you can't win in Sydney. If it goes one-all, and Sydney is the decider, the pressure they will bring to bear upon you will be unbelievable.' He couldn't have been more prophetic because the pressure was intense and all credit to the squad, who responded magnificently. There was a feeling everybody was against you – the whole country, politicians, showbiz stars, rugby league, commentators, press and television. It was as if the Lions were so inconsequential they didn't exist. It built and built and built. And the Aussies are good at it because they will do anything they can to ensure their environment is strongest for their team. To a certain degree, this must be admirable and I wish we as a nation had a more overt, collective desire to will our teams on.

Recollections of the game were that it was a tough, good contest and one I always thought we were almost destined to win after all the trials and tribulations. Obviously I wanted us to win from a professional standpoint, but I was praying to win for Graham's sake, because the effort he put in was phenomenal. He probably did too much, but the desire and character he showed were unquestionable, and it would have been fantastic for him to succeed. Jonny Wilkinson had overcome his leg injury and scored a super try and, looking back, that period was a coming of age for him. The character he showed at that level, in that setting, was absolutely fantastic and history has shown he was evolving as a young man. Even now, after the amazing World Cup success, he is still evolving at 25 and probably won't be at his best for another 8 years. By the time he's 32, he'll be at his fastest and at 33 his strongest. From his experience of playing the game at that level, the closer he gets to the big games the less selfish he becomes. So while striving to become an even better player on a day-by-day basis he realises that, at any given moment, if not needed to play one of the lead parts, he will step back into a supporting role if it's in the best interest of the team.

The Australians were gracious in winning, but highlighted the 'Austin Healey outburst' and continually thanked us for giving them the edge. Of course, Sod's law prevailed because the star of the game was Justin Harrison, who had been the butt of the 'joke'. In a crucial lineout near the end of the game he went totally against his captain John Eales' orders when he was told not to contest for the ball. History tells us he did compete, won the ball and prevented us from winning the game. One of those things, and whether the Healey/Butler 'wind up' had anything to do with it is neither here nor there. Fate does have a knack of repeating itself, as fabulously illustrated two years later in 2003, when Jonny Wilkinson scored his dramatic drop-kick to win the World Cup for England – again in Australia, but this time after *he* had been the butt of relentless derision. There has to be a lesson learned here.

I have attempted to describe this Lions tour from my own perspective and much of it may seem negative, but lots of positive things came out of the experience. It showed beyond doubt that we were the best rugby nation in the world. Physically, we were so much better than them, markedly so, and if we had been fresh there would have been no contest, to the extent that future Lions tours will have to be looked at very carefully, because there was such a clear difference between the two sides. Certainly in the physical area we must question how we can send a whole British team to play one nation when one of the British teams, England, is already better than the rest. Here we were literally a team of cripples and still nearly blew them away. The First Test was magnificent. To witness at first hand the frightening pace of the game was remarkable, so much so that the Aussies couldn't cope with it. The Second Test should have been in the bag before half-time and in the Third we were so very nearly there. So, overall, it was a great performance by our squad, by any standards.

Things have definitely turned full circle. Before we were professional, the Aussies were. They cheated and were streets ahead. On our showing, even though we were finally beaten, we have caught them up in the past seven years. On a good day, on a neutral pitch with everything else even, we will always beat them because of our superior physical capabilities. We also have more players to choose from. We have the players, some wonderful athletes, but we need better management structures in place. Sadly, when Graham Henry returned to the Welsh team, he was misled over the reasoning why we had lost the Lions tests. He actually thought that, from a physical capability, the Australians were fitter than us aerobically because Rod Macqueen, their coach, had intimated as much on a television programme, saying because they came back at the end of the second game and toughed out the third one it was their aerobic fitness that saw them through. This is arrant nonsense. The reason why they came back was because we were knackered and patched together, and also they had played together for so long that, when tired, their connective teamwork was better because every player knew what their inter-skills were going to be in response. We had only six weeks to sort it out and, when we were tired, we resorted to type, and passes and moves which were ingrained in club rugby took over. Player A, expecting player B to be at point C, found him not to be there.

When Graham returned, he had this on his mind and should have clenched his fists and said, 'Right, let's go for it. Let's put all our eggs in one basket, and that basket is going to be pace, speed, agility and power. Forget all about this plodding lark, let's make them short, sharp, bright sessions.'

If Scotland, Wales and Ireland want to compete at this level, they have to forget about aerobic conditioning, and do all their work on pace and skill. Rugby has changed at the top level. It's Bang! Bang! Stop. Bang! Bang! Stop. Bang! Bang! Stop. For a man who strives to get better at all times in all that he does and puts so much effort in, Graham was definitely misled and conditioned to train them in exactly the same way. Subsequently, Wales slid into a team being beaten and humiliated game after game, and Graham paid the price for that. I am his friend and I have to say he got it wrong. To use an analogy, sometimes speed is only important if you're running in the right direction and if you extrapolate that to effort, hard work and great attitude is only of any use if you're doing the right thing. Unfortunately Graham's efforts were misdirected by others around him. He was consumed by the politics and the fact he was under such immense pressure. He became isolated in a job that should have been joyful for him and ended up being unhappy and unfulfilled.

Successes on the tour were Jason Robinson, Rob Henderson, Phil Vickery, Richard Hill, Martyn Corry, Scott Quinnell, Brian O'Driscoll, Neil Back, Tom Smith and, of course, Jonny Wilkinson. It seemed like the end of Jason Leonard's Lions career. He did very well to play a couple of games and ended on a high. Incredibly, he went on to play a significant role in England's progress over the next two years, culminating in their World Cup success. As the most capped player in rugby, he is a legend and example to us all, and it couldn't have happened to a nicer guy – of course, he is married to a Geordie lass. It was great to work with these people and a pretty special honour. Success in management terms was to go so close to winning. Coaching was all right, but nothing out of the ordinary. Phil Larder is professional and able, but he gave the players too much contact, resulting in too many unnecessary injuries. Some of the discipline wasn't good, but I blame management for that and it seemed that some were only there for the ride, their hearts not striving for success as much as they should have been.

There were lessons to be learned: they should have had a two-week training camp prior to travel, then a week off, then back in the middle of the week ready to go. Other than that, more agility, better communication between everyone to avoid the cliques forming. Having said all that, I wouldn't have missed it for the world. Medical back-up was superb and

Mark Davies, the physio, great. Doctor James Robson was superb and the rub-a-dub man, Richard, was popular with the players, especially the English contingent, but to be fair I didn't really get to know him. All in all it was a positive experience for everyone, but regrettably badly reported by the media, and a share of the blame must lie at our doors because we didn't handle them properly. The media took umbrage at that and weren't as supportive as they should have been.

But isn't life strange, because we now have to look forward to British Lions Tour 2005, Henry v. Woodward, the final confrontation? And mouth-watering it really is certain to be – the clash of the titans. The way this unique situation has panned out will never ever occur again, where the former British Lions coach is now coaching New Zealand. Make no bones about it, no southern hemisphere coach will ever be in charge of the Lions again and it possibly shouldn't have happened the first time – not because Graham Henry wasn't capable of doing the job, he was more than able, but because the people he had to pick from and the troops working for him weren't right behind the idea and didn't have the bottle to say that from the outset. Had they done so, the matter could have been settled, but what should have been 'all for one and one for all' was never the case. Having said that, Graham didn't show his full hand, not out of any deceit, but because he attempted to compromise in order to help the others there.

Consequently, he knows inside out the English coaches he will be up against on the 2005 tour. He endured an intensive course with them for three months, ten hours a day, talking non-stop rugby. He'll know all their strengths and weaknesses, and have huge admiration for their strengths, but because he's a clever man he'll attack their weaknesses and learn from his own experience of having worked so closely with them. Of course, Clive's coaches will know Graham, but because he didn't show all his cards there are more advantages in Graham's toolbox.

In his neck of the woods, and doing it his way, Graham has to be the main man. He keeps winning leagues and cups and that cannot be accidental. When he came to Britain, his record with Wales was pretty damn good and the only time he faltered was when he began listening to other people and danced the dance of politics. I would like Graham to be a bit more selfish, but unfortunately, once you get to his age, the traits are set. The only problem I see is that the people round him can influence his decisions. So if they're good people, brilliant! If not, it could spell trouble. But at the end of the day his knowledge and experience is a great base. He certainly knows how to win games.

Clive Woodward isn't really a coach. He is more a new-age manager. I read recently that he suggested that he could be England's football manager and there is no doubt he could do it because he puts the right people in place. Forwards coach, backs coach, fitness adviser, nutritionist, psychologist, visual coach, throw-in coach, scrummage coach, and this is his backroom staff. He gets all those perceived to be the best in the business and puts together a massive team. Then, having the luxury of such a large pool of players to pick from, he selects the strongest squad, so eventually he has to win something. Tactically, I think he is reasonable and the Clive Woodward Lions squad will be all right, but not a team of genius. They will be solid and hugely competitive, but I don't know if they will have the cutting edge to beat Graham's All Blacks. Graham's strategy, if he gets it right, could just be brilliant because on the physical side of things he's got superb athletes.

Personally, I'm a little bit surprised Clive Woodward took on the job. I think that maybe he would have weighed up the whole situation and thought he had nothing to gain from it. I thought he was shrewder than wanting to rise to the bait in order to show that he should have been in charge of the 2001 Lions. Unfortunately, I think perhaps ego has taken over, having won the World Cup and also a fantastic England winning sequence. Bearing in mind what happened in Australia, he probably thinks he is the man to put it right. Perhaps he is – only time will tell. However, I think the All Blacks will be a better side. They are a very young, vibrant team and will take some beating.

Clive Woodward deserves enormous credit for being at the head of a playing organisation that proved itself to be the best in the world during the 2003 World Cup held in Australia. Putting it quite simply, the object of the game is to score more points than the opposition and that's what Clive's England team did. It was a very player-led team and, once again, Clive deserves the praise and plaudits that came his way for allowing that power base to grow. That power base and ownership actually took some six years to develop fully, but once it had, England were the best team, probably by some considerable margin, the year before the World Cup began. Since that heady success, however, the strength of the squad has diminished as players have left, and maybe (in some cases) lost focus concerning their *raison d'être*.

There is now a need to facilitate the building of a new England team, but this won't (can't) happen overnight, and whoever leads that journey will need to be in it for the long, hard haul. I get the impression that Clive is not really up for that challenge for that long in this sport at this stage of his career. He probably needs a different stimulus and that looks like it will be soccer. Can he be successful? Of course he can. As a manager/facilitator, he'll appoint coaches, trainers and players, and his success will be governed by the quality of those appointments. If he's astute enough to back the right coach, he's got the opportunity to make a noticeable impression in the round-ball game. If he doesn't, or he arrives at a club who don't have much money to buy quality players, then his soccer career could be painful and short-lived. With good people around him he'll survive, without them he won't, much like the other managers who work in professional sport, strangely enough!

His philosophy of having almost as many coaches as players will be new in the football world. Specialist coaches for throw-ins, goal kicks, free kicks, corners, goalkeepers, defensive coach, attacking coach, midfield coach, weight-training coach, running coach, balance expert, nutritionist, psychologist, human resource facilitator, lifestyle coach, etc. etc., may raise a few eyebrows . . . oh, all right then, a vision coach. I'm teasing a little, but this is a philosophy that soccer will find hard to come to terms with, especially if Clive doesn't have a very talented and effective group of players at his disposal . . . the rest of the 'backroom' philosophy may not have the time to take hold, as a string of defeats and the associated pressures invariably brings the sack, no matter how illustrious the name you carry. On a personal level, good luck to him, because he is showing courage and ambition, and choosing to take a road less travelled. I sincerely hope he is rewarded for his adventurous spirit.

Back to rugby now, and I must say I need to voice a concern about the England rugby regime Clive has left. My gut feeling is that the formula is too prescriptive, too utilitarian in nature, and there are too many cooks. If you have a marvellous team of players who actually run the team performance themselves, you can be successful in spite of this preparatory regime, not because of it. Whoever takes the reins as head coach now must personalise the regime, must shed some of the backroom staff, must choose a small, elite group of coaching staff and get close to this new team and evolve as a group who have a collective purpose. We need to get emotional – controlled, professional but emotional – to get the best out of our national personality. If we are to have a chance of retaining the World Cup, we must begin this process now.

British rugby is now very much in a period of transition and the recent Six Nations Championship in 2004 has shown that. England have shown just how much they miss the likes of Jonny Wilkinson and Martin Johnson. Winning is everything. The World Cup is in the bank and that is fabulous, but things move on and everything has to be constantly appraised. However, I certainly don't dismiss Clive Woodward's vast experience and superb record, for, like Graham, he certainly knows how to win.

The two men have very different personalities and styles. Graham is very much hands on, whilst Clive is more the businessman, putting the overall framework in place, placing people in the slots and then everything is ticked methodically. On that basis, he is confident and expects to turn up and win. Graham is also very thorough. But which one embraces the human element? I'm going to suggest that Graham Henry will be the one to succeed in what will be an epic battle. New Zealand have the home advantage and it can't be stressed how important a psychological factor that is. Here they are up against the old enemy who are now world champions. What motivation! What a scalp!

Clive comes across as focused and calculating, while Graham always has a glint in his eye and a good sense of humour – always mischievous, but never devious. Also he's more inclined to do it as it is, and when the time comes to tell someone they have to go he does it with that human consideration. I may be wrong, but on the evidence shown publicly, Clive will chop people ruthlessly. There has to be a place for that, but I sometimes wonder about his style, especially when he has been quoted as saying England would have won the World Cup without Jonny Wilkinson.

Compare that to Graham Henry who said that whichever world team had Jonny in it would win.

So Clive has a factor that leaves chinks in his armour and I think his premeditated control will make him predisposed to selecting almost a full England team for the Lions, except for that Irish wizard, Brian O'Driscoll. I can understand the thinking behind that, because he will want to select his strongest team. However, this could create problems within the fabric of rugby union in Britain, if it is to be representative of the Lions of Britain and Ireland.

So, on paper, it looks like the best coach in rugby versus the best manager. Who will come out on top? You could flip a coin, it's that close to the wire, it really is. If you were to push me, I'm afraid I'll have to go with Graham Henry.

Blackie is and always will be the most positive and happy colleague I have ever worked with. His unique brand of conditioning and well-being was a breath of fresh air and I miss him dearly.

Apart from his inimitable wealth of experience in his field of sport, it was his knowledge of pretty much everything that excited me, and I can remember lying on a beach in Portugal, pre-World Cup in 1999, and sharing our love for the golden era of the silver screen. We talked in great detail about all the beautiful belles of a time gone by, the likes of Virginia Mayo, Maureen O'Sullivan, Deborah Kerr, Janet Leigh, etc., but you know what I mean?

We sat on that beach and put ourselves in our own little dream world and envisaged what it would be like to be a leading man opposite these almost picture-perfect screen goddesses. It was a moment shared and that moment was our life! That was the most magical hour I can remember as only Blackie and I sat and reminisced as if we were Spencer Tracey, James Stewart and Cary Grant!

My favourite quote from Blackie is about me. He once said, 'Gibbsy has great balance and agility for a centre, but he just loves running through brick walls!'
Scott Gibbs – British Lions, Wales

I was first introduced to Blackie in the autumn of 1998 when he was appointed Welsh fitness adviser by Graham Henry. It was Graham's first appointment since he had started the Welsh coaching position and what a major appointment it turned out to be! Blackie was a breath of fresh air, but more importantly his contribution was immense. Many people over the years have questioned whether Blackie is a psychologist or fitness coach and my answer is both!

Blackie is unique. Graham tended to leave him to his own devices and sometimes you would see Graham walking away in disbelief when he saw 22 rugby players with their eyes closed meditating. That was Blackie.

During my term as captain of Wales, Blackie worked very hard not only with the squad but also with potential World Cup squad players who had lost their form or desire for whatever reason. Leigh Davies was a classical example.

Blackie became your mate, but you always knew where to draw the white line. He had respect from all the squad. You worked hard, but you enjoyed the sessions. They were varied, planned (I think) and, more importantly, in tune with what Graham wanted to achieve.

Blackie had a major impact on Welsh rugby because he cared. I use that particular word because it sums up Blackie. Anything he could do for you, at any time of the day, he would. Blackie made sure he was there for you.

Wales toured Argentina in 1999, won the Test series 2–0, the only northern hemisphere team to achieve this accolade. Why? Blackie ensured the right environment to be successful. How many injures on a gruelling six-match tour? None! Why? Blackie made sure every one of the 37 playing squad was looked after, treated properly and ensured that, if they weren't 100 per cent fit, they didn't train.

How good is Blackie? Very! Just look at what Wales achieved during his term in office. The 11-match-winning run. He certainly helped me through some difficult times whilst I was captain and I like to think he made me a better player for it. As I said earlier, Blackie is unique and Welsh rugby was the major loser when he departed in 2000.

Rob Howley – British Lions, Wales

Steve Black is a professional of the highest standard, a man of integrity, dedicated and fully committed. Also, he is a bloody nice bloke, who cared for those around him and made them all feel a part of something special. The effect he had on this group of Welsh rugby players and management team will stay with them forever. It is a pity that some people out there did not know the full story; they could learn a great deal from him and his professional attitude.

Alun Carter – British Lions, Wales

Coming back from tour I was sitting in the lounge at Heathrow waiting for my flight to Newcastle when I met an old friend, Steve Bainbridge, himself a former England and Lions international. Steve and I had gone to school together and he said he had been watching the Lions Tests and thought we had done very well. It was a sobering moment, returning to home soil and talking to someone who understood what I had experienced. Flying back to Newcastle, I was in a reflective mood, thinking about how I had arrived at this incredible moment in time in my life. I had experienced heady moments of rugby history and it seemed like a distant dream, but as soon as the wheels hit the landing strip I was brought slap-bang back into the real world with a bump. Jet-lagged to hell and completely knackered, I went directly to Kingston Park to begin Newcastle Falcons' forthcoming season's preparation. Ten minutes into the session on the field it was as if I'd never been away.

Chapter Eleven

THE SHOW GOES ON

Listening to reason always means listening to what
someone else has got to say. Most people ignore most
poetry because most poetry ignores most people. You
might as well fall flat on your face as lean over too far
backwards.

Anonymous graffiti on a Hertfordshire flyover

Having attempted to put my story down, I suddenly realise how much
more complicated my life is because I constantly put myself under
pressure even though it has a detrimental effect on my health. I can't help
it. I have a worm inside driving me into seemingly impossible situations,
as if I have to test myself out every day. So I continue to go with gut
instincts because my main aim is to achieve and, by doing so, I will then
have given my family the best opportunities on offer. This is the overriding
goal and after that comes my own motivation to give 100 per cent to those
I am working for or with.

The ability to get the best out of yourself and others is a skill that some
have naturally, while others must work hard at it, but it's a skill
nevertheless. Achieving it will differ slightly from team to team and
individual to individual, but each and every method must be underwritten

with a mixture of love of that sport and caring for that bunch of players. While the 'big stick' type approach is definitely in the toolbox, and undoubtedly effective from time to time, in general people respond better to a kind word than they do to ranting and raving. Similarly, if that 'ranting and raving' includes longer and more intensive sessions, then the coach has probably strayed outside his recipe for success and mediocrity is the likely outcome.

First and foremost, successful teams need good players. It isn't possible to produce a team to challenge for a title if they do not have a benchmark of ability to play towards in competitive situations. It's also possible to gather together a wonderful bunch of players yet fail to gel them into an effective team on the park. Yet you can have, say, the fourth or fifth best squad of players talentwise, but by implementing sound coaching methods get them realistically competing for championships.

One of the top business gurus in the USA over recent years has been Harvey Mackay. I attended a conference in San Francisco when he said something that not only made an immediate impression, but has stuck with me since. He said, 'You would never have trouble with any employee if, at the onset of the relationship, you told them, and have them agree to, exactly what would be expected in all aspects of their job.' Sport is most certainly part of that process. So many performers come to me and say they're out of favour yet they don't know why. When an explanation eventually filters through, they say, 'I wasn't told that.'

Communication is the key and most people just aren't very good communicators. So what should we communicate? In any sport you must practise the basics – reliable basic skills are vital. If you're a kicker, you must practise kicking. The same with passing and tackling technique – only one way forward: practice. Of course many so-called experts will say, 'How revolutionary is that?' and 'Everyone knows that.' Well, if that is the case, why don't they do it? Second, you have to enjoy the preparation, and tied in with that package comes enthusiasm which then becomes infectious and is the perfect recipe for team success on a regular basis.

During the course of my life I have been incredibly lucky to work with the best in the business, and some perhaps not quite the best, but in every given set of circumstances I have always endeavoured to give it my top shots. Often I take out of that situation or relationship more than I put in. The reason is that I like people, I like them to succeed, I like to see them grow as human beings, but, most of all, I like to hear them laugh. Those rewards far outweigh any financial gains, though I'd be foolish if I didn't enjoy the financial rewards as well.

In this book I have attempted to put down some of the benchmarks of my life and career to date with honesty and integrity, but I accept that these are my views and many of those involved may beg to differ about events or situations. For instance, my spell at Wales was wonderful, despite the outcome. Even now, I still feel that, had we been given the right support from the Union, Wales would have gone from strength to strength as a top international team. I honestly believe that, but politics and the old guard prevailed, and subsequent events have proved that something in their system is going very wrong. I found I had a strange but total affinity with the Welsh people. They recognised me as a Geordie first and an Englishman second. I think by that they meant that my pride as a Geordie matched theirs as Welshmen.

My association with Kevin Keegan is where this journey in professional sport really began and I will always be indebted to him for the major breakthrough. When I first met Kevin and Terry McDermott at Newcastle United I told them I thought I could improve the players in many different ways, including their biomechanical movement and their energy systems, but most of all I was confident of putting a smile on their faces. Being happy is such an important factor in life. If you enjoy something, in all probability you will do it quite well. Initially I was on a three-month trial, but after two weeks Kevin jacked up some publicity and announced he wanted to take me on, which was a great fillip. I wasn't receiving much money, but I enjoyed it immensely, because money wasn't the driving force and I was now swimming in deeper and more interesting waters.

I was involved in several special projects and Kevin recognised that I operated best on a one-to-one basis with athletes. For example, I first worked with a lad called David Roach, a Geordie boy who had great talent. He was 16 when I took him under my wing. We'd go down to the beach to train and he really made great progress. Unfortunately, the magnetism of the dark side of life was greater than that of becoming a football star for him, which was a great shame. He was a sad loss to the game because he could have become another Paul McGrath.

Then I formed fantastic relationships with Lee Clark, Robbie Elliott, Steve Watson and Alan Thompson who all went on to do extremely well. I am proud of all of them. Lee Clark was especially close and I love him to bits – a great character whom I also coached when he was at Sunderland and Fulham. A fabulous spirit in the dressing-room, a good professional and someone who has grown in stature as a person, he was totally dedicated and suffered some dreadful injuries, but always grafted hard to make it back. Steve Watson is yet another terrific lad and wonderful athlete. We currently see Lua Lua and others doing cartwheels and gymnastics on the field, but at 16 years of age, at St James' Park, with a full house, Steve was doing handsprings with the ball leading up to the throw-in. This was an unbelievable measure of his ability and confidence, and quite dramatic when he did it. Robbie Elliott is out of the same mould, again an out-and-out professional and lovely personality. Alan Thompson is totally crackers, but yet again a great player. He gets very nervous before games, unbelievably so. I saw him play against Liverpool in the reserves and he ran past the referee and threw up all over the place. Every game, in the dressing-room, it could be anywhere, all over, Black Forest gateau, the lot – but what a fabulous player. I remember him coming back from the World Youth Cup and his first partner in the 'N's team up front was me and I said, 'Now either you've made it, Tomma, or I must be getting better.' We got on really well and I'm delighted that he's gone from strength to strength at Aston Villa, then Bolton, where he scored in the Cup final against Liverpool, and now at Celtic. It has been a privilege to have been a part of his career.

What can you say about Blackie? Certainly nothing bad. He remains the only man who can make me cry with laughter at the same time as almost throwing up with exhaustion at the end of another hard session on Tynemouth beach.

As a fitness coach, he was the main reason behind me getting back to form fitter than ever, after two very poor seasons. This was at a time when my career could have gone either way at the age of 19. After a full summer of training I returned to pre-season training not only fitter, but again knowing that I belonged in the top flight and playing for 'the Toon'. Previously I had begun to doubt that.

The help he gave me mentally was every bit as good as the help he gave me physically. Maybe more so. All this was done not as a job for Blackie, but because he cared about myself, Lee Clark and Rob Elliott. He knew we were capable of more and made us believe it. He wanted to make us better players and, as a result, better people.

It was also a great honour to work with Glenn McCrory and the Newcastle Falcons who were some of the best athletes I've ever worked with, and also the most dedicated, not to mention a great bunch of lads.

Blackie will always be a very special friend to me and my family. He even spoke at my wedding and, as he always does, stole the show. The only thing I've ever done for him was wake him up every now and then, but he knows that if he needs anything from me or help in any way, he only has to ask. But that will never even come close to repaying him for the time and help he's given me.

He is simply 'the Top Man'.

Steve Watson – Everton FC

We used to have a lot of fun and, at times, Kevin thought I was barmy because I loved having a laugh with the lads. For instance, I'd take them amongst the trees at Durham training ground and tell them, 'Look, the configuration of those trees isn't by chance. They were planted with a purpose many years ago – to draw in diffused light in order to maximise on the thoughts and guidance of Druids.' Kevin would get exasperated and shout at me to 'get on with it', but it was all good banter and really an integral part of my approach to enjoying the whole exercise. Otherwise, what's the point?

Sir John Hall would also rise to the bait. He'd come to the training ground and ask what I was doing with the players and I'd say, 'We're all going to an Italian restaurant, have a nice meal, a sing-song and a lie down.' He'd give me a quizzical look because I think he expected me to say I'd run them up and down the hill for an hour and a half to make them sick. Again, it was fun, but Kevin would come and ask what the hell I'd been telling the chairman who was wondering what I was being paid for. We were top of the League, played 13 and won 13, so I told him to tell Sir John to make up his own mind because the proof of the pudding was the one he was eating.

BLACKIE

This was in 1992. Newcastle United were in the First Division and Kevin hadn't been there long. It was wonderful to be part of the team that broke through into the Premiership, regaining their rightful status in the football world. The squad were first class, with the flamboyant and no-nonsense Barry Venison, Pavel Srnicek, a fine athlete, Andy Cole, a prolific crowd-pleaser and goal machine, and many other terrific players.

It would probably be boring and difficult for me to list all the athletes I have been involved with, some for a short period, with others forming a more sustained relationship. My work also covered a multitude of sports. Quite simply, success boils down to several simple factors – ability, recognition of that ability, a clear focus, determination, a lot of confidence and a little luck.

For instance, I worked with Paul Eales, the golfer, then ranked 60th in the world, and I developed an excellent relationship with him. Now, I know very little about golf but I very quickly recognised his big problem was confidence. He allowed things to distract him. So we worked on precision, instilling into him that he knew he was doing things right and would do them well – simple visualisation of success. The difference between Paul and the top winning golfers like Tiger Woods and Ernie Els is wafer-thin, but unfortunately Paul was analysing everything I said to him. People were telling him this or that was wrong and because his confidence wasn't as strong as it could have been, or commensurate with his undoubted ability, he seemed to allow some negative thoughts to affect his game. For example, he might hit a ball perfectly 99 times and then slice the next one. Now, I don't know anyone yet who was born perfect. OK, Rocky Marciano, the boxer, had 49 fights and 49 wins as a professional, but he did lose some as an amateur, so a duff shot is perfectly understandable and acceptable because that is what life is all about. Basketball's greatest player ever, Michael Jordan, lost so many games it was unbelievable. Some of the finest runners such as Seb Coe, Steve Ovett and Ron Clarke lost races. Paul, however, would concentrate on that failure, analyse it and focus on putting it right instead of forgetting all about it and reverting back to type, which would have ensured far more successful shots than poor ones. In a way, he'd almost forgotten how successful he generally was when tested, so I endeavoured to instil into him that he must ignore that failure because great champions don't even consider it as an option.

Having travelled the sporting road for so long, I would like to think I have been of some assistance to most of those athletes I have been connected with, but, by and large, the bulk of them wanted to succeed anyway. While football was my first love, I have been totally consumed by rugby and I have to say that many of the finest athletes I have met come from this sport. I was lucky to be there at the start of the professional game in England and it has given me a wonderful opportunity to expand my theories, with some spectacular success. I am frequently asked who is the finest sportsman I have ever worked with and that is difficult to answer, because many dozens fall into the top calibre and nearly all for the same reasons. Their skill, humility and personality sets them above the norm, but most of all there is an indefinable quality which registers with the public, a magnetic charisma. For example, Paul Gascoigne – Gazza – is probably one of the finest footballers of his generation. It was a pleasure to work with him prior to his going off to play in China in 2003. I coached him one-on-one for several weeks and was impressed by his fantastic work ethic and commitment. When he left for China, he was in excellent condition. OK, his faults have been documented ad nauseam via the tabloids, but I would still place him up among the greats. Having him stay and train with me for six weeks in late 2002 was a marvellous experience, not just professionally, but because it gave us the opportunity to forge a deeper and more lasting friendship.

I have recently been getting help from a top psychologist for my problems and he asked me who had designed my regime and how I was in such good shape. I told him that Steve Black had done it and the psychologist said, 'Well, that guy knows more than me.'

Not too long ago, I was on a downward spiral for several weeks and realised that, if I continued to live the way I was, there would be no return. My weight had gone down to 11 st. and I was frightened that I was going to die. I desperately needed to get my life back on track, and David McCreery said I should see Steve Black.

I didn't know what he could do for me, but within one day of meeting him I knew that this was the guy to help me. He talked to me and then put me onto a strict regime and immediately I began to feel good about myself.

Blackie was incredible and invited me to stay with his family – far more than I deserved. His care with me and style of approach was fantastic, and after eight weeks of training me, I was in better condition than if I'd had three months' pre-season with a club.

Blackie got me mentally focused and fitter that I ever imagined could have been achieved in such a short time. He trained me hard and I didn't know if I could stick with the regime he set me, but I have. My weight is back and I feel better physically and mentally than I have for years. This is all down to Blackie, who is a phenomenal person in every way. I owe him so much. I love the guy and he saved me from a life sentence.

If any guy is struggling with his life or career and feels he has nothing to live for, all I can say is see Steve Black.

Paul Gascoigne – former England international footballer

Of all the players I trained, to pick out any would be unjust but I can't help but mention the likes of Neil Jenkins, a true great and one of the finest rugby players produced by Wales – a terrific lad, with humility and an amazing work rate. Neil was the complete pressure athlete who kicked over 1,000 points for Wales, yet retained his modesty. Scott Quinnell, Scott Gibbs, David Young, Chris Wyatt, Rob Howley, Colin Charvis, Garin Jenkins, Jon Humphries and the much-underrated and overcriticised Craig Quinnell were all top players not just in Wales but on the world stage. Great characters like Doddie Weir, Ben Evans, John Bentley and Jonathan Edwards give you so much pleasure as a fan as well as a coach.

Blackie is probably the most genuine and down-to-earth guy I have ever met. Even though he never trained me as a sportsman, he has done so much for me in so many other ways, it's impossible to list them all. It does not matter who he is with, even if it were the Queen, he will invite you into the conversation and certainly make you feel part of the group.

Recently, he invited me, together with Gazza, to a tribute rugby match to participate as the kickers, and even though we were both apprehensive about it, he immediately brought us into the fold and made us completely at ease with his fantastic personality. In the build-up, we had a training session with Jonny Wilkinson, which was one of the most incredible experiences of my life. To train with him and Jonny in that setting, and to witness the relationship between them, was a privilege and I only wish that I'd had Blackie's support during my playing career. It is not just his physical ability but also his mental and motivational skills, all hooked up with his fabulous off-the-wall humour, that makes him a total one-off. On one level he is so normal but on another so uniquely different – that makes him so very special.

Peter Beardsley – former England international and ex-Newcastle United

There are so many athletes who spring to mind, but the greatest of them all has to be Jonny Wilkinson. He possesses everything and has so much more. I have been privileged to be with him right from the start. His application and dedication can only be described as phenomenal. This lad is without doubt one of the greatest sportsmen ever to come out of Britain. The toughest? A certain Jedburgh knight, Gary Armstrong.

I still take great pleasure out of working with a terrific bunch of young players at Newcastle Falcons, but the 2002–03 season with them probably proved to be the most stressful of my career. The 2001–02 season had ended with Pat Lam, Inga Tuigamala, George Graham, Doddie Weir and Gary Armstrong leaving the club. Suffice to say they were missed, not only for their on-field contributions, but also for their general presence and effect. Characters like that are difficult to replace – so we didn't! Seriously, our young team needed to be getting the best guidance and motivation if they were to compete successfully week after week. To be able to deliver that support, we needed to have a coaching team who were firing on all cylinders, thinking on the same wavelength, full of enthusiasm and enjoying their jobs.

For that to happen, a team of people needed to interact optimally and this is only possible after a period of adjustment and compromise. It takes time. If you have a well-established team with a strong and tested subculture, then a gelling of a new coaching team can be accommodated. If your team are young and relatively inexperienced, then it can't. At the Falcons, we had a meeting of two clear subcultures – the northern and the southern hemispheres. Andy Blades joined us from ACT Brumbies after a hugely successful playing career culminating with a World Cup-winner's medal in December 1999. Andy has some great ideas concerning the game in general but in his early days at Kingston Park his style of delivery was obviously suited to the Australian market, where it's tried and tested and has been successful.

Rob Andrew, Steve Bates and I were inexperienced in accommodating a coach from a different hemisphere – he was a different coaching animal altogether. Our English courtesy didn't help Andy's transition, our effectiveness, or, more significantly, the team. By the time the penny had dropped, we were six points adrift at the bottom of the League and Steve Bates, our head coach of seven years' standing, took the brunt of our collective ineffectiveness. I think that Rob, Steve and Andy could have worked together very effectively, if we'd handled the situation better. Hindsight is a great thing. However, the learning process – about each other – was taking place on the job, and with our inexperienced team there wasn't really a great margin for error in the preparation stakes for this new coaching set-up. Crazy, but it goes to show that we're learning all the time and will continue to do so, no matter how long and at what level we've worked.

Losing Batesy coincided with us winning the battle to train at a more controlled and functional setting at Darsley Park, the Newcastle United indoor training centre which Freddie Shepherd so kindly allocated for our disposal, along with signing five good players and the subsequent effect of winning games. Since then, we've started to look like a formidable team on and off the field, and that augurs well for the future.

At the end of 2003–04, we finished the season on a high, having won the national cup competition, the Powergen Cup, for the second time in three years after a marvellous game against Sale Sharks at Twickenham. The last two domestic years at the Falcons were possibly as stressful, eventful and professionally demanding as the previous seven combined!

Newcastle Falcons have now begun to develop and grow as an established Premiership team. All the young lads are beginning to come through and there have been many success stories, despite the disappointments. We have a new stand which holds 10,000 spectators and, through the success of the World Cup, and Jonny Wilkinson in particular, rugby is now firmly on the North-east map, with a terrific fan base. We fill the stadium to capacity for every big match. The atmosphere is great and it is a pleasure to go to work every day with a highly motivated squad. The 2004 season was a bit of a curate's egg and there is no doubt we missed the expertise of Jonny, who was out with a long-term injury. However, we went on to win the Powergen Cup without him and that puts us into Europe. The thought of it is mouth-watering – with Jonny back, of course. Premiership rugby is a tough battleground and all the teams in it have begun to consolidate a level of competitiveness whereby every match you have is a veritable Cup final, unlike the early days. It is anybody's game and the level of athleticism and ability throughout the sport has moved onto another level. I strive to take the players further yet, as there is still an enormous amount of room for improvement. Fortunately, pre-season for 2004–05 has gone fantastically well and I really do think we can be leading contenders for the League title this year. New experienced additions to the squad, such as Matt Burke, Colin Charvis, Samo Settiti, Mike McCarthy, Luke Gross, Andy Long and, last but not least, a certain Mr Jonny Wilkinson, will definitely improve our lot this season alongside youngsters like Matthew Tait, Andy Buist, Geoff Parling, Stuart Mackie, Ed Williamson and Ollie Phillips, to name but a few who will collectively push to get into that first-team 22 throughout the season and will continue to learn how to handle themselves in game-like situations off the rugby field.

What can you say about Blackie that everybody hasn't already? Well, he eats loads, he smells, he's a bad driver, he's got terrible jokes, he's small, he's going bald, he used to be Elton John's partner, he was on the Titanic *– only joking on some of the above!*

On a serious note he is one pure dead brilliant guy. Words are unable to describe the man. Words are also hard to find to describe what he has done to the game of sport. On a personal note, he changed my total perception about training. I detested training when I was in Scotland and it was only when I joined the Toon in '95 that I enjoyed and looked forward to training. My Five Nations player of the year and British Lions selection was undoubtedly down to the big man and nobody else – cheers, Blackie!

He somehow has the ability to get the maximum out of body and mind in order for that person or team to strive for excellence. He doesn't take failure or failures easy, and very seldom does he get it.

He is a great man, one of the best. I owe a lot to him and miss his banter and smile. Onwards and upwards!

Doddie Weir – British Lions, Scotland, Borders

A top man and a great friend. I have known Stephen for over 15 years and worked with him at extremely close quarters, especially at Newcastle Falcons. In all of that time, despite brickbats and problems, he always comes up with a smile, a joke and a positive spin on life. He is a winner in all senses of the word and it is a joy to know him.

Martin Brewer – Falcons physio

Barmy.

Stuart Grimes – Newcastle Falcons, Scotland

Blackie is the most honest, straight-up bloke I've ever met. There aren't enough words to describe the effect he has had on those around him.

Jon Dunbar – Newcastle Falcons, Scotland

Funniest man I've ever met. You can turn to him for help and advice in any situation, and I feel honoured to have him as a friend.

Joe Shaw – Newcastle Falcons, England 7s

One of the worst people to take to the cinema.

Hall Charlton – Newcastle Falcons

A great man and a great character. The backbone of this club from the start and for years to come.

Epi Taione – Newcastle Falcons, Tonga

Outside my family, the single most important person in my career inside and outside rugby, and one of my closest friends with it!

Mark Wilkinson – Newcastle Falcons

Trains you till you are sick, but you still love him in a non-sexual way!! He's been a father to me in the rugby world.

  Liam Botham – Newcastle Falcons, England

An inspiration to us all. An exceptional man who is loved by everyone. Once you've met him, you'll never forget him.

  Angela Harrison – club masseuse

I have a lot of time and respect for Blackie. His knowledge of professional sport and his personal experience have helped us tremendously as a team, on and off the field. There is no end to his enthusiasm and the energy he puts into the team – one of the driving forces behind our strengths, our weaknesses and us, whom he knows personally. What a great guy to have on our side!

  Marius Hurter – Newcastle Falcons, South Africa

Blackie has an ability to come up with a humorous, yet totally off-the-wall comment, no matter how serious the moment – a top bloke.

  Gareth MacLure – Newcastle Falcons

Impossible not to like Blackie. He is one of those people who commands attention when they walk into a room. That's if he remembers to turn up on time.

  Steve Brotherstone – Newcastle Falcons, Scotland

Always looking for the positive in every situation. For someone with so much experience, his thirst for knowledge is amazing. He has helped me focus on seeking solutions rather than just identifying problems. He gives energy to everyone around him.

  Andrew Blades – Australia

The most positive man I know. Whatever the situation, there will always be something positive saved.

  Tom May – Newcastle Falcons, England

BLACKIE

Larger than life, big heart, one of the best storytellers in the North-east. A good friend to know.
    Jamie Noon – Newcastle Falcons, England

Very unorthodox in his inspiring methods and always makes you feel good.
    Micky Ward – Newcastle Falcons

Inspiring in all aspects of life.
    Matt Thompson – Newcastle Falcons, Scotland

Brilliant, barmy Blackie!
    Craig Hamilton – Newcastle Falcons

A chilled-out entertainer.
    James Isaacson – Newcastle Falcons

Having only met him a few months ago, it has amazed me how much of an influence he has had on me as a person. Totally respected by his peers, he is a great man.
    James Grindal – Newcastle Falcons

He is an inspiration to all. He has that rare ability to get the best out of each individual and his enthusiasm and larger-than-life personality rubs off on everyone else. One of life's true characters.
    Phil Godman – Newcastle Falcons

Beyond description, beyond understanding, beyond compare. A motivational guru, part-time psychologist and somebody who looks after everyone he meets.
    Phil Dowson – Newcastle Falcons, England 7s

A great person, truly inspirational. He helped me grow as a person and I have a huge respect for him. A brutally honest person who has a positive effect on everyone he meets, even though I do hate him during pre-season.
    Rob Devonshire – Newcastle Falcons

An inspirational character who has the ability to get anyone he trains to give 100 per cent from start to finish. Personally, I've wasted around two days of my life listening to his amusing, but pointless stories.
  Ian Peel – Newcastle Falcons

A fantastic motivator with a large handful of crazy humour, he gets the best out of you for every training session.
  Hugh Vyvyan – Newcastle Falcons, England

Here at Kingston Park, things are looking healthy for the club once again.

Preparing teams to play well is not rocket science. While you've got to treat full contact work in training with respect and common-sense caution, the basic premise is that training should be at game intensity or above for relatively short periods of time and geared specifically towards the exact way you want to play the game. It has to include lots of simulated match-play to ensure that players and coaches know how to immediately change focus between attack and defence, and get used to exploiting each situation. Skills should predominate, practised in game-like situations, although I accept that as long as it never takes the place of high-intensity training, regular passing and kicking drills are a positive addition to any player's regime. This type of training can and does improve the confidence and mental strength of the participant.

Forty-eight hours before a game is crucial, and energy should be conserved and consolidated during this time. Play to your strengths. Let senior players practise what they're good at and don't waste time trying to change the match-intensity functional skill base of your senior players.

Southern hemisphere players generally have a better early exposure and learning environment than British players. Their basic skills are generally better than those of their British counterparts and because of this they respond to, and get more benefit from, technical training regimes as adults. That's why, if we are to appoint technical coaches from Australia and New Zealand, it should be for our youngsters and not our senior teams. Southern hemisphere technical coaches aren't effective with adult British players, and because the players invariably find the training drills difficult to successfully complete, these coaches only slow the training field down to a speed whereby what the players learn cannot be transferred to the field of play. They also make the players feel inadequate by invariably telling one and all how incompetent they are! So, to all the technical coaches from all those regions Down Under, by all means come over and share your expertise, but come and help our youngsters develop better basic skills and help our coaches who operate at youth level. Don't waste our time coming over to improve our senior players' skill levels. You can't do it and you mess up the senior team's chances of winning games. Southern hemisphere coaches whose main bent is strategic are as welcome as we would be there. That's only fair.

There are some excellent sports science and sports studies courses at colleges and universities in the UK. We should give them a chance to show that British coaches can make all the same decisions as our foreign friends from France, New Zealand, South Africa and Australia. Everyone uses the same textbooks and research papers now, all saying the same thing. They have not been any different now for around the last ten years, and even then the difference was in terminology, not concept. Why the sizeable misrepresentation in this area?

A couple of points for conditioning coaches to ponder. Do any of you understand that it is different getting an athlete ready to compete in the Olympics, fight for a world boxing title or run in a one-off marathon than it is getting a rugby, soccer, hockey, netball or basketball team ready to play week in, week out? The number of soft-tissue injuries I see suggests that many of you don't. Get players too close to optimal fitness week by week and they'll break down, the team will get beat and you'll get sacked! People pressurising you into subscribing to fads from Del-Boy-type characters won't save your job or further the cause of peak performance.

Finally, fitness testing. Where do I stand on its usage with elite-level games players? Up until senior level it has enormous merit, not only as an ongoing research document and collation of normative data, but also as a guide and motivational tool for the young athlete to develop both physically and mentally. At these younger ages, the players should make fairly constant and at times significant gains which will show up during testing. The most important aspect of training and testing at this time is to condition the player mentally to the fact that he or she must continually strive to improve in all aspects of the programme formulated with their coach.

At senior level the system should have filtered out those players who do not appreciate the benefits of a professional training programme. And the actual results of the tests mean nothing in themselves – for example, you can be a great player if your percentage body fat is 14 per cent or 9 per cent, if your 100 metre time is 10.8 or 12.1, etc. Check it out. Name your best international select team and look at their fitness test profile. I'll guarantee you it isn't the best at their club, never mind the world.

Trying to be as good as you can be is everything, and I feel that cements the characteristics that make up the sporting personality. It is more important than any fitness test result. Because of the role ego plays in the make-up of any athlete, they invariably strive to get better at the variables they are being tested at rather than focusing on becoming better and more effective players. I can't believe the number of coaches who say such-and-such has results from their fitness test to show they've improved significantly across the broad spectrum. They have not necessarily improved as players! So, all you conditioners out there, train them to make them better rugby and soccer players, not to give better fitness-test results. You'll be rewarded for your trust in them.

Appendix One

STING . . . STUNG . . .
YOU MAKES YER CHOICE

'Any advance on 1,700 . . . come on now . . . it's going to go for 1,700 quid everybody. OK, that's it, bidding finished. This sock is sold to Sting!'

The scene was the Variety Club of Great Britain's tribute to Sting held at Newcastle Civic Centre on Friday, 7 May 2004. The place was stuffed to the rafters and I was logged in to do the auction at the star-studded Geordie event. The top table was groaning with celebrities, people like Robson Green, who was on great form, back to the Dudley lad we all know, Jimmy Nail, Peter Beardsley, Freddie Shepherd, Rob Andrew, Jack Charlton, Sir Bobby Robson, Mark Knopfler, Sting, Ray Laidlaw, Jonathan Edwards, Jools Holland, Glen McCrory and Alan Shearer. It was chaired by Bob Gladwin and compered by Bill Steel.

Jools Holland and others gave a potted history of their relationships with Sting, which was relayed on large screens right around the Civic Centre. Jools told of living with him in a flat where they shared three socks – one had gone missing and he suspected Sting had stolen it. All good crack. Mark Knopfler, Jimmy Nail and others spoke about the effect he had on them and it was progressing quite nicely . . . then it dawned on me. I decided to find that appropriated piece of hosiery, so I sent Peter Beardsley to find a sock and he did just that.

Before I began the auction, the crowd was milling and rumbustious so I started by singing a Geordie version of 'Don't Stand so Close to Me'. This had no effect, so I raised my voice: 'Hey! You've got 30 seconds and if you don't sit down, I'll take the lot of you outside and give you a good hiding.'

It seemed to do the trick. Then I told them of my secret relationship with Sting, how our paths had crossed and a deep friendship was forged. It went as follows.

'There's a wonderful holiday camp beside Berwick called Haggerston Castle and I went there one year. It generally takes about 45 or 50 minutes, but if you get stuck behind a tractor, and especially as the main roads aren't particularly good going up to Scotland, it could take forever. But eventually I arrived and got changed, only to find I'd made a dreadful mistake. I had put a jacket on and, as it was quite sunny outside, I started perspiring and was forced to take it off. This was only wasted time, but at the end of the day there's one thing you can't salvage anything from – wasted time.'

The room went deadly silent as the audience began to wonder where the story was going, or whether I'd flipped my lid. I continued.

'But ladies and gentlemen, I have to tell you, there was a buzz in the air . . . a buzz, there was a definite buzz, there was definitely something there. So I went for a paper, I can't remember which paper it was, but it doesn't really make any difference. I think it was the *Berwick Herald* . . . no, it was *Scotland on Sunday*, which is very strange because it was a Monday and they must have had one left over . . . sometimes newsagents do this. Then I went to the coffee shop and had a coffee. Well, I say coffee, but it was a latte, all milky with two sugars. I'm a diabetic now . . . had I known I was a diabetic then, I probably wouldn't have had the two sugars, because it would probably have been irresponsible. But there was a buzz, a magic in the air, and now I'm going to say it . . . Sting and I . . . well, we didn't actually bump into each other because he was in LA recording an album.'

Sting, his wife Trudie Styler and Jimmy Nail had tuned in to what I was saying and were absolutely creased with laughter . . . and I continued talking total nonsense. The atmosphere for the auction was set.

'Jimmy has told you Sting is such a kind person and I can tell you he is. One day I came in from work and found the back lawn cut and trimmed. I hadn't cut it . . . all the borders were done . . . then, on entering the house, the kitchen had been freshly painted and a new carpet fitted in the hallway. I don't want to embarrass him, because I didn't actually see him do it, but me and my wife would like to think that it was Sting.'

I then opened up with the sock . . . and ended by selling Ian Peel for sex to a guy for £1,000, provided Ian wore a blonde wig and could guarantee a good night out on the town. The Geordie spirit and wallets did the Variety Club charity proud that day and we raised £215,000 for underprivileged children.

So it wasn't really nonsense after all, and here was me, a lad from Benton in this high-octane gathering, which may seem surreal, but, you know what?, it seemed absolutely normal to me.

Appendix Two

BLACKIE'S BEST MAN GIGS!
... in chronological order

PETER ASHCROFT – One of the best crossers of a ball in his house. Met Peter when I was four years old and he's still a good pal. I think that says it all. One of the best-intentioned people I know.

LAWRENCE FAWCETT – Best mates for years and years and we still laugh at each other's jokes! Jam-packed full of good values and integrity. Not a bad left foot either.

3BOB MORTON – Knocked about together 30 years ago and still see each other daily. Mischievous with a soft underbelly, I love his company.

RONNIE FAECHIN – In the same class at school, eight years of age. Smashing lad, good singer but not the best goalscorer who ever lived, no matter what stories he tells my sons.

PAUL McCARTHY – I've known Paul since he was knee-high to a grasshopper. His dad, Jimmy, was one of my mentors/heroes. Very talented footballer/Powderhall sprinter and friend.

KELLY SCOTT – Stephen's and Mark's soccer coach and one of the world's most enthusiastic people. He and his dad, Butch, did great things for youth football provision in the east end of Newcastle. Now a successful businessman.

MIKE HOOPER – Talented goalkeeper who wanted to be a rugby player, and his personality and physical attributes would have lent themselves to the oval ball environment readily. So talented in so many areas, I hope he reaches his potential in an area he enjoys. A lovely lad.

Appendix Three

BLACKIE'S BLUEPRINT FOR SUCCESS

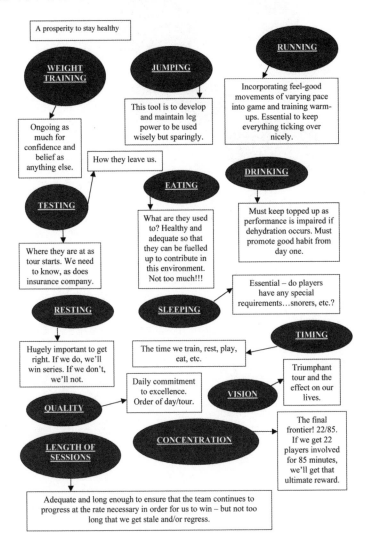

A prosperity to stay healthy

WEIGHT TRAINING

Ongoing as much for confidence and belief as anything else.

JUMPING

This tool is to develop and maintain leg power to be used wisely but sparingly.

RUNNING

Incorporating feel-good movements of varying pace into game and training warm-ups. Essential to keep everything ticking over nicely.

How they leave us.

EATING

What are they used to? Healthy and adequate so that they can be fuelled up to contribute in this environment. Not too much!!!

DRINKING

Must keep topped up as performance is impaired if dehydration occurs. Must promote good habit from day one.

TESTING

Where they are at as tour starts. We need to know, as does insurance company.

SLEEPING

Essential – do players have any special requirements…snorers, etc.?

RESTING

Hugely important to get right. If we do, we'll win series. If we don't, we'll not.

The time we train, rest, play, eat, etc.

TIMING

Triumphant tour and the effect on our lives.

QUALITY

Daily commitment to excellence. Order of day/tour.

VISION

CONCENTRATION

The final frontier! 22/85. If we get 22 players involved for 85 minutes, we'll get that ultimate reward.

LENGTH OF SESSIONS

Adequate and long enough to ensure that the team continues to progress at the rate necessary in order for us to win – but not too long that we get stale and/or regress.

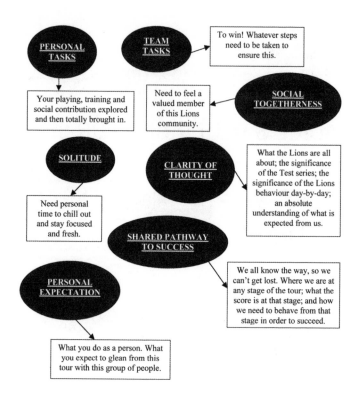

PERSONAL TASKS

Your playing, training and social contribution explored and then totally brought in.

TEAM TASKS

To win! Whatever steps need to be taken to ensure this.

SOCIAL TOGETHERNESS

Need to feel a valued member of this Lions community.

SOLITUDE

Need personal time to chill out and stay focused and fresh.

CLARITY OF THOUGHT

What the Lions are all about; the significance of the Test series; the significance of the Lions behaviour day-by-day; an absolute understanding of what is expected from us.

SHARED PATHWAY TO SUCCESS

We all know the way, so we can't get lost. Where we are at any stage of the tour; what the score is at that stage; and how we need to behave from that stage in order to succeed.

PERSONAL EXPECTATION

What you do as a person. What you expect to glean from this tour with this group of people.

Steve Black, British Lions Preparation Checklist, April 2001